CRASHING THE IDOLS

CRASHING THE IDOLS

THE VOCATION OF WILL D. CAMPBELL
(and Any Other Christian for That Matter)

WILL D. CAMPBELL
RICHARD C. GOODE

 CASCADE *Books* • Eugene, Oregon

CRASHING THE IDOLS
The Vocation of Will D. Campbell (and Any Other Christian for That Matter)

Copyright © 2010 Will D. Campbell and Richard C. Goode. All rights reserved. Except for brief quotations in critical publications or reviews, no part of this book may be reproduced in any manner without prior written permission from the publisher. Write: Permissions, Wipf and Stock Publishers, 199 W. 8th Ave., Suite 3, Eugene, OR 97401.

Cascade Books
An imprint of Wipf and Stock Publishers
199 W. 8th Ave., Suite 3
Eugene, OR 97401

www.wipfandstock.com

ISBN 13: 978-1-60608-127-3

Cataloging-in-Publication data:

Campbell, Will D.

    Crashing the idols : the vocation of Will D. Campbell (and any other Christian for that matter) / Will D. Campbell and Richard C. Goode.

    xiv + 230 p. ; 23 cm. — Includes bibliographical references and indexes.

    ISBN 13: 978-1-60608-127-3

    1. Campbell, Will D. 2. Baptists—Clergy—Biography. 3. Social Action. I. Goode, Richard C. II. Title.

BX6495 .C28 G66 2010

Manufactured in the U.S.A.

CONTENTS

Preface | vii

Reconciled!
by Richard C. Goode

Formation of an Iconoclast | 3
Life within the Steeples and Ivory Towers | 9
Formal Civil Rights Work | 15
Crashing the Idols of the National Council of Churches | 26
The Committee of Southern Churchmen | 40
A Campbell Credo | 52
Living Hope | 59

Race and Renewal of the Church
by Will D. Campbell

Are We Still the Church? | 73
The Nature of the Problem | 83
The Gods of Law and Order | 92
The Humanistic Detour | 100
The Christian Concern and Starting Point | 111
Accomplishments and New Dangers | 121
The Church: Prophet and Conservator | 130

Incarnating Radical Christianity in the American South: The Importance of Will D. Campbell
by Richard C. Goode

Beyond H. Richard Niebuhr's *Christ and Culture* | 145
Beyond Mark Toulouse's *God in Public* | 155

A Campbell-Inspired Radical Alternative | 167
Problems with the Principalities and Powers | 173
What Is the Radical Difference Being Incarnated? | 189
Rethinking Sect | 199

Conclusion | 203
Bibliography | 207
Scripture Index | 217
Subject Index | 219

"God has called you to smash the images erected which have become more important than God himself."

—Will D. Campbell[1]

PREFACE

THE OPPORTUNITY TO SOJOURN intellectually with the marvelously provocative Will D. Campbell has been a real joy and education. Over several years I have had the opportunity to read and visit with Will. On a few occasions I have sat with him at his log cabin office in Mt. Juliet, Tennessee. Will has also graciously participated in academic classes some of us have offered at the Riverbend Maximum Security Prison in Nashville. The invitation from Cascade Books to work on this project, therefore, came as quite a gift. Lipscomb University has enhanced the experience by generously funding a sabbatical to work on the project.

As discussions about the Will Campbell project unfolded, I kept my friend Harmon Wray informed because Harmon had introduced me to Will in the first place. Harmon's fellowship with Will went back to the 1970s when he worked with Will and Tony Dunbar in the Southern Prison Ministries. For more than a decade Harmon piqued my interest about Will, sharing stories and anecdotes, and informally guiding me through Will's corpus of writings. Harmon, moreover, helped connect several of my intellectual mentors. I had read Thomas Merton, for example, heard of Campbell, but was largely unaware of William Stringfellow. It was Harmon who showed me how the three often fit together in rich and complementary ways.

---

1. Campbell, "Christian Concern: Fourteenth Amendment or First Commandment?" Although committed to gender-inclusive language, I have chosen to retain much of Will's original terminology.

Beyond his own personal experiences, Harmon's wealth of knowledge about Will came from his own dissertation project. As a PhD candidate at Vanderbilt, Harmon investigated the work of Clarence Jordan and Will Campbell. In retrospect, however, Harmon may have been too close to his subjects to take on such an academic task. As the old cliché goes, there are two kinds of dissertations—good ones and done ones. Because he so revered Jordan and Campbell, Harmon was especially cautious and deliberate to get the story right. Additionally, Harmon's widespread interests and spirited activism constantly distracted him from the dissertation project. Somewhere in the 1980s, the window for completing that work closed. After years of living with the Jordan-Campbell project, Harmon never finished it.

The fact that Harmon's dissertation remained incomplete, however, hardly impeded his work. He was a stalwart advocate for society's marginalized and disinherited. His credo was similar to that of Eugene V. Debs, who announced to a federal court in 1918, "While there is a lower class, I am in it, and while there is a criminal element, I am of it, and while there is a soul in prison, I am not free." Harmon lived that pledge. Through the Vanderbilt Divinity School, for example, Harmon, Janet Wolf, and I created an academic program at the Riverbend Maximum Security Institution. Eventually Harmon became the unflagging Director of the Vanderbilt Program in Faith and Criminal Justice.

Then, on July 23, 2007, Harmon suffered a massive stroke, succumbing the next day. A week later, our "Glad River(bend)"[2] community gathered for a memorial service to grieve our loss and celebrate Harmon's life and work. I recall looking across the sullen faces in Riverbend's chapel that evening. Will was especially silent, starring off into the distance. The loss of Harmon was just beginning to sink in. It continues to do so.

Sometime around Christmas 2007, Judy Parks, Harmon's partner of many years, called to say that that while going through Harmon's voluminous collection of books, periodicals, clippings, and writings she found something of Harmon's dissertation manuscript. The document contained an introduction to the project, followed by an initial biographical sketch of Jordan and Campbell. Handwritten into the margins, Harmon included phrases like "develop this in the analytical section." Unfortunately, no such analytical section followed. Harmon's prelimi-

---

2. Campbell, *The Glad River*. Perhaps Will's finest book, which he has preferred to classify as "not non-fiction."

nary thoughts have provided good inspiration for this project, although I have gone in directions that Harmon would undoubtedly question.

The architecture of this volume is rather straightforward, seeking to address three basic questions. First, who is Will Davis Campbell? Second, what has he said? And third, why should we consider what he has said and done?

With two autobiographical volumes,[3] two full-length biographies,[4] and numerous essays and interviews of Campbell available, the first section of this book does not seek to offer a comprehensive biography. Rather, "Reconciled!" offers an interpretive preamble to the man who has raised so many interesting and unsettling questions. As the *Nashville Scene* has asked:

> So who is this bootleg preacher who makes the Baptist elite clam up? This man who has no faculty seat at any divinity school, no church building—and certainly no television pulpit—yet challenges one of the most powerful religious bodies in the country and has written books and essays that make renowned theologians sit up and take notice? Who is this redneck farmer with no organization who became a major figure in the civil rights struggle? This integrationist who reaches out to Klansmen? This Christian cleric who marries, baptizes, and buries Catholics, Jews, heathens and the unchurched alike? This hillbilly guitar strummer with no press agent who becomes friends with some of the most famous—and infamous—country music stars of all time?[5]

What *do* we make of Will? Is he "conservative" or "liberal"? Do such categories have any utility for a Radical like Will?[6] Is he really the "*gentle iconoclast*" described by the *Wittenburg Door*,[7] especially when he calls a high-ranking Baptist official a "hypocrite and a jackass"—and to the official's face at that? Will has sought to tell any Christian who will listen,

---

3. Campbell, *Brother to a Dragonfly*; and *Forty Acres and a Goat*.

4. Connelly, *Will Campbell and the Soul of the South*; and Hawkins, *Will Campbell: Radical Prophet of the South*.

5. Sweat, "Nothing Sacred."

6. When capitalized, "Radical" refers to the unstructured fellowship described in Bradstock and Rowland, *Radical Christian Writings*; Inchausti, *Subversive Orthodoxy*; and York, *Living on Hope While Living in Babylon*. Comprised of Catholics, Anglicans, Anabaptists, and others across Christian history, these Radicals dig down to expose the root of injustice, chauvinism, racism, militarism, and materialism, while highlighting Christianity's alternative *shalom* of equality, reconciliation, peace, and sacrificial love.

7. Flynn, "Interview with Will D. Campbell."

"You have been called to sound the alarm, to crash the idols, to reply 'No, but by God's Grace, we are no longer mad, we are about our Father's business.'"[8] The purpose of this volume's biographical sketch is to address a few of these questions, while hopefully prompting several more. Seeking to make part 1 as narrative as possible, I have limited the use of such technical apparatus as footnotes. Material in the text boxes elaborate on topics of related interest.

Perhaps the best entrée into Campbell's body of writing is his first major work, *Race and the Renewal of the Church*, published in 1962. Long out of print, we are pleased to offer it here, for in this short book Campbell's reconciling iconoclasm comes into focus. Before the publication of *Race and Renewal*, Campbell had immersed himself in a variety of events and actions, becoming what Gayraud Wilmore called "a pioneer trouble shooter." By '62, for example, Campbell had already participated in events spanning from Oxford, Mississippi, and Clinton, Tennessee, to Little Rock, Nashville, Montgomery, and beyond. With the publication of *Race and Renewal*, however, Campbell reached an audience that would seldom find itself in such clear crisis situations. Most Christians, of course, would neither be an Elizabeth Eckford integrating Central High School in Little Rock, nor one of those stalking Autherine Lucy because she sought to integrate the University of Alabama. Instead of bombing schools, or having their churches burned, most Christians were living quiet, law-abiding lives; well-adjusted citizens according to the sociological and political conventions of society. Campbell suggests, however, that at the end of the day, this silent, all too compliant majority of "Christians" may be the most dangerous group of all.

What passes for "Christianity" in the U.S., Campbell asserts, is seldom more than "good, conventional, American citizenship." As he told *The Wittenburg Door*, the so-called "good Christians are the ones who behave the way a good boy or girl learns to behave in a Sixth Grade Civics class." The church's message is no more scandalous, and our discipleship is no more serious than a mild curriculum for children,[9] which allows "Christians" to confuse courtesy, compassion, humanitarianism, and fidelity to the federal government with the outrageous proclamation of the gospel. Too often what passes for Christian teaching in the U.S. is some tepid "be good, polite, and don't rock the boat" encouragement.

8. Campbell, "Christian Concern: Fourteenth Amendment or First Commandment?"
9. "Will Campbell: Door Interview," *The Wittenburg Door*, 11.

If this is all the church has to recommend, Bob Eckblad challenges, "the church is basically providing the state with a massive obedience program."[10] Such a civil religion might make for a kinder, more urbane and democratic America, but it is not God's *kerygma* (proclamation). In *Race and the Renewal of the Church*, Campbell illustrated how the so-called "right" and "left" often work from the same misguided assumptions. First, each in their own way operates from a "human point of view," engaging neighbors according to society's prevailing sociological and political categories (e.g., race, class, gender, nationality). Second, both the "right" and the "left" make humanity the measure of all things, which is, according to Campbell, blasphemy against the sovereign God. Third, the "left" and the "right" both presume that political activism is *the* way to make a difference in the world.

Campbell's unrelenting work, therefore, has deconstructed an institutionalized, acculturated church that has all too conveniently aligned with, and sought to wield the power of, the civil government in the name of piety and justice. As Christians, our ministry of reconciliation is too easily sidetracked by political coalitions pledging to side with the "good guys" and against "bad guys." As disciples, our mission is derailed when we see as our principal end the cause of American freedom and liberal democracy, or the defeat of the racists and assorted bigots. As Campbell has illustrated, our work is for Christians to interpose the gospel's alternative reality in the place of social convention and political science. In the place of paternalistic activism, saccharine tolerance, or legislated integration, Christians are to *be* what God through Christ has made us to be—an oddly redeemed, socially awkward, beloved community. Christians are commissioned to tell of that radical reconciliation, not only with our lips, but in our lives. "God has created this new humanity, this new creation—the church—'to preach good news to the poor, . . . to proclaim release to the captives and recovering of sight to the blind, to set at liberty those who are oppressed, to proclaim the acceptable year of the Lord' (Luke 4:18–19 from Isaiah 61:1–2). If the church regards people from a human point of view in the pursuit of this mission," Campbell warned, "it neglects the calling and the charge that the Lord has laid upon it."[11] Articulating this message in the 1950s and '60s, Campbell foreshadowed many "Yoderwasians" (the school of

10. Eckblad, *A New Christian Manifesto*, 66.
11. Campbell, *Race and Renewal of the Church*, 79.

thought influenced by the writings of John Howard Yoder and Stanley Hauerwas), who lament the church's surrender of the very *kerygma* the world so desperately needs (i.e., a proclamation beyond common sense, political science, or natural law).

Part 3, "Incarnating Radical Christianity in the American South: The Importance of Will D. Campbell," explores the ongoing importance of Campbell. Harmon and I used to have lively conversations about "the place" of Will in American religious history. If Harmon were here, I'm sure we would have another lively conversation or two about the essay's claims and architecture. Harmon would have said things very differently, and I would love to hear what he would argue and how he would say it. I suspect, for example, he would want to see more detail about the Anabaptist heritage itself. However, I have chosen to keep the focus more on Will and his cadre of *Katallagete* contributors, connecting their viewpoints to some of today's more contested debates. Will has often confessed his intellectual and spiritual connection to the Anabaptist tradition, and I take him at his word. Thus I have tried to explore some of the ramifications of his life and work as a self-professing Radical—especially in light of current conversations about political theology and the public square. In this way, I trust the essay answers the all-important "so what?" question.

Admittedly, the architecture of this volume may surprise those who know and love Will, for this is not a "biography" in the classic sense. Clearly Will's life and work is at the center of both this and the companion volume.[12] Nevertheless, the larger intent is to better appreciate the genius of Radical Christianity by looking again at the life and work of Will Campbell. Instead of a solitary witness, Will has been a voice for a vital, important Radical tradition. By hearing the story of Will, in other words, we might discern a more comprehensive narrative.

Although my training has been in the academic field of history, I have no pretension of objectively reporting "just the facts." Certainly by the third section, if not well before, the reader will realize that I have little interest in being an unbiased chronicler. This book should be read as an extended essay, i.e., an apology for Will and the Radicals. Toward that goal, part 3 offers a portrait of what I have sometimes called "Mr. Campbell's neighborhood," a depiction of the Radical tradition or community into which Campbell fits. Thus, the presentation in the

---

12. Campbell, *Writings on Reconciliation and Resistance.*

final section often cites Campbell's colleagues as much as it references Campbell himself. For those needing to hear more from Will, *Writings on Reconciliation and Resistance* will provide sources to support the thesis presented here.

This project would not have been possible without the inspiration, support, and encouragement of several individuals. First, and most obviously, Will Campbell, who has been most generous with his time. Thank you, Bro, not only for your immediate support of, and participation in, this project, but for incarnating reconciliation in our all too divisive world. Second, my wife, Ms. Candyee Goode, who merits that wise blessing on behalf of "writers and the martyrs who must live with them." Third, on behalf of Harmon, I would like to recognize the community at Riverbend. I will undoubtedly miss a name or two, but for Harmon, Janet, and me, our dear brothers there—or those who have passed through RMSI—have been a remarkable family. To Rahim Buford, Eddie Hartman, Grant Henderson, Thomas Hicks, Mark Higgins, Al Hughes, John Johnson, Ed McKeown, Glen Mann, Nathan Miller, Ulysses Owens, David Phipps Jr., Kevin Richards, Charles Rutledge, Jorge Sanjines, Dean Shoemaker, Fred Sledge, Sam Taylor, Michael Waldron, and Tom Warren, we offer our humble thanks for sharing your life with us. You have often been Christ for us, a living community that incarnates reconciliation.

I would also like to thank Dale Johnson for reading a draft of "Reconciled!" and Jonathan Melton for reading a draft of "Incarnating Radical Christianity in the American South." Craig Katzenmiller and Benjamin Oliver have also helped with various details throughout. A special word of thanks to Christopher Spinks and Ted Lewis of Wipf and Stock for inviting me to take on the project, and for their editorial advice and guidance along the way.

Richard C. Goode
Feast of St. Mary Magdalene, 2009
Lipscomb University
Nashville

Reconciled!

Richard C. Goode

In his 1983 novella, *Cecelia's Sin*, Will Campbell chronicled the final days of Cecelia Geronymus, a sixteenth-century Dutch Christian who is all too conscious of her inevitable arrest and subsequent martyrdom for her Anabaptist faith. Pressed by time and strangled by the tightening noose of persecution all about her, Cecelia labors night and day to complete a history of her Anabaptist community before it is too late. Although her calling, she believes, is to record for God and posterity a history of the Radical witness, almost daily the executioner complicates Cecelia's mission by systematically extinguishing her living sources. In the very process of recording the narrative, however, Cecelia slowly experiences an epiphany, a revelation that the facts of the story she so zealously desires to save are nowhere near as important as the dynamic community itself. "Writing the story," she learns, "is not the *Story*."[1] Her sin, we learn, is that of many writers, theologians, and especially historians. Too often we presume that our life, both individually and collectively, matters only to the extent that we *make history*. While we have breath, therefore, we strive to record, capture, and preserve our successes—to chronicle our accomplishments, establish our importance, and prove that we have made a difference. We *made history*. Should we fail to narrate our story, history will soon forget us, and we will be lost forever. "The writing of the story," however, "is not the Story."

---

1. Campbell, *Cecelia's Sin*, 81.

THE FORMATION OF AN ICONOCLAST

On July 18, 1924, Will Davis Campbell was brought into the world, one of four children of Lee Webb and Hancie Bea "Ted" Parker Campbell. The Campbells' sixty-acre cotton farm, located in the Piney Woods section of Amite County in southwest Mississippi, was near the county seat town of Liberty. Stretching back to the 1890s, the county had been the scene of two forms of poor, rural, white rebellion: on the one hand, the reactionary vigilante violence of the "whitecapping" terror against wealthy merchant and gentry creditors and their poor black workers; and, on the other, a more respectable economic and political agrarian reform movement led by the Southern Farmers' Alliance and the Peoples' Party. Populism was not above racism, however, and in the early and middle twentieth century, Amite County and the Piney Woods region of the state would also distinguish themselves as the scene of strong Ku Klux Klan activity—becoming perhaps the most racially repressive section of the most segregated state in the Union.

In that political setting, Will Campbell grew up in a milieu centered on kinship and a fighting spirit. One hundred years before Will's birth, the East Fork Baptist Church—the home congregation of the Campbells—had been the site of the second organizing convention of the Mississippi Baptist Association, which opened with a sermon by Rev. Davis Collins from II Corinthians 10:4,

> For the weapons of our warfare are not worldly, But have divine power to destroy strongholds.

One year after Will's birth, the Ku Klux Klan visited the East Fork Church, providing not only a cash donation to the congregation's work, but also a leather-bound Bible for the pulpit. Engraved into the Bible's leather cover were the letters KKK. Eventually Will would preach from this Bible.

A sickly child, Will later suspected that around the age of five he had been dedicated to the gospel ministry by his family as part of a deal they struck with God when he narrowly averted death from pneumonia. Will has imagined his father bargaining with God in terms like, "Well, look at him [Will], he's not worth anything so if you want to pull him through you can have him."[1] At the early age of seven, Will was baptized by immersion in the East Fork of the Amite River. Also, about this time, Will had a second conversion experience. Most of the boys in Campbell's extended family played at Grandpa Bunt's house. "I can still see him," Campbell often recounts. "He always sat out on a tree stump, whittling and chewing Prince Albert tobacco." One Sunday afternoon the Campbell boys were verbally taunting an elderly African-American gentleman, who had recently been released from prison. "Hi nigger, hi," the boys jeered. "Grandpa Bunt called us all around him," Campbell later recalled, "and very calmly said,

> 'No Hon.'—he called everybody 'Hon'—'There ain't no such thing as a nigger.'
> 'Yeah, John Walker,' the boys responded.
> 'No, he's a colored man.'

"And I never forgot that. Now, I don't know why. My brothers and cousins and others, it didn't seem to affect them. And I'm not saying that it was a Road to Damascus experience, but it was something I never forgot."[2]

Along with his older brother and close friend, Joe, and the rest of his multi-generational extended family, Campbell grew up in Depression Era Mississippi. They may have been poor in material things, but they were rich in love and experience; in retrospect, neither "happy" nor "unhappy." By the age of sixteen, Will had graduated from East Fork Consolidated High School and had experienced, in the Southern Baptist tradition, the "call to preach." Although reared in a patriarchal tradition, he notes that the women in his life mediated his call to the ministry. He explored preaching while still a student in high school, but his formal recognition of "the call" came when he was seventeen. The East Fork Baptist Church ordained him to the ministry by the laying on of hands. This time the primary men in his life took center stage: his father, his uncle Luther Campbell, cousin D. Elisha Moore, and the local preacher. In retrospect, Campbell has always found this moment defining for his life. Years later he told Kenneth Gibble, "Hanging on my wall is a plain piece of paper full of misspelled words and typos that the Baptist preach-

---

1. Caudill, "An Oral History with Will D. Campbell."
2. Wray, "Interview of Will D. Campbell," 18–19.

er who ordained me typed up on that occasion." Campbell noted that it "hangs on my kitchen wall, glued on top of my college and seminary degrees and other alleged honors." "It's signed by my daddy and uncle and cousin and the country preacher. And nobody can take that away from me," Campbell asserts. "That piece of paper is my marching orders."[3] In 2008, those orders still hung on Campbell's wall over the mantle of his fireplace. His ordination occurred, of course, only after he had satisfactorily answered a battery of questions concerning the verbal inspiration of Scripture, the virgin birth of Christ, the existence of a literal hell, and the plan of salvation. That he became a Baptist was no surprise, given that the denomination comprised the entire church-going population of Amite County. The county was so Baptist, in fact, that the principal of Will's public school led a daily chapel, and on Fridays discussed the previous week's lesson published by the Baptist Sunday School Board. Once a Holiness family came drifting through, Campbell recalled, but didn't tarry long in the county.

Filling in one Sunday for a preacher in McComb, Mississippi, Will met Tom Sharp, an executive with Standard Oil, who almost unilaterally determined Campbell's early postsecondary education. After hearing the young Campbell preach, Sharp simply called Dean Weathersby of Louisiana College and enrolled Will. Although he has confessed that he was "about as prepared for any kind of college work as a skunk is for a garden party,"[4] in 1942 Will's father and Uncle Pur drove him over to Louisiana College, a Southern Baptist institution at Pineville, Louisiana. Here Will got his first taste of higher education, studying at Louisiana College for about a year. During that academic year, Will financially supported himself by working at a clothing store and preaching on the side. Campbell also served as the business manager of *The Wildcat*, the college's student newspaper. By 1942 the U.S. was, of course, fully involved in World War II, and Will's brother Joe had already been drafted. In solidarity with Joe, and in a burst of patriotism, Will waived his 4-D draft deferment—which he considered a "classification for ministers, ex-cons, feeble-minded folk and so on"[5]—and enlisted in the Army. Although he envisioned himself charging headlong on to hotly contested battlefields, he actually spent his three years of military service as a surgical techni-

3. Gibble, "Living Out the Drama," 570–71.
4. Caudill, "An Oral History with Will D. Campbell."
5. Ibid.

cian in the South Pacific Medic Corps, assigned to the 109th Special Hospital. Will remembers his initial joy when on August 6, 1945, his unit received word of the U.S. nuclear strike on Hiroshima. Having watched the *Enola Gay* depart only hours earlier from Saipan, Will had cheered the revelation of the bombing because—as he later recalled—he simply wanted to go home.

> ### CAMPBELL: A PACIFIST?
>
> As with many issues, Campbell's position on this question is complex. In a 1976 interview, for example, Campbell admitted "I am not a pacifist; I am not a non-pacifist." Either way, he is an Army veteran vocally critical of his one-time employer.
>
> In 1974 *Katallagete* dedicated an issue to nonviolence. Introducing the collection, Campbell editorialized:
>
>> First, if we cannot find it possible to refrain from violence, we can at least refrain from celebrating it, from being proud of it. . . . We can make our national days of feasting and jubilation days of fasting and repentance. . . . To do otherwise is sure and certain blasphemy. Second, we of the Faith, we who claim to take our cue from the Christ, can cease to ask the State on every and on each occasion to tell us when our violence is permissible, when it is moral, ethical and all right. Even as we cease to do so, Caesar will say "But your Christ was not non-violent." We do not say that Christ was non-violent, at least in our culturally defined use of the term. We say only that he was, and is, the Christ. "Ah, but your Messiah was no pacifist. He took a whip and drove folks out of the house of worship." And so He did. We are not contending that the Messiah was a pacifist. Again, not as we have permitted "civilization as *we* know it" to define and interpret. We are contending only that He was, and is, the Messiah. And then, parenthetically, add that it is a long way for sure from a leather strap to chase chicken peddlers out of the church house to dropping forty thousand tons of bombs on a tragic little country on His birthday.

Although he would later become a staunch critic of the U.S. military, these years were formative for him. For the first time in his life Will saw beyond the hegemonic South and experienced authentic diversity. In the military he rubbed elbows with "everything from good solid Cajun boys from the bayous of Louisiana, to a Marxist type from Brooklyn." He also frequently conversed with Chaplain Stephen Crary, a graduate of New

York City's Union Theological Seminary, who "had some keen thinking and insights on the whole question of race."[6] During 1943 Will read two books that restructured his view of the world. Frederick Douglass's *My Bondage and My Freedom* was the first. To this point Campbell had never heard of Douglass, but as he read, Will was "overwhelmed." "It was for me, epiphanal, a deliverance, and from that moment on I knew my life would never be the same." The second was Howard Fast's historical novel *Freedom Road*, which Will's brother, Joe, encouraged him to read. Set in Reconstruction South Carolina, the story chronicled the formation of an exceptional community of marginalized ex-slaves and poor whites, all struggling to survive. Fighting for greater economic and political power, for a time this *ad hoc* integrated fellowship rallied successfully against the landed gentry. Once President Rutherford B. Hayes withdrew federal troops from the South and formally ended Reconstruction, however, the planters used the Ku Klux Klan to crush the multiracial alliance. The heroic, yet failed, coalition of Southern poor whites and blacks struggled against their common adversaries—whether in white mansions, white robes, or in the White House. They gave Will a metahistorical perspective. "I knew that the tragedy of the South would occupy the remainder of my days," Campbell recalled. "It was a conversion experience comparable to none I had ever had, and I knew it would have to find expression."[7]

In addition to Fast's fiction, an all-too-real object lesson in racial bigotry occurred early one morning, about 3:00 am, when Will was awakened to assist in an emergency surgery on a young black child with a ruptured spleen. During the operation Campbell inquired what had happened to the boy. He learned that the patient was a houseboy who had been violently kicked in the back for dropping his planter's ashtray. "I got to thinking about that. Well, you know, I'm from Mississippi and I was eighteen years old, and I remembered similar incidents" of scorn and abuse. Will recalls that by the time he was mustered out of the Army he had become "a zealot about race and race relations."[8]

Heading back home to the segregated South he would be serious about racial justice and harmony. He began living out his decision even as the troops were transported back home, slowly making their way across the continental U.S., toward the Jim Crow South. Foreshadowing

6. Ibid.
7. Ibid.
8. Wray, "Interview of Will D. Campbell," 19.

the new trajectory of his life, Campbell chose to bunk with two African-American friends—an act of principled defiance against cultural protocol. Leaving behind "what his mamma dedicated him to the Lord to be," he could no longer be the "traditional preacher, with three revivals a year, moving on up the ladder and winding up as the pastor of the First Baptist Church of Sumrall, Mississippi." Folks at home immediately realized the change in Will, but initially thought "he'd come around and be alright." According to the Southern definition of the term, never again would Will Campbell be "alright."[9]

After the war, Will Campbell married Brenda Fisher, the young woman he had begun courting at Louisiana College. She came from a family of Louisiana farmers and Southern Baptist preachers, and had pledged never to marry a man who planned to pursue either career. The newlyweds soon moved to Winston-Salem, North Carolina, where Will used the G.I. Bill to pay for his education at Wake Forest College. He chose Wake Forest because some of his Army friends had spoken so highly of the Baptist school. Wake proved another formative experience. For nearly every paper Campbell submitted in his major-field English classes, he focused on race. Eventually his exasperated major professor assigned Campbell to read Thomas Dixon's *The Klansmen*, noting that Dixon was a noteworthy North Carolina writer and Wake Forest alumnus. It was his professor's way, Campbell concluded, of saying "Come off all this [racial] nonsense." Will would not be diverted from his calling, however. As a "young and foolish prophet,"[10] Campbell recollects, he persisted in challenging the South's social convention. Despite his conflicts with the faculty, in 1948 he graduated with a degree in English, and from there the Campbells moved to New Orleans. In the Big Easy, Will undertook a year of graduate study at Tulane University. Then in 1949 they moved to New Haven, Connecticut, for Will to study ethics at Yale Divinity School under Southern-born social ethicist Liston Pope. It was also during his time at Yale that Roland Bainton first introduced Will to the genius of the Anabaptist tradition. Will still envisioned ultimately returning to the Deep South as a fully credentialed Southern Baptist clergyman, and after three years of what he was later to call his "pseudo-sophisticated period," Will graduated in 1952 from Yale with a Bachelor of Divinity degree.

9. Caudill, "An Oral History with Will D. Campbell."
10. Wray, "Interview of Will D. Campbell," 19.

LIFE WITHIN THE STEEPLES AND IVORY TOWERS

A FTER GRADUATION FROM YALE, the Campbells headed south where Will accepted a call as pastor of a Southern Baptist congregation of three hundred members in the lumber mill town of Taylor, Louisiana. On the surface, Campbell provided pastoral care to a stereotypical small town, middle-class Southern Baptist church whose primary concerns seemed, to Campbell at least, dreadfully mundane and self-centered. Surviving minutes from Taylor's congregational meetings during the time of Campbell's pastorate suggest that the congregation's chief business was institutional maintenance. Congregational energies and resources were committed for routine budgeting issues such as installing a stained-glass window in the church baptistery. After weeks of negotiations, the church decided to substitute a painting for the stainedglass, and to use the remaining funds to purchase carpeting for the rostrum and aisles. Other bureaucratic decisions included the appointment of Will as the chairman of the Visual Aids Committee (with authorization to purchase a projector), and the hiring of an African-American woman to staff the church nursery during services (so long as her compensation did not exceed $2 per Sunday). Beyond the Taylor church's week-to-week routine, however, Will managed to generate some controversy when he joined picketing workers at a paper plant in Elizabeth, Louisiana. He also exhibited his progressive proclivities by frequently preaching against racial discrimination and McCarthyism's anti-communist hysteria, visiting Grambling University, and actually paying the family's maid minimum wage.

Campbell recalls that the parishioners at his first and only institutional pastorate tolerated his views, liked him well enough, and were "good people." But he felt "less than free" and more than a little patronized by the congregation. Reciting the perspective of his parishioners, Campbell recalls them saying, "You wouldn't believe our little preacher, he is the cutest thing: He talks about our kids going to go to school with niggers: He is a card, you know. He is a character, you know, he's sort of our mascot. We love him and won't pay any attention to him. We don't believe all that."[1] Besides, the congregation found pride and prestige in having one of only three Yale-trained preachers in the state of Louisiana. Events beyond Taylor, however, began to influence his pastorate. The U.S. Supreme Court's 1954 *Brown v. Board* school desegregation decision forced issues to the surface. Strongly committed to racial unity and harmony, Campbell "knew what was coming, and that I would not be able to survive it." Moreover, he was questioning the efficacy of the pulpit in educating anyone. "I think I was already beginning to see that the only way you teach anybody is precept and example," Campbell recalls. "What you say up there in the pulpit, that's probably *the* poorest way to communicate with a congregation."[2]

Will and Brenda were eager to get back to Mississippi anyway. Having emphasized the "religion and higher education" track in his studies at Yale, he jumped at the invitation to oversee campus ministry at the University of Mississippi. On Independence Day 1954, Will tendered his resignation to the Baptist church in Taylor and took the Director of Religious Life position at Ole Miss. Although he felt the congregation was sorry to see him go, he recalls that his resignation was accepted with no opposition.

The move from the local congregation to the larger vocational context of Ole Miss proved both wise and fortuitous. Here Campbell could take advantage of a more academic arena to respond to the South's visceral and illogical reaction to the *Brown* decision. As he would later write in *Providence*, the post-*Brown* era launched

> an epoch of moral mischief, indescribable repression, social and political unrest, at times approaching anarchy. A recalcitrant white citizenry, invidious legislation, killings, riots, and vigilante judiciary would leave the body politic in sordid disarray. Words seldom heard before became commonplace: state's rights, interposition, nullification, massive resistance, miscegenation, amalgamation. The groundswell saw the region's most urbane and intelligent legislators and governors passing panic statutes

---

1. Caudill, "An Oral History with Will D. Campbell."
2. Ibid.

as futile and ludicrous as a scholarly search for the hypotenuse of a circle.³

By early August 1954, the Campbells had relocated to Oxford, Mississippi, presuming that they had found their niche and would be there for the rest of their lives. Soon, discussions of school desegregation not only monopolized the attention of the university and state at large, but also gave rise to individuals like Judge Tom Brady, whose *Black Monday* spawned White Citizens Councils in Mississippi and throughout the South. Such backlash against the *Brown* decision actually clarified Campbell's vocation and focused his time and energies at Ole Miss. His work in the area of race relations earned him not only the ire of Mississippi's segregationist forces, but also the condemnation of the "good men" of the university administration who were still unwilling to stand up to the bigots and reactionaries. One of Campbell's first efforts involved Providence Farm, an interracial intentional community in Holmes County, Mississippi—a kindred spirit with Jordan's Kononia Farm near Americus, in southwest Georgia. Another centered on his bid to bring Episcopal priest Alvin Kershaw to campus to speak during Religious Emphasis Week—derisively called on the university's frat row "Be Good to God Week." Kershaw had recently made headlines when he won $32,000 on the popular TV game show "The $64,000 Question." When asked what he might do with his newfound fortune, Kershaw had announced that he and his wife would donate part of his winnings to a few agencies "laboring for justice and brotherhood in the world." In a subsequent interview, Kershaw listed CARE, UNICEF, and the NAACP as specific examples of such worthy agencies. "As Southerners," Kershaw explained, he and his wife "felt a deep responsibility in the desegregation work of the NAACP," and had been active members in the organization for several years.⁴

> ### CLARENCE JORDAN AND THE KONONIA COMMUNITY
> Clarence Jordan (1912–1969) was a Georgia native who earned an undergraduate degree in agriculture from the Univ. of Georgia, and a PhD in Greek from the Southern Baptist Theological Seminary in Louisville,

---

3. Campbell, *Providence*, 5.

4. Kershaw, "Open Letter to the Student Body of the University of Mississippi," undated. Will D. Campbell Papers. McCain Library and Archives.

> KY. Perhaps best known for his "Cotton Patch" paraphrase of the New Testament, in 1942, Jordan launched an intentional Christian community in Sumter County, Georgia. This "Koinonia" community would be God's demonstration plot—the living embodiment of what the church was literally called to be in the mid-20th century American South. Because Jordan advocated complete and unwavering integration, pacifism, and biblically based communal ownership of property, his neighbors burned Koinonia's buildings, shot at Koinonia families, and sought to boycott them out of existence. When Jordan died in 1969, for example, Kononia members had to take his body to Americus because the Sumter County emergency medical services honored the boycott and would not come to the Farm. The coroner even returned Jordan's body nude, with his possessions in a paper bag. In life and death, Jordan was a prophet without honor—Campbell's kind of churchman. Knowing him well and loving him deeply, Jordan provided Campbell with endless hope and inspiration.

Not long thereafter, Jimmy Morrow Jr., Rankin County's representative in Mississippi's lower house, learned that Kershaw was on Campbell's list of speakers for Ole Miss's Religious Emphasis Week. Although Kershaw's topic was to be the "religious insights of contemporary literature" and not the NAACP or the issue of segregation, Morrow filed a "vigorous protest" with Gov. White, Governor-Elect Coleman, and Ole Miss Chancellor J. D. Williams. The *Jackson Daily News* also ran a bald threat announcing "a protest against the appearance of Mr. Kershaw has been filed by the headquarters of the Mississippi Citizen's Council, and it can be stated with assurance that the Citizen's Council will see to it that Mr. Kershaw does not appear before the student body of the University of Mississippi." Mississippi's segregationist forces were mobilizing against Kershaw and Campbell.[5]

Campbell recalls the evening when the Ole Miss campus police arrived sometime after midnight to escort him immediately to the chancellor's residence. Upon arrival, Campbell found not only the university's chancellor, J. D. Williams, and the vice-chancellor present, but as much tension as he had ever felt in a room. The administration's unequivocal

---

5. *Jackson Daily News* editorial, November 9, 1955. Will D. Campbell Papers. McCain Library and Archives.

order was for Campbell to rescind Kershaw's invitation. Campbell obfuscated, arguing that he lacked the authority to comply with the administration's request because the student body's Committee of One Hundred had officially designed the Religious Emphasis Week program. Thus, Campbell suggested, the Chancellor would need to take his "request" to the Committee of One Hundred. In fact, the committee had essentially rubber-stamped the slate of speakers Campbell had put in front of them. The Ole Miss administration, of course, abided none of Campbell's diversions and reiterated their *order* to withdraw Kershaw's invitation.

Campbell complied with the university's dictates, but he had one more card to play. He created a "sympathy strike," asking all the invited speakers to withdraw from Religious Emphasis Week.[6] Campbell also networked with local ministers to confirm that they would refuse any offer to fill the speakers' void. With all the speakers having joined the Campbell-led boycott, Campbell then dramatized the protest by convening silent sit-ins in Fulton Chapel during the times when the sessions were originally scheduled. Each morning he positioned two empty chairs on the chapel stage, and had them fixed by spotlights. Campbell and fellow dissenters then sat in Fulton Chapel silently "mediating upon the things that had brought us to such a sad day." According to Will, each day some 500-800 protesters joined him in silence in Fulton Chapel. Although the collapse of "Be Good to God Week" proved a coup for Campbell and an embarrassment for the university administration, his days in Oxford were clearly numbered.[7]

Other racial "incidents" followed, including an innocuous pingpong match on campus between Campbell and a Baptist clergy colleague who happened to be African-American. The "audacity" of Campbell to socialize with African-Americans on campus led to further harassment, and drew additional unsolicited lectures from administrators. Evidently Dean Les Love kept instructing Will that an "educated" individual knew how to adapt to circumstances. Tensions culminated a few days later when someone placed human feces in the punch bowl at a student party

---

6. One of the invited speakers who joined Campbell's boycott of Ole Miss's Religious Emphasis Week over the Kershaw affair was Birmingham's Rabbi Milton Grafman. Leader of Temple Emanu-El, Rabbi Grafman was also one of Birmingham's eight white clergy members who, in 1963, published an open letter to Martin Luther King Jr., suggesting that King's Birmingham campaign was unwise and ill-advised. This open letter signed by Grafman prompted King's classic "Letter from a Birmingham Jail."

7. Caudill, "An Oral History with Will D. Campbell."

Campbell coordinated at the YMCA. Finding it "difficult to adjust to fecal punch," Campbell began to reconsider his latest professional assignment. Moreover, he told Wake Forest friend and mentor, McLeod Bryan, he had already come to see the "Y" at Ole Miss as little more than "a public relations gimmick for the University to convince the downstate mothers and Delta tycoons that their sons and daughters are in a good clean healthy atmosphere when they come to Oxford." By October 1, therefore, Campbell had chosen "of his own free will and accord without reservation, hesitation, equivocation or secret evasion" to resign. Perhaps as one of the more telling pieces of Will's severance package, the Ole Miss Board gave Campbell a nice Samsonite suitcase.[8]

In fact, the year 1956 proved a watershed year for Campbell. In addition to his campus ministry work at Ole Miss and its attendant controversies, he was beginning to make critical and promising contacts with a number of individuals and groups in the emerging modern civil rights movement, e.g., Martin Luther King Jr. and the Montgomery Improvement Association. This was also the year in which his brother and closest friend, Joe, now a pharmacist in Meridian, Mississippi, began a habit of drug abuse that would lead to a decade of addiction, personality change, domestic violence, the destruction of Joe's marriage, and—finally—Joe's own self-destruction. As is clear from Campbell's sensitive and revealing account of these years in *Brother to a Dragonfly*, Joe's deterioration was a wrenching, exhausting, and immensely painful process for the younger brother. During this period Will reversed his previous dependence on Joe, becoming the stronger, more mature leader of the two. Perhaps this role generated some of the fortitude Will would need during the civil rights decade to come. Leaving Ole Miss in 1956 also marked a change in vocation when will took a newly created position with the National Council of Churches of Christ (NCC).

8. Campbell, "Letter to Dr. McLeod Bryan," 6 January 1959. Will D. Campbell Papers. McCain Library and Archives.

FORMAL CIVIL RIGHTS WORK

On December 1, 1955, the very day Rosa Parks refused to give up her seat on a Montgomery bus, the NCC's General Board announced that civil rights concerns were overwhelming its Department of Racial and Cultural Relations. Little could the board anticipate how quickly the challenges would now emerge. The board wisely authorized its Division of Christian Life to seek new funding to hire an additional staff person, someone located in the South, to help the decidedly un-Southern NCC respond to the needs of the moment. With an initial three-year grant in place, the NCC launched its Nashville-based Southern Project in October 1956. Will Campbell would be the "Associate Executive Director of the Department of Racial and Cultural Relations of the Division of Christian Life and Work of the National Council of Churches of Christ in the USA." Despite the impressive title, Campbell's NCC job description was remarkably vague. The document outlining Campbell's position, entitled "Plans for the Southern Project," proved a catch-all list of responsibilities. Because of the lack of clarity, Will's Southern Project ended up providing aid, support, and counsel to almost anything churches and denominations were, if anything, already doing. Among other things, this meant the NCC expected Campbell to:

1. serve as a liaison between "persons and groups subjected to economic pressures as a result of race tensions";
2. "gather facts regarding race relations in the South," and to disseminate such information to denominations and inter-denominational agencies engaged in social action. This included developing a roster of churches in the South that had been active in advancing race relations. By January 1960, Campbell had developed an honor roll of forty-two such congregations and their ministers;
3. hold and attend conferences on race relations;

4. function as a resource person for literature and materials on race relations, and if necessary write the necessary literature himself.¹

Will was, in other words, the NCC's ombudsman on all things related to race in the South. The NCC's J. Quinter Miller, for example, queried Campbell about Martin Luther King Jr., inquiring, "What is your general appraisal of Martin Luther King's standing in both the Negro and white communities of the south? Would you think of him highly as a speaker for the General Assembly of the National Council in Saint Louis in December?"² No small challenge for Campbell, drafting a letter of recommendation for Martin Luther King Jr.

Years later Campbell reflected that the job came without concrete instructions. Events were so fluid at the moment no one could write a clear job description. Relishing his newfound freedom as well as the excitement and drama of the time, Campbell became a kind of itinerant troubleshooter in the civil rights movement. Although in retrospect Will sometimes discounts his role, in fact he was living his ministry of reconciliation. He was a prophet of justice to the New South, a mediator between distrustful groups, and an interpreter of events always pointing, full of hope, toward the Beloved Community. Will's self-created job description was to serve as a "missioner to the Confederacy, bridge between black and white, challenging the recalcitrant, exposing the gothic politics of the degenerate southland; prophet with a Bible in one hand and a well worn copy of W. J. Cash [*The Mind of the South*] in the other."³ He became a trusted advisor to many in the movement, a wise strategist closely in touch with the overall picture, and a skilled and sensitive pastor between conflicting parties. This meant Campbell spent considerable time interpreting the rapidly unfolding civil rights events to mostly white, mainline churches north and south—churches that still presumed civil rights to be a so-called "black concern."

The choice of Nashville as Campbell's headquarters was strategic. In an August 1957 memo sent to "All Human Relations Personnel in the South," Campbell noted that Nashville was a tactical "target city," which he jokingly noted was probably a "euphemism for 'let's all get shot

---

1. "Plans for the Southern Project," undated. Will D. Campbell Papers. McCain Library and Archives.

2. Campbell, "Letter to J. Quinter Miller," dated 14 February 1957. Will D. Campbell Papers. McCain Library and Archives.

3. Campbell, *Forty Acres and a Goat*, 5.

together.'" On the one hand, Nashville was sufficiently "Deep South" to have a variety of racists with which to contend. Among these he listed as "potentially most dangerous," John Kasper and his "fifty to seventy-five hard core followers." The Ku Klux Klan had a presence in town, but its "three hundred to five thousand" adherents were largely unorganized, and luckily distrusted Kasper and his cronies. Nashville was also home to the Tennessee Federation for Constitutional Government, comprised of Dixiecrats from the 1948 presidential election and other "white collar race baiters." The fact that Donald Davidson, an English professor from Vanderbilt University, chaired the Federation lent the organization an air of respectability.[4]

John Seigenthaler Sr. has often described Jim Crow Nashville as a city as segregated as any in South Africa at the height of Apartheid. Nevertheless, Nashville had a variety of community resources upon which Campbell could draw. Unlike other Southern cities, for example, Nashville had two African-Americans serving on the city council, with African-American turnout already representing about 30 percent of the local vote. Nashville's religious community also included several progressive leaders representing the Jewish, Catholic, and Protestant traditions. Fisk University's Charles S. Johnson had hosted a Race Relations Institute for some twenty years before Campbell arrived, drawing notable progressives to town annually. The Nashville Community Relations Conference represented some six hundred citizens who in the mid-50s actively supported the implementation of the Supreme Court's *Brown* decision. And then there was Kelly Miller Smith Jr., who had moved to Nashville in 1951 to take the pulpit of the First Baptist Church, Capitol Hill. The influence of Rev. Smith on Campbell is incalculable.

Campbell quickly immersed himself in his new work. From his Nashville base, for example, in the fall of 1956 Campbell drove to Anderson County, in eastern Tennessee, contacting all the white ministers in Clinton, soliciting their support and participation in the desegregation of Clinton's city schools. Hardly given to blind optimism anyway, Campbell was chastened by the effort, finding few ministers ready to join the work. "One man I spoke with was the Baptist minister there [Paul Turner], and I came away thinking 'of all the people I've talked to, here's a man who's never going to move away from his great big million dollar steeple. He's

---

4. "Memorandum," dated 20 August 1957. Will D. Campbell Papers. Southern Baptist Historical Library and Archives.

got it made.'" Much to Campbell's surprise, however, Turner soon risked life and profession to escort nine black children to school in Clinton. For his efforts, some of the good citizens of Clinton beat Turner "half to death."[5]

Even in this initial engagement, Campbell manifested a distinctive trademark. He avoided both political power plays, and an easy demonization of the so-called "other side." "In any concern for social justice," Campbell told the NCC in his 1959 report, "the soul of the racist must concern us as much as the suffering of the victim, and when it does not we are being something less than Christian." "How shall we work with the segregationist?" Campbell asks. By proclaiming that the gospel "was and is a message of redemption. The gospel was and is, God was in Christ, reconciling the world to himself . . . God was in Christ reconciling the world to one another and thus to himself. . . . God was in Christ loving him, accepting him, forgiving him . . . even if he is not yet able to love and accept his brother as himself. Tell him this," Campbell concludes, "and if he hears it, believes, it, and accepts it as his gospel he is a lot closer to an integrated church in an integrated society than if he is told that he 'ought' to be a good boy and obey the law."[6]

Campbell tried to be loving and consistent, even with the segregationist ringleader in the Clinton contest, John Kasper. For spreading his racist invective, Anderson County authorities charged and tried Kasper. Campbell noted, "I very much opposed the charges, you know. It seemed to me they were infringing on his freedom of speech. There was no doubt that his freedom of speech started riots in Clinton and Nashville, but freedom of speech can lead to all kinds of places."[7] One of those "places" where honest and respectful dialogue might actually lead could be "reconciliation." Instead of utilizing the power of government to coerce, defeat, and silence the segregationist, Campbell preferred to hear and learn from individuals like Kasper. For Campbell the common ground for productive engagement was neither public policy nor constitutional rights, but commitments like "grace, redemption, and judgment." Instead of a patronizing brow-beating of the racist, Campbell sought points of theological rapprochement. So, he thanked

---

5. Caudill, "An Oral History with Will D. Campbell."

6. Campbell, "The Church in the Midst of Changing Racial Patterns," dated 3 December 1959. Will D. Campbell Papers. McCain Library and Archives, 3.

7. Wray, "Interview of Will D. Campbell," 15.

the segregationist for "forcing us to re-examine the nature of God and man, the redemptive purpose of Jesus Christ and the judgment of God."[8] Here, Campbell believed, were the essential means by which to expose prejudice as a matter of bad cultural formation, and an opportunity to reassert reconciliation as integral to Christianity's *kerygma*—rather than a political tactic or legal strategy.

Even while seeking opportunities to thank racists, Campbell worked hand-in-hand with his colleagues to address the reality that Jim Crow was a persistent member at far too many churches. Campbell worked with Howard "Buck" Kester in 1957, for example, to convene the "First Conference on Christianity and Human Relations." Headlining the program would be Morehouse's Benjamin Mays and SCLC's Martin Luther King Jr., who could powerfully articulate the gospel of lived reconciliation. Never ones to put a candle under a bushel, Campbell and Kester invited President Dwight Eisenhower, Vice-President Richard Nixon, U.S. Attorney General Herbert Brownell, as well as 4,500 religious leaders. Unfortunately no federal officials accepted their invitations, and only three hundred Southern clergy attended the conference that met at Nashville's Scarritt College for Christian Workers. Despite the much smaller than desired turnout, the conference further connected Campbell to the work of the Southern Christian Leadership Conference (SCLC), which King now chaired.

Campbell had been the only white person admitted to the SCLC's organizing meeting in Atlanta the previous January. At first Campbell encountered some resistance to his presence, but Bayard Rustin personally intervened noting that the future of the organization might utilize the services of someone like Will who could transcend America's racial boundaries. Campbell often downplays his benefit to the SCLC, but the SCLC was of unquestioned importance to Campbell's work. His relationship with the civil rights organization and its affiliates (e.g., the Nashville Christian Leadership Conference) earned him access to events and crises as they were breaking out.

Among these erupting crises were two school desegregation episodes during the fall of 1957. One was in Nashville, the scene of considerable violence. The other, of greater national visibility, was the effort to desegregate Central High School in Little Rock, Arkansas. In Little Rock, Will was one of two white Southern clergymen to escort the nine black

---

8. Campbell, "The Church in the Midst of Changing Racial Patterns," 3.

children through the gauntlet of irate white citizens and the Arkansas National Guard. Ironically, Campbell already knew many of the National Guard personnel because, at that time, he was a chaplain in the Tennessee National Guard and the two state Guards had recently drilled together in Gulfport, Mississippi. Although President Eisenhower finally resolved the crisis by forcing Arkansas's governor, Orval Fabus, to comply, the school desegregation conflicts—and other civil rights confrontations—continued unabated across the nation for the next dozen years or more. Campbell seems to have been present at most of these hot spots, working quietly for racial justice and reconciliation.

Back in Nashville, Campbell was a key behind-the-scenes agent in the 1960 trailblazing sit-in movement, designed and launched in Nashville. The "Children," as older Nashvillians sometimes dubbed them, were students from schools like Nashville's American Baptist College, Fisk University, Meharry Medical College, and Tennessee State University. The principal Nashville corps, mentored by James Lawson, included John Lewis, Diane Nash, Bernard Lafayette, James Bevel, C. T. Vivian, and Marion Berry, to name a few. Baptized in fire by the 1960 sit-ins, these went on to form the Student Nonviolent Coordinating Committee (a birth that Campbell observed with Ella Baker and others), and to sustain the Freedom Rides in 1961. Campbell's role in the Nashville story was strategic and diplomatic, laboring closely with his friend, colleague, and movement leader, Kelly Miller Smith. At one point when the violence in Nashville seemed most explosive, Smith and Campbell tried to convince John Lewis to take a couple days off from marching and protesting. "Let things calm down and cool off some," they encouraged Lewis and the student leaders. Campbell remembers that he was the last to speak and tried to reason: "John [Lewis], you have agreed that to have demonstrations is more than apt to result in serious violence or loss of life, yet you still say 'We're going to march.' It seems to me that it's just a matter of your own hubris, you know." Lewis, Campbell recalls, would have none of it. "I never knew 'til I read his book, *Walking with the Wind*," Campbell confessed, "it never hit me what that young fellow, who was seventeen years old, said—that our vocation is to do what we are called to do at that point. It never hit me what a radical statement that young fellow had made. The response to their vocation—we are called to march, we are called to break down the wall of separation between black and white people in America. Whatever forces try to stop it we can't control that. It's not our business."⁹

As the tension escalated and the demonstrators were arrested, Campbell served as eyes and ears for the movement, gathering information and keeping unofficial lines of communication open within the community. He could talk easily with Nashville police, for example, learning which students had been arrested and where they were being held. In his interview for the Nashville Civil Rights Oral History project, James Lawson detailed how he and others relied on Campbell as their eyes and ears on the streets, watching the protests and taking notes—wisely counting on Campbell's surveillance for "needed courtroom testimony." Given the state of justice in Nashville at that time, having a white defense witness could help make a black defendant's case. Occasionally, Will's role was as simple as letting the student activists use his NCC telephone credit card, so they could continue their work. At other times, Campbell served as an unofficial "Human Relations advisor" for the community. He could be the liaison between the Mayor's office and the Movement leadership, or between the merchants who owned the targeted lunch counters and student protesters.

Campbell also entered the fury raging at Vanderbilt University over his friend James Lawson. A Methodist minister, Lawson had spent time in the early 1950s as a missionary in India studying Gandhi's philosophy. Inspired by King's success in Montgomery in 1955, Lawson then returned to the U.S. where King and The Fellowship of Reconciliation's A. J. Muste personally encouraged Lawson to move to Nashville—a moderate Southern state capital ripe for activism. Arriving in this self-proclaimed "Athens of the South," Lawson enrolled in Vanderbilt's Divinity School. He also contacted the NCC's representative, Will Campbell, and it was at one of Lawson's visits to Campbell's office, that the young seminarian met Dorothy Wood—Campbell's secretary. Jim and Dorothy soon married, but not without some protest from Will. "I knew Jim Lawson would be in trouble until the day he died, and I didn't think she was strong enough to take that, but I was bad wrong," Campbell later acknowledged.¹⁰ Lawson soon began to offer Nashville's students "extracurricular" classes in the theory and practice of nonviolence. His syllabus took students through

---

9. Wray, "Interview of Will D. Campbell," 24.
10. Ibid., 16.

an investigation of both biblical and Gandhian approaches, studying and practicing nonviolent responses to brutality. Lawson was intentionally working to replicate in Nashville the nonviolent successes Gandhi achieved a generation earlier in Nagpur, India. Once the students were schooled in nonviolence they then chose their mission—the desegregation of Nashville's lunch counters. As the students initiated their strategic plan by sitting in at targeted restaurants in February 1960, Nashville's James Stahlman retaliated by pressuring Vanderbilt chancellor, Harvie Branscomb, to expel Lawson. Stahlman was not only the owner-publisher of *The Nashville Banner* (the city's conservative newspaper), but also a member of Vanderbilt's Board of Trust. Although Lawson was in his final semester at Vanderbilt and poised to receive his BD degree, the chancellor succumbed to pressure and expelled Lawson from the Divinity School. Lawson was inclined to comply with the Board's decision and withdraw from Vanderbilt, but Campbell encouraged Lawson not to go too quietly. Drawing on his own experience at Ole Miss four years earlier, Campbell challenged Lawson to force Vanderbilt's hand. Make them "run you off," Campbell counseled Lawson.

On one level, the "Lawson Affair" ended with the expulsion of Lawson and the departure of the Divinity School's dean, J. Robert Nelson. On another level, the episode forced the Vanderbilt community to clarify its identity and mission from that point forward. As Will Campbell would later confess to Harmon Wray, "We were all just ordinary people fighting it out and in the end there were no heroes."

Since the early 1960s Campbell has always downplayed his role in the civil rights movement, yet others have stressed his contributions. "If there's any unsung hero of the Civil Rights Movement," fellow Nashvillian George Barrett has noted, "it's Will Campbell." Looking back at the movement, Wallace Westfeldt, former network news producer, likewise concluded, "Will was, to me, the most remarkable person in the world" because Campbell was constantly at the center of events. Bernard LaFayette, one of Nashville's student leaders, has also sung Campbell's praises. "Myles Horton, Glenn Smiley, Clarence Jordan, Will Campbell. These men were the practitioners of the Christian faith," LaFayette has noted. "We always consider him [Will], not based on skin color but based on the Christian principles under pressure, this is how Will Campbell is going to act. . . . Under the worst situations, down in McComb [MS] or wherever it was, Will would show up. I guess the Lord had these people like angels, who have reached such a spiritual maturity that they are the benefactors of the whole human family and they see themselves as that."[11]

> ## GEORGE BARRETT
>
> Often finding himself in need of legal services in the '60s, Campbell frequently found support from fellow iconoclast George Barrett. Like Campbell, Barrett has a storied resume. Even before his collaborations with Campbell, Barrett established his reputation by defending the Highlander Folk School from legal challenges. In 1960 Barrett represented students arrested in the sit-ins, and continued his advocacy on their behalf when he and Campbell traveled to Montgomery in 1961 to protect the savagely attacked Freedom Riders. Barrett oversaw the legal transformation of the Fellowship of Southern Churchmen into the Committee of Southern Churchmen. When Anthony Towne submitted his incendiary "Revolution and the Marks of Baptism," Campbell turned to Barrett for legal advice on potential federal prosecution and retribution if *Katallagete* published the essay. Barrett, moreover, helped Campbell and the Committee develop a strategy to sue the state of Tennessee and the University of Tennessee Board of Regents when the state planned a major building campaign for the University of Tennessee–Nashville, while the facilities at nearby, and historically African-American, Tennessee State University languished.
>
> As kindred spirits and friends, when George's mother, Ms. Annie Barrett, passed away in the mid 1960s, Campbell and the Committee paid for the funeral Mass to be said at the Abbey of Gethsemani, Fr. Thomas Merton officiating.

When it came to the civil rights movement, Campbell seemed nearly ubiquitous. Early in 1961, for example, Campbell was part of a delegation of white Southern progressive leaders who met with the new Attorney General, Robert Kennedy, to discuss civil rights issues. The Attorney General assured Campbell and others that the new administration had a fine working relationship with FBI Director J. Edgar Hoover, and that the federal government would be using new electronic listening devices to detect Southern subversives. Campbell astutely sensed that Kennedy's assurances actually supported his long-time suspicion that

---

11. Interviews in the Nashville Civil Rights Oral History project, appended to Wray's "Interview of Will D. Campbell," 43–51.

state and local law enforcement authorities had been surveilling black leaders and white progressives, and not simply segregationist subversives, in this manner for some time. This revelation affirmed Campbell's inclination that the federal government was at best selective, and probably ambivalent toward civil rights.

Despite his services to the cause, Campbell still wrestled with feelings of inadequacy, i.e., being little more than another guilty bystander—especially when racists unleashed their fury on the protesting "Children." In his memoirs he would write:

> Perhaps I was also bothered that while others have been killed, jailed, or beaten, my participation in the Movement had been from a relatively safe distance. In fact, other than a few rejections by old friends and relatives, occasional threats and late night phone calls, I had not suffered at all. I rationalized that there were many roles to be played by many different individuals, and that my role was one of reporter, observer, liaison, between black and white, negotiator between merchants, mayors, media, and Movement. But as I sat with my friend [T. J. Eakes] that windy March afternoon, heard the story of brutality told with a voice of dejection and loneliness, smelling the foul symbol of bigotry wafting from [the police-inflicted wound on T. J.'s] head, the justification was cumbersome.

Perhaps looking for some absolution from his imaginary African-American confessor, Campbell conceded to T. J., "You know, sometimes I get tired of working behind the scenes." Refusing to assuage Campbell's guilt so easily, Eakes responds, "Yeah, I guess it does get kind of crowded back there sometimes."[12]

Clearly, Campbell refused to see the movement as an abstract political philosophy, or policy issue. Campbell was much more interested in discerning the human crisis at hand than debating the finer points of public administration and theory. This comes through in the introduction to his September 19, 1963, convocation address at the Pittsburgh Theological Seminary. The previous Sunday morning a bomb had ripped through Birmingham's Sixteenth Avenue Baptist Church, killing four young girls. As an impromptu preface to his formal presentation, Campbell scribbled the following thoughts.

---

12. Campbell, *Forty Acres and a Goat*, 105–6.

I suppose some of you expect me to say something about Birmingham, since I am an American Christian. And I had thought that I would, until yesterday when I tried to figure out what it would be. What do you say about four children getting killed while trying to worship God? "I'm sorry?" I didn't go to the funeral yesterday. I had a reservation and an airline ticket, but I didn't go. For, you see, I killed them along with your help. So I didn't go. There is something at once damning and redemptive in looking at what one has done, but I couldn't stand the damnation, so I stand before you without the redemption. I foxed the police experts whose theory is that one always returns to the scene of the crime. You see, I'm smarter than they are so I didn't go. And you didn't go either because you are smarter than they are too and you helped me, your cousin from Mississippi, do it. So, here we are, both of us, refusing to face the damnation, without the redemption. Where do we go from here?[13]

13. Will D. Campbell Papers. McCain Library and Archives.

CRASHING THE IDOLS OF THE NATIONAL COUNCIL OF CHURCHES

EARLY ON IN HIS work with the NCC, Will Campbell thought the most liberal, progressive, and ecumenical religious organization in the country would provide the freedom he failed to find in the parish or the academy. He thought he had found a new home, one with the most compassionate, righteous, and courageous men and women—black and white, Northern and Southern—of his time. Increasingly Campbell realized that the NCC reasoned in simplistic patterns—thoughts not dissimilar to those of the segregationists.

In fact, seeds sown back in 1955 at the Providence Cooperative Farm were germinating in Campbell's consciousness. On the surface, the all-too-predictable, bigoted reaction of Holmes County to that experiment in godly justice seemed to incarnate "the good fight" in the "evil South." Like Jordan's Koinonia, Campbell believed Providence was closer to the church, the actual incarnate body of Christ, than anything the "steeples" had to offer. Providence was "ecumenism in bootleg vestments;" "an unlikely assemblage. Presbyterians, Disciples, Southern Baptists. In a house whose doors had been open to Protestants, Jews, and Catholics. Atheists and doubters. Foreigners and native born."[1] Even though Providence seemed like the closest thing to heaven on earth that he had found, Will came to realize that he still could not easily damn those five hundred "rednecks" who voted to expel God's Providence from Holmes County, Mississippi. Far from condoning their actions, he began to see in "the enemy" his own "convoluted birthright." "I knew that those who had attended the mass meeting in Holmes County where my friends had been summarily tried, convicted, and sentenced to exile, were no different from those from whose loins I had sprung in Amite County, Mississippi. I knew their essential impulses were honorable."[2]

1. Campbell, *Providence*, 18.
2. Ibid., 111.

Will began to rethink original sin, "a doctrine I had been taught but never really believed before." In the process, Will realized that these five hundred bigots were not the real powerbrokers.

> Many of them were poor laborers and sharecroppers, individuals who were little better off than the Negroes they were there to oppose. Called "rednecks" by the insensitive, they had competed with the Freedmen and women following the Civil War, and the competition for bread and status had never abated. It is the tragedy of the poor, white, rural working class of the South, those called rednecks, my people, to choose the wrong enemy.

If he could simply dismiss the racists as inhuman or "just wicked," Will would need to have no sympathy for them at all. "Still," he confessed, "I was haunted by the thought that all of them were there [at the meeting to close Providence] out of certainty that their cause was just, right, and necessary, with minds muzzled by something as deep and faraway as the Edenic fall and as near at hand as the rhetoric of election year." Mississippi's powers manipulated the "rednecks," just as they had the African-Americans.[3]

In its own way, the principality known as the NCC thought and acted in a similar fashion. The NCC presumed that if its "good" institution and agents could devise the right strategic plan and implement it with effective technique, then *it* could defeat the "bad" segregationists. Such institutional self-righteousness, of course, never squared with Campbell's theological orientation. Why not trust the gospel, Campbell wondered. Campbell wrote to Grover Bagby of the NCC's General Board of Social Concerns, describing the situation in Birmingham and articulating his concerns. Having marked his letter "Confidential," Campbell sarcastically lamented,

> We just can't quite trust the power of the Gospel message. There just *must* be something we can add, some gimmick, some technique, some strategy. Just this once I wanted to rely *only* upon this [the gospel] and if it wasn't enough then let it not be enough. I am more and more convinced that it is enough if our witness to it is faithful. I am likewise more and more convinced that it is all we have to offer as the Church.[4]

---

3. Ibid., 22–23.

4. Campbell, "Letter to Grover Bagby," November 5, 1964, Will D. Campbell Papers. McCain Library and Archives.

Because God had already achieved reconciliation, God had already overcome the deficient and misguided. "The question is not 'Will the churches unite to build a kingdom?'" he argued. "The question is 'Here is a kingdom already. Will we enter it and bid others to enter it, reminding them that it is a kingdom beyond caste?' This is my quarrel with the NCC," Campbell concluded. "There is too much trying to create a kingdom and not enough bidding" for all to enter humbly into the casteless, reconciled community that God has *already* created.[5]

Campbell increasingly learned that even the movement could degenerate into a contest of self-assured principalities and sanctimonious powers. While straining to resolve their preferred "justice" issue of the day (e.g., where one could get a hamburger or seats on public conveyances), the contending parties left unattended the larger issues of rank economic exploitation and division. In other words, civil rights institutions often failed to unite the "pulpwood hauler and the pulpwood broker, the sheriff and the blacks in the street, none of whom are wielders of much power."[6] Many presumed the civil rights movement to be some profound revolution. Campbell began to discern that the powers-that-be indulged the poor to fight in the movement so long as their fight was among themselves. Campbell, therefore, ruefully asked:

> Why didn't the Movement picket the City Club and the Belle Meade Country Club instead of F.W. Woolworth? Why didn't we know that it was they who could make a difference, who would finally decide? Why did we incur the wrath of the boys who had come to town to get their hair cut at the Barber College for a quarter and who, finally, would not even be a party to the truce? Why didn't we go to the clubs and tell them that we had come to break bread with them? And when they refused tell that we were Lazarus there to gather the crumbs from the table of Dives? Were we demanding of the patricians that they force the plebeians of all colors to eat together while they remained unaffected behind the dividing wall of affluence?[7]

To the extent that the NCC, or another institution or agency, pitted one group against another according to race or class—no matter how laudable the cause or devious the offender—it was divisive and unChristian.

---

5. "New Sermon of the Church," undated. Will D. Campbell Papers. McCain Library and Archives.

6. Campbell, *Forty Acres and a Goat*, 250.

7. Ibid., 273.

In the early 1960s, Campbell's speeches and writings—notably *Race and the Renewal of the Church* (1962)—increasingly took on this deeper, more nuanced, and biblically prophetic tone. Campbell saw himself as a reporter, but in fact he was a prophet exposing the educational and political idols American Christians tended to worship. Thus, his message became that of the non-aligned churchperson witnessing to the communion of saints what he saw, in explicitly biblical and theological language. Campbell saw, for example, the ubiquity of sin, the idolatry of progress, and the apostasy of churches.

In the mid-1950s, Campbell's experiences with the Ole Miss administration along with the Religious Emphasis Week and the fecal punch episodes had revealed to him that academic chaplaincy was not his vocation—the ivory tower could never deliver the social transformation and reconciliation he had sought. Similarly, two events in the early 1960s helped to crystallize for Campbell both his vocational homelessness and the impotence of the NCC to provoke the needed social conversion. When he wrote a brief article about the Albany Movement for the 19 September 1962 issue of *The Christian Century*, some within the liberal church took issue with Campbell's description of the campaign. Ms. Miriam Brattain of Riverside Drive in New York City, for example, wrote Will lamenting "What a queer article!"[8] What bothered Ms. Brattain and many other good liberals was Will's audacity to call the notorious Albany sheriff, Laurie Pritchett, "a good man." Campbell even seemed to side with Pritchett's indictment that the "praying-in" Northern clergy, whom the sheriff arrested, ought to "go back and preach to your own congregations, convert your own cities before you come here to convert us." Campbell further shocked readers by highlighting the "complexity of human sin" manifested on the streets of Albany. Instead of a simplistic depiction of the Albany campaign as an assault of "the good" against "the evil," Campbell was nuanced and ambiguous. He explained how after watching Sheriff Pritchett arrest scores of clergy, he "hurried back to Cedar Street, back to the headquarters of the Albany Movement" where "[e]verything seemed the same—well oiled, efficient, polished. No worse off. No better off." Campbell then wondered aloud and quite cryptically: "The *church*! What about the church? Well perhaps. And maybe." Instead of the shout of victorious triumph, Campbell struck a

---

8. Personal letter to Will Campbell, dated 16 October 1962. Will D. Campbell Papers. McCain Library and Archives.

tone of uncertain tragedy. A message unlikely either to sell copies of the *Century*, or to promote the movement.

As Campbell would later note, too many white liberals in the civil rights movement failed to look beyond the immediate symptoms of injustice to see the larger tragedy of human sin. "In a tragedy you really don't take sides with any satisfaction. Who are you going to blame in all of those things?" In classic tragedies, by the end of the drama, "everyone is involved and may be lying dead on the stage." All are at some level innocent and guilty—none with an easy, clear, good choice. Once one appreciates "tragedy," "you quit blaming one side or the other. You quit choosing up sides, and you start to minister wherever the hurt is, as best you can."[9] Campbell's iconoclastic vocation was coming ever sharper.

Campbell also ruffled liberal feathers in the Albany campaign when he and Andrew Young chose to bail out the arrested Northern clergy with all *deliberate* speed. In the Albany Movement, numerous clergy had flown in to Atlanta and bused the 180 miles south to Albany, zealous to have a "Sheriff Pritchett arrest" added to their movement vita. In fact when they arrived in Georgia, the clergy deposited their bail money in a special account so as to expedite their release. Campbell and Young thought this tourist approach to civil disobedience "did not count." Having gone to all that trouble, Young and Campbell thought it down right inhospitable both to the sheriff and the "tourists" themselves to bail everyone out so quickly. Such an immediate release would not only deny the arrested clergy their full measure of participation in the movement, but offend Sheriff Pritchett who had gone to such trouble to find the clergy accommodations in some of the most rank and disgusting jails in southern Georgia. Young and Campbell, therefore, chose to provide the protesters some unscheduled contemplative time. "Some of them, sure enough, were awfully mad when we got them out," Campbell remembers. These clergy members who came simply to add a new line on their civil rights résumé said, "Now look. We agreed to come and be arrested. We didn't agree to come down here and stay overnight in this nasty, rotten jail [with] no air conditioning, no cigarettes, no beer, nothing but Georgia heat."[10]

Campbell received some critical comments on his work in Albany and on the *Christian Century* article, but at the time that seemed like a

9. Caudill, "An Oral History with Will D. Campbell."
10. Ibid.

mere ripple. The more serious, and more revelatory, event came with the NCC's National Conference on Religion and Race. Held in Chicago, January 14–17, 1963, the conference was to commemorate the centennial of the Emancipation Proclamation, and to provide religious representatives an opportunity to speak with one voice about racial harmony and integration. Some 650 delegates representing 70 religious groups attended this major conference, jointly convened by the Social Action Department of the National Catholic Welfare Conference, the Social Action Commission of the Synagogue Council of America, and Campbell's own Department of Racial and Cultural Relations of the NCC. Campbell's assigned topic was "The Inner Life of the Church and Synagogue" and, in accordance with instructions, he provided an early copy of his text for the benefit of the press.

Will's manuscript, however, utterly scandalized his NCC superiors when they saw it. Instead of celebrating the Emancipation Proclamation, the U.S. Constitution, or the federal machinery promoting integration, Campbell centered his remarks on the sovereignty of God, the universality of human sinfulness, and the theological irrelevance of race. In the presentation Campbell had the audacity to call for repentance from both the *integrationists* in the churches (the self-assured "good guys"), as well as *segregationists* throughout society (the all-too-obvious "bad guys"). Wanting to protect the celebratory spirit of the conference, Campbell's NCC superiors forced him to strike from his prepared remarks one segment of his manuscript deemed particularly disconcerting:

> [I]n our generation white children will be marched into gas chambers by dark skinned masters, clutching their little toys to their breasts in Auschwitz fashion. Our generation may well see senile whites forced to dig their own mass graves by a heavily pigmented Eichmann. If we doubt this we have only to examine the Jewish and Christian understanding of the nature of man, and the pages of human history to see it as more than a slight possibility.[11]

Presumably, it was fine to point out that blacks were equally good with whites, but Will found himself absolutely forbidden to express the corollary—that African-Americans could be equally fallen.

The gall and presumption of the national organization struck Campbell yet again. First, the contested passage was a quote directly from his

---

11. Campbell, "The Inner Life of the Church and Synagogue in Race Relations" (manuscript). Will D. Campbell Papers. McCain Library and Archives.

Race and the Renewal of the Church, released months earlier (see page 75 below). Had no one in the NCC bureaucracy bothered to read the book? If they were already aware of the passage, was it not disingenuous for his NCC superiors to balk at his point in this speech while ignoring it in print? Second, Campbell knew African-American leadership to be "sophisticated, superior, and nonviolent," but white liberals at the NCC had created a fictional, desirable African-American, "pretending as if all black people looked like Lena Horne and had minds like Ralph Bunche." Campbell realized that the fabrication said more about the NCC than the African-American community, and was its own "bigotry in the extreme." "If black people are equally good, black people are equally bad." Otherwise blacks are not really equal, and the goal is not reconciliation.[12]

The NCC organizers told Campbell that he could believe such ideas back in Tennessee, but he could not say them at this convention in Chicago. Campbell yielded to NCC censorship, but offered a pregnant pause when he came to that portion of the manuscript during his oral delivery. The press, of course, had Campbell's original version and had been laying wagers on whether Campbell would actually stick to his manuscript. Under the headline "That Awful Fatalism," *Time* magazine reported in its 25 January issue the excised portion of Campbell's presentation, along with Episcopal layman William Stringfellow's comment that "The most practical thing to do now is to weep." (Stringfellow had also chastised the NCC conference as "too little, too late, and too lily-white.") Responses came quickly. In a letter to *Time*'s editors, (printed in the 15 February issue) Richard Greenleaf explained that Stingfellow was both "controverted in the auditorium and widely denounced in the corridors," while Campbell was simply "ignored." Rev. P. Edgar Williams of Chicago likewise lamented, "I'd hate to think that the best hope we have to offer our people is the philosophy of the Rev. Will D. Campbell." Beyond this unfavorable press, the more formal and long-term consequence of the episode was the strong recommendation that Campbell "go easy," and that he run his manuscripts and speeches through the NCC's Office of Information, "just to make sure we are not playing into the hands of the enemy."[13]

---

12. Caudill, "An Oral History with Will D. Campbell."

13. Campbell, "Letter to R. H. Edwin Espy, Associate General Secretary of the National Council of Churches," dated 27 May 1963; and an unlabeled, undated manuscript. Will D. Campbell Papers. McCain Library and Archives.

Campbell would not yield again. In the midst of the controversy, Campbell admitted to James Holloway, "The liberal brethren seem to be closing in on me a little more each day and I find that I have less patience with them than I do with even the fundies and even the racists." Campbell wondered aloud whether his reaction to the NCC revealed that he was "still a fundy of sorts at heart." Nevertheless, he decided not to "worry too much about it," and instead, "just enjoy disliking the liberals."[14] Later Campbell recalled, "Look, I've worked in the state of Mississippi which was supposed to be one of the more backward, one of the more repressive and fascistic outfits in the country. Nobody ever asked to see a speech I was going to make. They may put shit in my punch; but they're not going to ask me to [submit manuscript drafts for approval], and I'm not going to do it for the allegedly most enlightened, liberal, free organization in the country."[15]

It had happened again, now for the third time. In succession, a local congregation, a university campus, and now an ecumenical religious organization, had each seemed to promise initially the experience of community, fellowship, and freedom for faithful and effective ministry. But in each case, disappointment followed. Will simply could conform neither to the "right" (congregation and university), nor the "left" (the NCC). The NCC presumed he was like them—a liberal white advancing *their* civil rights work. Certainly Will cared about race relations, but not because he was a "white liberal." White liberals, Will discovered, were often too proud, too self-righteous about "God being on their side," and too infatuated with their own contributions to "the cause." Whenever trouble broke out, white liberals would "go racing over to the black community announcing: 'Look. Look. Look. Look. We're one of you.'"[16]

> ### "MILESTONES INTO MILLSTONES"
> Reflecting on civil rights achievements, Campbell warns,
>
> Milestones become millstones when they are celebrated more by the donor than by the recipient. And it is white people who tell the world of

---

14. Campbell, "Letter to James Holloway," dated 4 March 1963. James Holloway Papers. Department of Archives and Special Collections, University of Mississippi.

15. Caudill, "An Oral History with Will D. Campbell."

16. Ibid.

> our gains, not Negroes. . . . Those of us who have argued and worked for desegregation must have assumed that the injection of a few well chosen and well qualified Negroes into the living organism called white society would stimulate the production of sufficient antibodies to deliver us from the deserved wrath of God and wrath of Negroes. What would happen to the unchosen and unqualified did not seem to be a factor, the assumption being that *black* is the antigen and *white* is the living organism. . . . One can examine the milestones one by one and conclude that they are made of white clay, not black stone. The Civil Rights Acts leave the ghettoes intact and the white suburbs safe. The Voting Bill did encourage considerable numbers of Negro voters but it also helped insure the election of several racist governors. The War on Poverty employed a small number of middle class Negroes and a much smaller number of poor Negroes . . .
>
> *Katallagete* (Winter 1966–67)

Never seeking to be "an honorary Negro" himself, Will was unconcerned for accolades or expressions of thanks. He was not looking to make civil rights history. Although his attitude can be read as a kind of false humility, Will did not want to be "a leader in the civil rights movement." In fact, he has argued that, on one level, he "never had any interest in race relations, really." Instead of political and/or social reform, "I was interested in the perpetuation of the Christian faith." To be sure, the Christian faith—as Will has understood it—has volumes to say about race relations and reconciliation. But faithful reconciliation between the races is never measured by "some simple thing of getting black kids into the schoolhouses—as if that would make everything alright. I never believed that."[17] For all of his work in Little Rock, Clinton, Nashville, and beyond, Will came to the conclusion that white liberals had made an idol out of education and social engineering. "It is high time," Campbell warned, that the white liberal "abandon his idol for making civil rights the gospel . . . an idol more dangerous [than] the one the segregationists have worshipped."[18] If we can get "them" into "our" schools, the white liberals reasoned, then "we" will have done "our" part. We shall have overcome, and will live happily ever after. Behind such generous gestures,

17. Ibid.

18. Campbell, "White Liberals are Alright in Their Place," undated manuscript. Will D. Campbell Papers. McCain Library and Archives.

however, the black community would end up indebted to white liberals for reining in the bigots and Klansmen who had oppressed them for so long. Experience had taught Campbell that white liberals were willing to effect surface reforms, but avoided any substantive change that would threaten their own white privilege. At the end of the day, white liberals worked for an outcome that still left them holding the patriarchal power to make ultimate decisions for all of society. Such paternalism William Stringfellow called "the most virulent form of racism in the American inheritance." Instead of being a friend and advocate of the marginalized African-American, white liberals merely offered a different version of oppression. Leave it to Campbell to expose the lie. In late 1962, he wrote to Robert C. Dodds, one time director of the NCC's Planning and Ecumenical Affairs, that the NCC "had not yet learned to work with the predominantly Negro denominations beyond a sentimental and paternalistic level."[19]

Campbell's understanding of Christianity proved qualitatively different from that of progressive white liberals. To him, white mainline churches had identified too opportunistically with the rich and powerful; thinking and acting more like the "Red Cross, the UGF [the United Way], Boy Scouts, League of Women Voters,"[20] or some other civic-minded agency. The church simply aligned itself with the powerful and the rich, mildly counseling the powers-that-be to be compassionate, kind, and charitable with their power and affluence. Where was the unique, scandalous Christian *kerygma* in that? Who is ultimately being helped?

In his prophetic "Inner Life of Church and Synagogue" speech to the 1963 National Conference on Race and Religion, Campbell established that for 2,000 years Jews and Christians had every reason to transcend racial and ethnic barriers of all kinds. Reconciliation, harmony, and unity have always been at the heart of their common story and identity. Nevertheless, both Jews and Christians have compiled a failing record on race. Why? How had people with such a calling missed the obvious so badly, Campbell inquired. He proposed that on one level Walker Percy had rightly diagnosed the problem seven years earlier.

In his 6 July 1956 *Commonweal* essay, "Stoicism in the South," Percy maintained that educated, refined, genteel, old-money Southern whites

---

19. Campbell, "Letter to Robert Dodds," dated 8 November 1962. Will D. Campbell Papers. McCain Library and Archives.
20. Clancy, "Jesus in the Brush Arbor," 231.

had, for generations, overseen race relations, but only as long as they presumed it their paternalistic responsibility to do so. Refereeing the races, in other words, had been one of the political crosses these cultural patricians felt called to bear as part of their privileged birthright. Percy's ultimate point, however, was that the aristocracy's presumption, (i.e., the superior governed the inferior), was a version of Greek Stoicism, rather than a manifestation of Christianity's egalitarian *kerygma*. "How curiously foreign to the South sound the Decalogue, the Beatitudes, the doctrine of the Mystical Body," Percy bemoaned. Campbell could have hardly agreed with Percy more. Affluent Southern whites might practice a social ministry of keeping poor whites from abusing African-Americans, but only so long as both sets of inferiors remained in their assigned social roles, obedient to their superiors. When African-Americans became less deferential and more independent and autonomous—celebrating their biblical equality as children of God—the Southern aristocracy became at least distant and apathetic, if not openly hostile. Following Percy's lead, Campbell explained in his 1961 *Union Seminary Quarterly Review* essay that mainstream Protestant types had indeed reacted to racial problems, but most often with an eye toward conserving society's hierarchical arrangement.[21] Thus, Will concluded, "the South has always been more Greek" in its thinking and practice "than Christian."[22]

As if Old South Stoics were not bad enough, however, the new-money, upwardly mobile Southern white progressives were hardly better —or any more Christian. Unseemly entrepreneurial, opportunistic, and greedy for accolades, their humanitarian concern often established their own reputation. If these social-climbing humanitarian "Christians" could prove that they could effectively control the Southern racist better than the old Southern aristocracy, they would prove their social worth and relevance. They would merit, even if begrudgingly, the respect they so desired from the rest of society, parlaying that respect into rising numbers and power. Campbell's point, however, was that the new, progressives were no more Christian than the old, conservative Stoics. That such humanitarianism was no substitute for the proclamation of the Christian gospel was a central tenant of Campbell's *Race and Renewal*

---

21. Campbell, "The Role of Religious Organizations in the Desegregation Controversy."

22. Campbell, "Democracy and Original Sin," undated, Will D. Campbell Papers. McCain Library and Archives.

of the Church. Those meriting the "Christian" label, Campbell held, were those who comfortably related not to the privileged elite, but to the so-called whores and the scalawags. The Christian quest is not to acquire supremacy and strength, but to be used up in the service of God and humanity. "Jesus said to go and get rid of all that and then come back and they would talk about discipleship," Campbell reminds his readers. "To render ourselves powerless, poor and therefore, in this culture at least, no longer good, would be, in my judgment, the most responsible thing we could do."[23]

Taking his cue from the *kenosis* of Christ as read in Philippians 2, and historically lived in the Anabaptist communities, Campbell contends that disciples renounce the privilege of such power—even when the power is apparently sanctified for the greater good. As disciples, Radical Christians are pledged to the abdication of power rather than its acquisition. Instead of putting themselves and their own progressive social policies front and center, Radical Christians are more likely to abandon their privilege and annihilate their wishes—even foregoing their rights. Moreover, this abnegation is, in the Radical tradition, called "freedom." In "Whose Freedom?" Campbell explained how "Just going around seeking freedom can be a form of arrogance." Too often the quest for civil rights and equality was a search for superiority. "Every man is superior to me in the Christian understanding," Campbell counseled.

> I am his servant and God's servant. I find my life by losing it. . . . To be in Christ is to be free. To be in Christ is to be a slave. I am delivered from the old nature which told me that to be a man someone else must be less than I. I am redeemed from the old man who pushed me to cling to the old order. I am free not to hate and discriminate. I am released to love. But it is freedom that keeps me in chains to a sovereign Lord who alone calls the shots.[24]

No southern institution or "steeple" was ready to take on this kind of authentically sacrificial leadership, he thought; but he did know some individual renegade Southern white clergy who had. In his Spring 1964 article in *Dialogue*, Campbell celebrated D. W. Clark of Mansfield, Texas; Paul Turner of Clinton, Tennessee; Eugene Davenport and Thomas Reeves of Alabama; Gerald Kersey of Georgia; James Willis Vaughn,

---

23. Clancy, "Jesus in the Brush Arbor," 231.

24. Campbell," Whose Freedom?" 1965 manuscript. Will D. Campbell Papers. McCain Library and Archives.

Horace Germany, Duncan Gray, and Wofford Smith in Mississippi; and the twenty-eight young Methodist ministers of Mississippi who in January 1963, signed the prophetic "Born of Conviction" statement, which cost most signatories their pulpits. What did these, and those few like them, expect to gain from their true and faithful witness? "We expect in some cases to gain the only thing our Lord promised his followers," Campbell explains, "a cross; and the peace that comes with knowing that we have been his good servants."[25]

To emphasize the scandal of the idea, Campbell placed the following conjecture in the mouth of T. J. Eakes, his African-American friend and interlocutor.

> When you think about it, there's something pretty selfish about trying so hard to get *my* rights. Maybe the Christian thing to be doing is to be handing over the rights I already have. Jesus said don't resist evil. Said if you take away my sweater to give you my coat. That if the policeman hits me on one side of the head to turn the other side and let him hit that too. And if he makes me run a mile, run two. [Responding to Campbell's dissent that the Civil Rights Movement had achieved much by acquiring rights and wielding power, Eakes continues:] I'm telling you that as I read the Book, Brother Jesus is asking us to give up power, not get more. All those white cats you named under the big steeples, yeah they got power to give up. They got influence. And what's it good for? Somebody told me one time that the quickest way to lose your influence is to use it. Go tell'um, Brother Will. Go tell'em to get rid of some of it.... And when your folks drop their power, I'll tell mine to let it lie where it fell. Not to pick it up. Cause if they do they're in a peck of trouble.[26]

Unfortunately Christians do not trust themselves and their story enough to have the faith to forego power.

In a letter to the Associate General Secretary of the NCC, Edwin Espy, Campbell explained his resignation from the institution, asserting that his grievances were neither trivial nor bureaucratic. Instead, he found that he "had a totally different understanding of the nature of the Christian faith, the mission and message of the Church"—especially on matters concerning race. Told by his immediate supervisor that his Chicago speech had "made him sick at his stomach," and that "the Church

---

25. Campbell, "Rumblings of Rebellion among Southern White Clergy," 18–19.
26. Campbell, Forty Acres and a Goat, 95–97.

must rely upon the Social Sciences for deliverance," Campbell responded, "This I do not believe and this I cannot and will not promote." Here Campbell established a major distinction between the NCC as "progressive/liberal," and himself as a "Radical." Christian liberals/progressives thoughtfully synthesize the *kerygma* with the best scholarship of the era. Although no obscurantist, the Radical Campbell remained committed to the unique, peculiar, scandalous genius of the Christian proclamation. For all progress that political science might offer on the matter of civil rights, "I must go on saying that the Christian gospel has something to say beyond the humanistic and humanitarian dimensions."[27]

In his final reports to the NCC Will provided prophetic warnings. If the NCC and its white liberals continued to follow humanistic strategies and political science, "there is the very real danger that we ['Christians'] may accelerate the complete secularization of culture through our legitimate concerns for human rights." He had seen in Nashville and elsewhere that the sit-ins and the Freedom Rides were energized by the gospel, but the spirit was changing, and the youth "may now be lost to the Church" if the "steeples" continued to promote the stratagems of the state.[28] In a passage that shows his affinity to individuals like Jacques Ellul and Ivan Illich, Campbell argued that the need was not for better organization and "techniques." Instead, reconciliation occurred via "personal visitation and counseling, the kind of 'hand-holding' operation we did more of in the early years of the work. Likewise, I am still convinced that, particularly in the South, there is no substitute for the preaching of the Word."[29]

Radical faith renounces the Baals of "institution" and "activism." Such renunciation may make Radicals appear ineffective, inefficient, alienated and even disjointed from society—perhaps even a pitiful failure. Then again, one of the morals of Campbell's narrative is that such social and political "non-cooperation" may be the grace and hope of the Christian vocation.

---

27. Campbell, "Letter to R.H. Edwin Espy," dated 27 May 1963. Will D. Campbell Papers. McCain Library and Archives.

28. Campbell, "Five Year Report of the Southern Office," 1962. Will D. Campbell Papers. McCain Library and Archives.

29. Campbell, "Annual Report of the Southern Project," 20 March 1963. Will D. Campbell Papers. McCain Library and Archives.

THE COMMITTEE OF SOUTHERN CHURCHMEN

To MAINSTREAM SOCIETY WILL'S efforts may have appeared dysfunctional, but he has always known that he is part of a long, storied history both within Christian tradition and even in the South. The Fellowship of Southern Churchmen (FSC), for example, was an interracial community, initially convened in 1932 by a group of Christian socialists. In the 1930s, '40s, and '50s, the FSC focused their work on the labor movement, land reform, church renewal, and peace efforts. It was the FSC's Sherwood Eddy and Reinhold Niebuhr, for example, who had provided impetus for Mississippi's Providence Cooperative Farm, which had such a positive impact on Will. It was probably Howard "Buck" Kester (the FSC's first secretary) who invited Campbell to join the FSC in July, 1955.

> ## HOWARD "BUCK" KESTER (1904–1977)
> A student of Alva Taylor at the Vanderbilt Divinity School, Kester was a forerunner to key elements of the work Campbell would later pursue in the South. In the 1920s, Kester served as a field secretary for the Fellowship of Reconciliation. In 1934, Kester and others disappointed with the politics of FDR's New Deal, the unions, racial injustice, and the organized church, met at Myles Horton's Highlander Folk School in Monteagle, Tennessee, where Reinhold Niebuhr radicalized the gathering. There they formed the Committee of Younger Churchmen in the South, which would soon become the Fellowship of Southern Churchmen. They chose as their standard of faith Luke 4:18. In the late '30s, Kester worked full time for the Fellowship, where, among other duties, he investigated lynchings for the NAACP and the ACLU. By this time an ordained Congregationalist minister and a Christian Socialist by theological outlook, Kester went on to lead the interracial Southern Tenant Farmers Union (STFU) in Arkansas, a work detailed in Kester's 1936

> *Revolt among the Sharecroppers.* Campbell has described Kester's STFU as the "first, authentic, most valiant effort of poor white and poor black rural folk banding and bonding in American history."

As Campbell transitioned out of the NCC in 1963, a group of his friends and FSC members launched what he called a "little 'Save Old Campbell' movement."[1] The idea was to reorganize the old FSC into a new Committee of Southern Churchmen (COSC). Although by 1963 the South had plenty of agencies promoting civil rights, Campbell and the COSC reasoned that most civil rights organizations thought and acted according to legal and humanitarian criteria, i.e., "integrate because the Supreme Court and the Commander-in-Chief say so." In its "Preliminary Statement," the COSC envisioned "a ministry consciously and admittedly grounded in the belief that relating the Christian message to specific problems and the proclamation of that Gospel can be the most powerful and dynamic force in changing the South."[2]

As Flannery O'Connor famously noted, the South is a Christ-haunted region, which supposedly made Southerners more responsive to Bibles, revivals, and sermons than to Supreme Court decisions and Executive Orders. The South, in other words, required an approach other than court injunctions and legislation that would persuade the hearts and minds of its people to be and to do differently. "While we have no desire to perpetuate an irrelevant religious piousity," the COSC Proposal stated, "we believe people immersed in it can be faced with the moral dimensions and imperatives of the situation in the language with which they are most familiar, and by which they are most moved." "There seems little doubt now that institutionalized pulpits cannot do what must be done," the proposal continued. Progress required a circumvention of the "steeples."

> Any hope of influencing this [popular] segment of society lies in the by-passing of the institution and going directly to the people. This is not a suggestion for a moderate ministry to the moderates. Nor is it an effort to get harmony in a community in the usual sense of getting the parties in conflict to "communicate" with one

---

1. Caudill, "An Oral History with Will D. Campbell."
2. "Preliminary Statement Regarding the Committee of Southern Churchmen," 4 June 1963. Will D. Campbell Papers. McCain Library and Archives.

another, or say a prayer together in the same room. It is an effort to go directly to the mass of uninvolved and ignored Southern whites with a radical moral appeal in language and thought-forms with which they are familiar and which motivate them.[3]

In fact, nearly a decade later, Campbell described the COSC as "a small group of steeple dropouts"; individuals who were serious about their faith but who had no confidence in the "institutional, structured, steepled, canopy."[4] An "unstructured and unorganized" community, the COSC would be a group of some 30-100 women and men being God's reconciling presence throughout the South, encouraging their fellow Christians in the region to incarnate the reconciliation God had wrought.

On one level, this ministry would take the form of media-broadcast sermons and published literature. Eventually the COSC, for example, developed a library of twenty taped radio spots, played throughout the Deep South—especially when the situation most required a reconciling word (e.g., in and around Selma, 1965). COSC spots included such titles as "Southern Indirection," "Love and Justice," "The Southerner and the Past," "The Tragic Sense of Life among Negroes," "The Tragic Sense of Life among Whites," "The Burden of the Neighbor," "Change and Decay," "The Southern Sense of Guilt," and "Our People." The COSC also ran its "Southern Churchmen Speak" column in over one hundred newspapers in the region.

Additionally, the COSC established a preacher-at-large program so that clergy expelled from their pulpits by reactionary Southern congregations could sustain their witness in the South. The COSC would, in other words, put these clergy on its own payroll, allowing ministers to function like apostles and prophets to the South, rather than leaving for the North to find livelihood and income.

One of Campbell's responsibilities, therefore, became fundraising. Principally this meant locating funding for the COSC's nearly $40,000 yearly budget. Occasionally this meant raising support for those in need. In 1969, for example, Campbell and the COSC sent Fanny Lou Hamer nearly $3,700 to help on needed repairs to her house.

---

3. "A Proposal for the Fellowship of Southern Churchmen (Committee of Southern Churchmen)," 29 July 1963. Will D. Campbell Papers. McCain Library and Archives.

4. "Will Campbell: Door Interview," 6.

The COSC officially organized itself in Nashville on February 6, 1964, electing Kelly Miller Smith as its inaugural president, and affirming Will Campbell as executive director. Despite support and participation by many, James Branscomb confessed in a personal letter to James Holloway, "I fully know what you mean when you say the COSC is Will Campbell, period."[5] At its founding the COSC adopted a combination statement of faith, confession of sin, and a covenant of discipleship that incorporated the Pauline emphasis of reconciliation in II Corinthians 5:15–20.

> ### STATEMENT ADOPTED BY THE COMMITTEE OF SOUTHERN CHURCHMEN
>
> Nashville, Tennessee
>
> February 6, 1964
>
> We confess this message of faith and life of the Christian community (II Cor. 5:15–20) speaks directly to the broken relationships between and among men. The Church is the Church, when by the gift of grace, it lives this faith and proclaims this message in obedience to its Lord. In dying for all men, Christ destroyed every barrier which denies fellowship, brotherhood, and community between and among all men. Beginning in the Church, therefore, worldly standards must cease to count in relationships among men, or Christ's death and resurrection are mocked. . . . Having been entrusted with this service of reconciliation, we, as a Committee of Southern Churchmen, covenant to proclaim in faith and with our lives that Christ's reconciliation of all men is neither social stratagem nor political expedient, but the gift of God that has and does and will liberate men from bondage and death—forevermore, but also "while still in life" here and now.
>
> "In Christ's name, therefore, we implore you, be reconciled to God!"

An important part of the program of the newly reorganized Committee was the creation of a new journal, *Katallagete: Be Reconciled!* with Will Campbell as publisher and James Y. Holloway as editor. Campbell and Holloway had met in 1961 at Mercer University, and even though their friendship may have been rocky, their theological outlook was similar. Their collaboration produced numerous essays and made *Katallagete*

---

5. James Branscomb, "Letter to James Holloway," undated. James Holloway Papers.

a unique and high-quality theological publication. The journal could be simultaneously earthy and intellectual, attracting a diverse range of contributors and some of the finest writers in the U.S. and abroad. Among its offerings, *Katallagete*'s first issue contained the COSC Statement of Faith, a preface by President Kelly Miller Smith, two introductory articles by Holloway and Campbell, and an essay by James McBride Dabbs explaining the transition from the FSC to the COSC. The inaugural issue also included an expanded version of William Stringfellow's address to the annual meeting of the COSC.

> ### JAMES Y. HOLLOWAY
>
> A graduate of the Southern Baptist Mercer University, Holloway went on to earn a BD and MA in political philosophy from Vanderbilt University, and a PhD in theological ethics from Yale University. After studying under H. Richard Niebuhr at Yale, Holloway studied under Karl Barth in Basel, Switzerland. Holloway returned to teach at Mercer in 1964. In 1965, Holloway moved to Berea College in Berea, Kentucky. Soon after arriving in central Kentucky, Holloway and Campbell jumped a fence at The Abbey of Gethsemani to talk with the famous Trappist monk, Thomas Merton. Rumor has it that the trio (Merton, Campbell, and Holloway) might even show up at local taverns from time to time to hear good bluegrass music. In a more traditional theological vein, Holloway developed an appreciation for the French theologian, Jacques Ellul, introducing him to a larger U.S. audience.

In his essay, "The Orthodoxy of Involvement," Stringfellow developed the theological genius of the COSC. "The event of Jesus Christ which is the reconciliation of the whole creation in the fullness of time is in behalf of all men, and all men benefit thereby whether they realize it, desire it, or like it. It is," Stringfellow continued, "simply the gift of God acting, as it were, all by Himself, amongst men and in the place of men in this world." Humans may oppose, refuse, condemn, dishonor, and deny this grace, but no response can diminish the fullness and completeness of the reconciliation God wrought in Christ. Those consciously embracing this biblical reality of reconciliation "participate in the unconditional, extravagant, inexhaustible, expendable, incredible love of God. . . . To be a Christian, to be already reconciled, means to love the world—all the world—just as it is—*unconditionally*." The COSC would strive to avoid manipulating others by withholding love until the others acquiesce or conform to the COSC's point of view. After Easter, nothing more has been needed to make reconciliation complete. "Reconciliation is, simply, lived." It is lived by loving oppressed minorities, as well as oppressors like Selma's Sheriff Clark. It is lived by dying rather than defeating.[6] In the same vein, Jim Waits's article in the inaugural issue of *Katallagete* presented the principal eschatological vision of the COSC. "The singular task of the Church, the Committee asserts, is to *be* the Church, ministering within its own categories of faith. It is through the reformation of its own life that the Church will have its most significant ministry. For as inner integrity is secured, the Church's witness to the world will be manifest."[7] Announcing the birth of the project, Campbell reflected on the call of reconciliation in II Corinthians 5, distinguishing the Committee's position from that of both classic Southern, revivalist pietism, and the liberal social gospel. Campbell affirmed as God's true mission for the church—and, thus, as the message of the COSC—is not a "gimmick," a strategy, or a technique, but "an evangelism that sees all of life as incarnational; a social action that follows as naturally as breathing."[8] In its first three years, the journal published not only articles by its in-house Committee leaders, but also contributions by renowned authors such as Walker Percy, Markus Barth, Dan Berrigan, Leander Keck, Thomas Merton, John Lewis, Vincent Harding, Reinhold Niebuhr, Walter Lippmann, and Christopher Lasch. Not surprisingly, by the spring of 1967 *Katallagete* had some 3,000 subscribers.

Over the years, Campbell's and/or Holloway's *Katallagete* articles maintained the COSC focus, and created quite a stir, e.g., "Can There Be a Crusade for Christ?" "An Open Letter to Billy Graham," "Politics as Baal," and "Footwashing or the New Hermeneutic?"[9] During the early 1970s, Campbell and Holloway edited and published in book form several collections of essays that initially appeared in issues of *Katallagete*, e.g., *The Failure and Hope: Essays of Southern Churchmen* (1972), *". . . and the criminals with him . . . Luke 23:33"* (1973), and *Callings!* (1974). The second of these edited volumes is of special interest, as the volume

6. Stringfellow, "The Orthodoxy of Involvement," *Katallagete* (June 1965), 12–17.

7. Waits, "A Reformation and the Mission of the Committee," *Katallagete* (June 1965) 18.

8. Campbell, "The Day of Our Birth," *Katallagete* (June 1965) 5.

9. Most of these are included in Campbell, *Writings on Reconciliation and Resistance*.

consisted of writings by prisoners, ex-prisoners, children of incarcerated parents, a KKK Grand Dragon, and Vietnam War draft resisters. Campbell and the COSC used funds generated by the publication to hire Tony Dunbar to "minister to prisoners in the South." Dunbar was able to locate sufficient additional funding to launch the Southern Prison Ministry, a non-profit organization both performing prison ministry and working for criminal justice reform throughout the South, but especially in Tennessee and Georgia.

Katallagete's Winter '68–'69 issue focused on politics, and proved so provocative that *Christianity and Crisis* reprinted the title essay in an early 1969 issue. Responses in *Christianity and Crisis* were mixed, but most dismissed Campbell's and Holloway's claims as political-theological heresy. Given the national interest, Campbell and Holloway published *Up To Our Steeples in Politics*, in 1970, which reprinted many of the original essays from *Katallagete* and added a new introduction.[10] Appearing at the height of the volatile culture wars over such issues as the Vietnam War, the black liberation struggle, unrest over university governance, and counter-cultural lifestyles, the title essay—much like the book as a whole—presented a sharp and incisive critique on what the authors diagnosed as a messiah complex, or sheer idolatry, on the part of "the steeples" when it came to political participation. Campbell and Holloway indicted the church, in other words, for placing more faith in the power of legislation than in the gospel. Later Campbell revisited the thesis, and explained, "Our call is not to be Caesar; our call is to be in conflict with Caesar. And we will be in conflict, because of the nature of the two critters."[11] All in all, the *Up To Our Steeples in Politics* episode generated considerable heat and some light. In the longterm, the controversy alerted many to the COSC's *Katallagete* and to Will Campbell in particular.

Thrice burned by institutions, Campbell enjoyed the loosely structured COSC as his church, a fellowship that honored and sustained his eclectic vocation. For the first few years, Campbell and the Committee continued much of the work he had been doing with the NCC: public speaking, frequent travel to provide pastoral care and support for civil rights activists, and an outreach program to support Southern church folk who suffered as a result of their work for racial reconciliation. In

---

10. Campbell, *Writings on Reconciliation and Resistance*, 197–201.
11. Gibble, "Living Out the Drama: An Interview with Will Campbell," 571.

1966, for example, after a would-be assassin shot James Meredith during his "March against Fear" through Mississippi, Campbell made pastoral visits both to Meredith and the accused assailant. As both the Vietnam War and the antiwar movement began heating up, Campbell and the Committee sought to mobilize support from Southern clergy and laity for the peace movement. Forming or joining a political action committee against the war, however, did not seem quite right to Campbell. Advising "Caesar" on foreign policy in Southeast Asia was "somehow offensive to my Anabaptist genes." Nevertheless, he had no reservations trying to rescue some of "Caesar's" victims by providing them sanctuary at Dolan House on his Mt. Juliet, Tennessee farm, even personally taking draft dodgers to Canada.

Perhaps the best description of the COSC came in Campbell's unofficial response to Beth Braxton, who inquired into the mission and nature of the Committee. "What is the Committee of Southern Churchmen? I have not the slightest idea," Campbell answered.

> It doth not yet appear what it shall be. And when it doth appear, it will be the end of it. Whatever the MAN was talking about when HE said lose your life if you want to find it, I take it to mean that when we race around asking such College YMCA questions as "Who am I?" we will never find out. It doesn't matter a damn who I am. Maybe it is because I know it would make me puke if suddenly I should find out. Something happened back there with Jesus and all.... The Committee of Southern Churchmen, to those who observe us, is me and a part-time secretary. That is the office. Add to that about fifty or so people around the South who are what the charter (Caesar) calls the Board of Directors. They are in fact an extended staff of this office who do things like putting out a magazine (*Katallagete: Be Reconciled!*), driving an ambulance, upward bounds, head starts, cooperative vegetable farming, running a gift shop in the French Quarter and feeding the hippies, etc. We have no program.... I'm not trying to be coy, or cute, not talking more about what the Committee is. In short, it *is* what little we *are*. It does what little we *be*. I seldom do the same thing twice, so it is difficult to say what I do. But, o well, enough. Let it pass.[12]

During these early years of the COSC, several experiences influenced Campbell and brought him more closely in touch with the

12. Campbell, "Letter to Beth Braxton," undated. Will D. Campbell Papers. McCain Library and Archives.

inextricable bond of blood, culture, and spirit, which tied him to his own people, i.e., his family and the whole class of rural, Southern, poor whites. In February 1967, Will's brother, Joe, died. Officially Joe's death was attributed to coronary failure, but Will believed Joe had willed his death. "It might as well have been a gun or rope or hose from an exhaust pipe. He had to die. Life had become too much."[13] Will's grief was deep and enduring.

Eighteen months earlier, Joe and P. D. East had spent an evening together at East's home in Fairhope, Alabama—drinking, arguing, and grieving over the recent murder of Jonathan Daniels. A friend of Will's, Daniels was a young Episcopal seminarian from New England who in the summer of 1965 had been laboring for civil rights in Lowndes County, Alabama. Just released from a week's stint in jail for his work, Daniels was brutally killed when volunteer Deputy Sheriff Thomas Coleman fired his shotgun at a group of civil right workers in Hayneville, Alabama. As Will grieved and raged over Daniels' murder, P. D. East, an agnostic, reminded him of a conversation they had had years earlier. East had challenged Will to give him a summary definition of the Christian faith, to which Will ultimately responded: "We are all bastards, but God loves us anyway."[14] With the murder of Daniels, East now challenged Campbell's definition of Christianity. Was Will still so confident? Which of those bastards—Jonathan or Thomas—did God love the most, East inquired. Will remembers that East's question was nothing short of a conversion experience, comparable both to his reading of *Freedom Road* some twenty years earlier, and the lesson he had learned as a child from his Grandpa Bunt years before that. Now, just as he learned from both his Mississippi grandfather and from a Marxist novelist that African-Americans were never "niggers," Will was learning from his fellow Southerner, P. D. East, that their "kind"—which was also Thomas Coleman's kind—were no longer to be denigrated as "white niggers," as poor white trash, as "rednecks." Campbell's conversion experience, and the conclusions he has derived from it, were complex and multi-faceted, with personal, historical, sociological, and theological revelations all at work. In an expression reminiscent of Peter Maurin's and Dorothy Day's "personalism," Campbell told an interviewer, "What you do as a Christian has got to be the same," whether the person in front of you "is

13. Campbell, *Brother to a Dragonfly*, 259.
14. Ibid., 220.

going to cut your head off or pin a medal on you."[15] This is the ground of reconciliation. Every human bears the image of God, and must be treated as one would profess to treat God in the flesh.

By 1965, the era of the Selma March, Campbell had developed a keener sense of vocation. As he explained in a letter to Garry Oniki, a leader in the United Church of Christ:

> We are being less than Christian if we do not minister to those who oppose us. As a Southern White, the blood that is on my hands is not so much the [James] Reebs, [Jimmie Lee] Jacksons, [James] Cheneys, et. al., but the immortal souls of those who snuffed out their earthly lives. And I am convinced they did so in the name of Jesus Christ—something hard for one not familiar with the region to understand, unless, of course, he believes in original sin. . . . I know of no other way to reach those poor wicked sons of God. I can't imagine why He died for them (can't imagine why He died for anybody 'cepting me) but He did. . . . They might kill us, but they can't kill us for being from Boston or Detroit. And perhaps it is we whose time it is to die.[16]

KATALLAGETE! NO EXCEPTIONS. NO CONDITIONS

"I remember that during the civil rights movement, when I began proposing that the most rabid segregationist is as precious in God's sight as anybody else, some of my colleagues in the National Council of Churches would say, yeah, that *sounds* good. But what about those folks who stopped Mickey Schwerner, Andy Goodman, and James Chaney down there on a lonely, dark, Mississippi road, and then took them out and tied them to a tree and beat them till their blood mingled with the red clay of Neshoba County and finished them off with a bullet and dumped them in a government-financed dam? Are you going to go down there and tell them everything is cool, you're forgiven, it's all right, God doesn't hold your misdeeds against you? But *I* didn't say that. *Paul* said that, in Second Corinthians. 'God is in Christ, no longer holding our misdeeds

---

15. Caudill, "An Oral History with Will D. Campbell."

16. Campbell, "Letter to Garry Oniki," 30 March 1965. Will D. Campbell Papers. McCain Library and Archives. Will has practiced his commitment to pastor both victim and offender throughout his adult life. In the 1990s, for example, Campbell carried on a congenial correspondence with Byron de la Beckwith, the convicted assassin of Campbell's colleague, Medgar Evers.

> against us.' The most radical of *all* notions. *No* exceptions. *No* conditions. Now, I wouldn't have done it that way. I would have had a lot of exceptions. But it's not there. The New Testament has nothing to do with ideology that I can find. Jesus doesn't say I come to proclaim release of captives unless they're Kluxers or unless they're black or unless they live north of the forty-eighth parallel in Korea. . . . If you stop judging folks by human standards, then you've gotten rid of a considerable load. There goes geography, there goes race, and there goes a lot of things. And that is a pretty drastic piece of information, if you really took it seriously. I can see why they ran the apostles out of town before sundown."
>
> Mitchell J. Shields, "Travels with Brother Will,"
> *Atlanta Weekly* (April 19, 1981).

With this clarity of perspective, Campbell was ready when, in 1966, Stokely Carmichael and other more militant-sounding leaders in the black liberation struggle began to voice and practice a policy of racial separatism and black power. In fact, in a 1968 address to the Arkansas Council on Human Relations, Campbell took up the question raised by Stokely Carmichael, H. Rap Brown, and other Black Power spokespersons, whether the integration policies of the previous decade had been a form of genocide. Over time, Campbell asserted,

> Blacks began to see that we were willing, yes, even eager, to receive the Negro into *our* schools, *our* neighborhoods, *our* jobs, *our* clubs, perhaps, *our* churches (sometimes), and even into our families and bedrooms, but he saw that our understanding of the end of segregation was often identified with that kind of acceptance. . . . Integration as a term came to mean that we actively pursue that course that the two races will encounter each other in such a way that the white partner actually forgives the black fellowman for being black—that he makes him an honorary white man. . . . No more was required of Negroes than they learn their lesson. Keep their yards clean, keep their voices down, wash themselves at least once a day, enjoy the treasures of higher cultures, stabilize their courtship and marriage customs, just as the white man is alleged to have done. [This is] the beginning of genocide. It is not ovens and concentration camps. The beginning of genocide is the expectation of the majority that the minority become like themselves.[17]

---

17. Campbell, "The Faith of a Fatalist," 52.

Five years later, in an interview with *The Wittenburg Door*, Campbell equated the construction of federal housing projects with concentration camps. "It's not like Nazi Germany, as yet," Campbell acknowledged. "But the real paradigm for concentration camps in the technological society is the things we're doing in the name of progress. Am I saying let's not have progress? I'm just saying we don't apparently know what progress is."[18]

While regretting the growing chasm between black and white participants in the civil rights movement, Campbell appreciated Carmichael's point that whites sympathetic to the black cause might spend more of their energy focusing upon their own people, where the problem of racism was rooted. Within this context, Campbell's increasing openness and friendliness—all while maintaining critical judgment—to a number of Ku Klux Klan members makes sense. The non-aligned nature of the COSC allowed Campbell the time and space to pursue such scandalous reconciling ministries.

---

18. "Will Campbell: Door Interview," 12.

A CAMPBELL CREDO

Occasionally Will has been inclined to confess, "I'll help you up if you're falling on your ass, but I'm not going to tell you what you've got to believe, or how to live your life."[1] Those with a more "doctrinaire" or "fundamentalist" Christian orientation might hear him and conclude that Campbell lacks core commitments. Such an opinion, however, would be misinformed. As he explained in a *Newsweek* interview, "I believe that Christ is the Lord, goddam it. It's not that I believe in God, but that He believes in me, in us. And I'm willing to bet my life on that."[2]

The Greek imperative *katallagete* ("be reconciled") stands as a second central tenet for Will. This reconciliation is an accomplished fact, which disciples are then commissioned to live out. "Now if our misdeeds are not held against us that means we are free. It means we do not have to do anything," proclaims Campbell.[3] Elsewhere Campbell told an interviewer, "There's nothing I can do. I believe this concept began as a mistake of liberal Christians who assumed that we are going to go out and build a kingdom in which it will be possible for men to live as brothers. This is very fine sociologically and politically, but it's not Christian."[4] "We are not called upon to establish a Kingdom but to abide in one already established and to bid others to do the same. Just groove it, man. 'And He enlisted us in this service of reconciliation.'" This credo also reveals Will's ecclesiology:

> That what the "Church" is—those who accept this enlistment. And all St. Paul called upon us to do is to live as if what God did in Christ is true. But our programs, schemes, strategies, next steps in this, that, or the other say that Paul is a liar—that God did not

---

1. Lloyd, "Radical Grace," 15.
2. "Good Will," *Newsweek*, May 8, 1972, 84.
3. Clancy, "Jesus in the Brush Arbor," 230.
4. Bowman, "Prophet, Poet, Preacher-at-Large," 30.

really reconcile us to one another and to Himself. I believe that He did. Therefore, if I am reconciled there is no such thing as nigger, redneck, Pollock, spick, Injun, Mick, Mackerel-snapper, Kluxer, etc., etc.[5]

By erasing all "human points of view," the imperative in 2 Corinthians 5 also establishes our anthropology. "There you are. It is quite clear," Campbell told Walter Clancy.

If those categories do not exist—all those worldly standards, or human categories we place one another in—then the problem is solved. We just live what has already been done for us. If I am reconciled to someone then I sure Lord ain't going to lynch him, don't care if he lives next door to me, goes to Mass in Jesuit Bend, goes to school with my children, marries my daughters. That is the radical word from St. Paul.[6]

A practical expression of this second tenet of Campbell's credo has been his unconditional, critical love for all peoples of the South. As his appreciation of this "radical word of St. Paul" grew, Campbell would no longer allow himself to be used by the white liberal North as an instrument to call attention to the significant racial speck in the South's eye. He reduced his speaking engagements in the North, suspecting that Yankee audiences too eagerly relished his denunciations of an immoral, unjust South. "That's what they [the North] wanted. That's what we want. It doesn't mean that they're any worse than we are, but we want somebody to isolate the Jonah and say 'Here, we've got him and we've got him by both legs and his balls, and we're going to throw him out here in the ocean and then race relations will be alright.'"[7] Campbell, therefore, stepped up his one-man educational campaign against the elitist and derogatory terms like "redneck," "peckerwood," "woolhat," "hillbilly," and other epithets for poor, white, rural Southerners. Once referred to as "The Aquinas of the Rednecks," Campbell said he would prefer to be known as "The St. Francis of the Rednecks or the Pope John [XXIII] of the Rednecks."[8] Those disparaged as "crackers, kluxers, and woolhats," he told a meeting of African-American pastors and Jewish rabbis, are

---

5. Clancy, "Jesus in the Brush Arbor," 230.
6. Ibid.
7. Caudill, "An Oral History with Will D. Campbell."
8. Clancy, "Jesus in the Brush Arbor," 229.

often "born into the pathology of the white ghetto and are as powerless to get out of it as people born into the black ghetto."[9]

Taking a page from Fast's *Freedom Road*, Campbell has urged conscientious individuals to look past the pitiful extremist group like the Klan to the more menacing clan that really has the power—an "invisible empire far more subtle, far more insidious, more cunning and treacherous than a few hundred people gathered in a cow pasture around a burning cross." The powers with a vested interest in sustaining the status quo are not the "rednecks," but "the university-educated, the sophisticated, nice gentlemen and ladies who make broad their phylacteries in the Cathedral (be it of Rome, Canterbury, Geneva, New York, or Nashville), know where the salad fork goes, have good taste in literature, music, and philosophy but continue to maintain a system wherein a very few whites own and run it all, while all blacks and most whites run none of it."[10] The tragedy of American history, and especially Southern history, therefore, is not only the emergence of bigoted bumpkins, but perhaps more importantly the success of the principalities and powers to pit blacks, poor whites, and other marginalized peoples against one another—slaves against servants. Instead of the disinherited finding common cause and uniting to resist the white male capitalist oppressor—the real terrorist of American history—the elite whites have bated poor whites into seeing and fighting blacks as their enemy, and vice versa. Under the guise of "political relevance" and "social effectiveness," the steeples have aligned themselves with (i.e., served as chaplains to), these aristocratic powers-that-be; teaching a gospel of conformity to America's obscene social and economic conventions.

A third core principle in Campbell's credo is that all institutions are "inherently evil." Whether sacred or secular, public or private, academic or political, no institution is ever trustworthy. No institution is ever deserving of our faith and allegiance. Why? "All institutions, every last single one of them, are evil; self-serving, self-preserving, self-loving; and very early in the life of any institution it will exist for its own self."[11]

---

9. Campbell, "The Resurgence of the Ku Klux Klan, or Why America Needs a Resurgence of the Ku Klux Klan," undated. Will D. Campbell Papers. McCain Library and Archives.

10. Clancy, "Jesus in the Brush Arbor," 230.

11. Campbell, *Writings on Reconciliation and Resistance*, 151.

Institutions are simply incapable of the *agape* love incarnated by Christ, and to which disciples are called.

Nation-states, whether the United States of America or any other civil government, illustrate the self-interested, self-serving, and inherently evil nature of institutions. Architects of national policy and advancement frequently decide that individuals—real humans bearing the image of their Creator—are expendable. Administrators and bureaucrats send one group of God's creation to kill another part of God's creation, all in the name of "our security" or "our way of life." Patriotism, from this perspective, is a sin, no different from racism. On national "holidays" Campbell, therefore, rings the bells on his farm, but not to celebrate. The tolling is a lamentation:

> It is to lament the results of the doctrines of Manifest Destiny, the Jackson Harvest, the roll call of the Iroquois and Sioux, the Cherokee and the Navaho, Hopi and the Crow. It is to confess the ideas of racial and sexual supremacy which continue to dominate this land, the roll of generations of slaves. It is to acknowledge and bewail our manifold sins and wickedness, the patterns of greed, conformity and blind obedience to witless authority that would spell doom if left, like genocide, to follow their own grim logic.

Ever sensitive to choosing up sides, Campbell "grieves for the soldiers on both sides of a war that was to be a new birth of freedom, and the casualties of great Social Movements, like the ones which have claimed all of my own adult life, dedicated to somehow alter the legacy of original sin."[12]

THE SIN OF PATRIOTISM

"I believe God made the St. Lawrence River, and the Rio Grande River, and the China Sea and the English Channel, but I don't believe God made America, or Canada, or Mexico, or England, or China. Man did that. . . . It is doubtful that there has ever been a nation established for bad reasons. Nations are always established to escape tyranny, to combat evil, to find freedom, to reach heaven. Man has always been able to desire to build a heaven. But it seems he has never been able to admit that he didn't pull it off. So he keeps insisting that he did pull it off. And that is really what patriotism is all about. It is the insistence that what we have done is sacred. It is that transference of allegiance from what God

---

12. Campbell, *Forty Acres and a Goat*, 277.

> did in creating the whole wide world to what we have done with (or to) a little sliver of it. Patriotism is immoral. Flying a national flag—any national flag—in a church house is a symbol of idolatry. Singing 'God Bless America' in a Christian service is blasphemy. Patriotism is immoral because it is a violation of the First Commandment."
>
> Will D. Campbell, "I Love My Country: Christ Have Mercy,"
> *Motive* (December, 1969)

The inherent evil of institutions, however, is not limited to nation-states with large geographic claims and enormous treasuries. Campbell relates his experience with a smaller, supposedly faith-based, but no less fallen and self-centered institution. In 1969, Campbell got involved with Memphis's Methodist Hospital, a para-church institution under the episcopal jurisdiction of three Methodist bishops. The facility had an abysmal record on race relations, with hospital administrators frequently using the term "nigra" to refer to African-American employees, and refusing to share either elevators or equipment with African-American colleagues. These outrages, along with abusive scheduling demands, led the younger African-American staff to stage a walk-out. Campbell initially had no intention of getting involved, but as a board member of Tennessee's Council on Human Relations, as well as a member of the communion of saints, he decided to at least listen to both sides. He quickly found hospital administrators unreceptive to his reconciling efforts. "I could not understand how it was that I felt unwelcome in an institution bearing the name of the Lord I had sought to serve for twenty-six years," Campbell explained. "I have had occasion to sit in on many meetings having to do with America's racial crisis—with mayors, governors, merchants, industrialists, educators." Among these members of his own faith family, however, Campbell felt entirely unwanted. As Campbell appealed to Christian ethics, one of the Methodist Hospital administrators rebutted, "You can't run a hospital like that." Campbell recalled that those were "the same words I had heard from Delta planters, from Birmingham businessmen, from Southern mayors and governors. It was the same word the president of Harvard University had used when he called the police to club and pull the students from the ivied hall when they protested." "I had heard the words before," Campbell surmised, "but somehow it was different now. Not in here. Not in here.

Not in an institution dedicated to relieving human suffering in the name of the sad and lonely Galilean, in the name of my Jesus." Upon hearing the administrator's explanation, a colleague of Campbell's referenced the Methodist *Book of Discipline*. The administrator retorted that he knew the *Discipline*, but "the *Discipline* does *not* apply here." Campbell reflected on all the "mediating sessions I had sat through with those who claimed no loyalty save profit for the stockholders," and compared such an attitude to that presented by representatives "whose loyalty is alleged to be to Christ. I thought of the bishops and how they had reported, truthfully, that they really do not have much to do with the manner in which the hospital is operated. And the administrators had said the same. 'We're just doing our job. We don't make the decisions.' What an excellent defense for Judas that would have been." Campbell saw the embodiment of institutional evil. A non-human entity can dehumanize real individuals bearing the image of their Creator, and yet no one is ultimately responsible or culpable. "The bishops, the pastors, the board of directors, the administrators. Each one is doing his job as best he can. It would be so easy if we could find the one to blame and straighten him out." Campbell then concludes with the words of a country song:

> You can't find the one to blame,
> It's too smart to have a name,
> Cause it ain't flesh and blood we fight with,
> It's powers, and principalities,
> And Armageddon can't be far away.[13]

When it comes to institutions, therefore, Campbell's credo and experience makes him a Christian anarchist. In fact, in the late 1990s, when someone accused him of being a "yellow dog Democrat," Campbell responded "Actually I am a Christian Anarchist. In the Anabaptist cast. Or would be if I only had the guts."[14] Some may balk at this idea. Is Will really an anarchist? The short answer is "Kind of." Historically, anarchists have trusted unregulated individuals—rather than empowered institutions—to do the right thing. Campbell is too distrusting of human goodness to be that kind of anarchist. Instead, Will mixes some Reinhold Niebuhr with a little Roger Williams, steadfastly distrusting *both* humans *and* their

---

13. Campbell, "A Little More Memphis," 28–34.
14. Campbell, "Stetson," undated manuscript, 2. Will D. Campbell Papers. McCain Library and Archives.

institutions. Institutions are evil because they collect and compound the self-centered, avaricious, cut-throat, apathetic inclinations of the sinful individuals who comprise them. The more power institutions attain, the more likely they are to try and control, direct, or coerce matters in a sinful direction. By design, therefore, institutions *of all kinds* are more inclined to harm than to help—and Will bears the scars to corroborate his viewpoint. Campbell does not, however, languish in pessimism. In fact, he is optimistically committed to the enterprise of the powerless, unstructured church being the authentic Beloved Community. "All I'm saying," he told *The Wittenburg Door* in 1973, "is that you don't ever take them [i.e., institutions] seriously. And that you see them as the enemy. You know that they're after your soul."[15] Nevertheless, Campbell remains committed and ever hopeful in the accomplished fact of reconciliation incarnated among improvised communities of faithful believers.

---

15. "Will Campbell: Door Interview," 6.

LIVING HOPE

Not long after Will shifted his employment from the NCC to the COSC, he and Brenda bought a twenty-acre farm in Mt. Juliet, Tennessee, about twenty-five miles east of Nashville. Relocating the family there, they later purchased additional acreage, roughly doubling the size of the farm. Since that time Campbell has cultivated a small truck farm—mostly, he has said, for recreation—where he has used a small log cabin as his office. From this Mt. Juliet location he has pastored his congregation. "When people ask me what I do, I say I'm a Baptist preacher, but never on Sunday," Campbell notes. "Some of them get the symbolism of that and others don't," he confesses.[1] In 1972, Marshall Frady called Will's congregation a "pulpitless, roofless, unpropertied and uncodified" church. Then searching for the vocabulary to describe Will, Frady depicted him as "a solitary country-evangelist Quixote," a "populist John the Baptist" engaged in an "assiduous guerilla ministry."[2] That's about as accurate was one can be in describing Will and his church. He simply will not conform to the categories used in the *Handbook of Denominations in the United States*. Although reared as, and ordained to preach as, a Southern Baptist, Will has unflinchingly dishonored denominational lines. "What's the difference between [our own exploitation of the poor], the pope's jewels, and all those Lutheran and Presbyterian and Methodist steeples out there casting shadows on whores and pimps and addicts and bums?" he rhetorically asks. "The difference is simply one of taste," he concludes.[3]

> ### THE CHURCH
> I think it ["the Church"] does exist, but I'm afraid to look for it, because if I find it and name it, I'm going to run it, if I can. That's the evil of institu-

---

1. Gibble, "Living Out the Drama," 572.
2. Frady, "Fighter for Forgotten Men," 59.
3. Gibble, "Living Out the Drama," 572.

> tions. But Jesus said he would build his church in the world, and exactly where it is at any moment, I don't know. I don't think [one knows when she is in it]. I don't know when I'm in it. Take Gass's Tavern [Mt. Juliet, TN], for example. For many years it was just a little country beer joint. I've done a wedding for just about everybody there. I've buried numerous patrons who have died. I visit the ones who are in jail. Sometimes I get up on stage and pray for the sick. Now, I could make the case that that's my church, but I won't, because if I did, the next thing you know, we'd have a bulletin, or drink only Pabst. And I'd expect to be rewarded for all the things I did there. So I don't say that's my church, but that *is* the Church at work in my life. . . . If I believe that all institutions are inherently evil by definition, then I certainly can't assume that I can create a better one. I might have a good organization for a while, but, before long, any organization is going to become hardened and rigid. I think people *do* come together, like we do down at Gass's Tavern. It's when we institutionalize it—when we do it the same way every Sunday—that it becomes perfunctory and loses any meaning. I say this in spite of the fact that I like ritual, liturgy, and so on.
>
> Jeremy Lloyd, "Radical Grace: An Interview with Will D. Campbell."
> *The Sun* (May 2000).

Even without a formal denomination, Will has been a pastor. For years he continued the wide-ranging ministry he began during his NCC years. Campbell has filled numerous requests as a preacher, speaker, workshop and retreat leader, consultant, and even "theologian in residence" (although Will prefers not to be called a theologian). He has noted, however, that no "white steeple" in the Nashville area has ever invited him to preach. Lacking a formal congregation to pastor has hardly impeded his labors. He has provided more traditional pastoral care (e.g., weddings, baptisms, and funerals) than many "full-time ministers." Even in this capacity, however, he refuses to conform. He baptizes in a large container near his log cabin, and marries couples even though they may lack state-issued marriage licenses. Once asked whether marrying a couple without a license is legal, Will responded, "I don't know and don't care. What's the difference?" For these lawless couples he always provides extra counseling, because without "Caesar's blessing," he notes, the couples will lose certain legal rights. But he is not too concerned about the legal sacrifices. All that a marriage license actually provides,

Campbell maintains, is one partner's right to sue the other in Caesar's courts.[4] Why would the church be yoked with such an empty, divisive state formalities?

> ### I AM A CHRISTIAN PREACHER
>
> Well, first of all, it should be understood that I am not a reconciler. I am a Christian preacher, and I believe that all are already reconciled. . . . In 2 Corinthians 5, Paul said that Christ *has* reconciled us. Not he's *going to*; or, we can reconcile ourselves by being good boys and loving black folks or Klan folks or whoever. He *has* reconciled us and enlisted us in this *service of reconciliation*. Now that is what the church really is.
>
> Norman Bowman, "Prophet, Poet, Preacher-at-Large: A Conversation with Will Campbell," *The Student* (December 1970).

As another expression of his reconciling vocation, Campbell has frequently delivered eulogies for folks ranging from the famous to the nameless. Will seeks to be a compassionate officiant, speaking a healing word to a grieving family. One noteworthy example was Campbell's eulogy for Billy Carter (President Jimmy Carter's eccentric and often maligned brother), who succumbed to pancreatic cancer in 1988. At the end of the day, whether baptizing, marrying, or burying, Will Campbell's ministry fits his vision of the church—always *ad hoc, in Diaspora*.

A number of factors have, over time, contributed to Will becoming something of a well-known, Southern folk hero, or inspirational figure. His colorful individuality, salty candor, and prophetically edgy writing, earned a hearing beyond traditional "Christian" audiences. Stated otherwise, he spoke like Hauerwas and wrote like Claiborne before there was a Stanley or Shane. Moreover, his embrace of seemingly contradictory views and practices (e.g., a bourbon-drinking Baptist preacher, who ministers both to Black Panthers and Ku Klux Klansmen) has provoked fascination and interest. Doug Marlette of the *Charlotte Observer* enhanced Will's popular persona when in 1981 the artist began using Campbell as his inspiration for the Rev. Will B. Dunn character in his "Kudzu" comic strip. Campbell has also moved comfortably in country music circles, befriending and pastoring such stars as Tom T. Hall, Johnny Cash, Kris Kristofferson, and Waylon Jennings. Blessed with a wry wit and self-effacing presentation, Campbell often seems uncomfortable with any

---

4. Caudill, "An Oral History with Will D. Campbell."

high public image. His wisdom and authenticity, however, have earned his public status. He may outrage the "steeples," and confuse the "Caesars," but neither can summarily dismiss Will Davis Campbell.

To systematicians in the Academy, Campbell's theology may seem an unfocused, unwieldy, eclectic fusion. His close friend John Egerton has called Campbell's theology "unstructured, simple, fundamental, and profound. It is two parts Paul and one part Barth, an unlikely combination of Yale Divinity School and East Fork Baptist Church. You can find in it a little situation ethics, some agnosticism, a dash of literalism and a mixture of Reinhold Niebuhr, A. J. Muste, and Billy Graham."[5] Campbell may be uninterested in parsing dogmas, but he is no relativist. He will thoroughly upbraid the self-righteous, and excoriate the self-satisfied—often with the most memorable vocabulary available. Those who presume to have "it" most figured out, are in Campbell's book the most misguided and dangerous. Campbell is, Egerton notes, "a pessimist, a fatalist, and an apocalyptic prophet of doom" when it comes to the human potential for goodness and self-correction. We humans can neither fix nor endure the chaotic injustice we have created. As Campbell once informed a group of college students, "All your human efforts, all strategies, all techniques, all movements will fail; all human engineering will go lame, and only your understanding of the tragedy will remain—only your broken heart, ability to weep—because you have the capacity to understand."[6]

> ### A FIRE IN HIS BONES
>
> Lest one presume that Campbell's ardor has subsided with age, consider his prophetic outrage in the fall of 2004. A federal judge had just sentenced Campbell's friend, the seventy-three-year-old Don Beisswenger, to six months in prison for stepping over a line at Ft. Benning during a School of the Americas protest. The preacher in Campbell took to the pulpit—in this case the pages of the Nashville *Tennessean*—to denounce the principalities and powers. Toward the end of this "sermon," Campbell concludes:
>
>> This old world is reeling and rocking. We've been lied to and driven into a war of aggression by the leaders of our own government, who justify their actions with slogans.

---

5. Egerton, *A Mind to Stay Here*, 22
6. Ibid., 24, 30–31.

> "Destroy their weapons of mass destruction." Not ours, but theirs. "Destroy the regime of this vicious dictator." Not just any dictator but this particular one . . .
>
> Young men and women with serial numbers are doing the bloody deeds their commander-in-chief sent them to do, at the risk of their lives and the lives of the invaded, evil and innocent alike. Such a waste!
>
> How in the name of God can this be justified?
>
> And now Don Beisswenger is going to get his number and enter a prison here in the waning years of his exemplary Christian life.
>
> GREAT GOD!
>
> What are we doing?
>
> Will D. Campbell, "Nashville Eye." The Tennessean
(September 2, 2004).

With all these reasons to despair, Campbell is, nonetheless, compassionate, encouraging, and hopeful, especially non-judgmental of those broken individuals who have damaged their lives. Moreover, he will be a stalwart advocate for those injured by the principalities and powers. To sustain this hope in the face of humanity's self-inflicted tragedy, Campbell has crafted an intellectual genealogy, a list of heroes—some historical, others fictional—who by their irrepressible conflict with the principalities and powers jolt us into an appreciation of community/church as it can and should be. First and foremost on Will's list of heroes would be Christ, who "was among the most anti-religious ever to come along, for He came breaking the rules, smashing the idols, tearing down structures, and proclaiming freedom from all such."[7] Continuing that tradition of reconciling iconoclasts, Campbell points to the following:

> The non-violence of Martin Luther King, the lone courage of Roger Williams standing against the religious intolerance of the New England establishment, the inspiration of those who at the foundation of this democracy stood for a principle of equal rights over the prerogatives of monarchs, the raw fortitude of Harriet Tubman and those since who have conducted the train on the lingering tracks of racial and sexual supremacy, the redeeming iconoclasm of our artists and their subjects from Hawthorne's Hester Prynne to Twain's Tom Sawyer to Ellison's Invisible Man

---

7. Clancy, "Jesus in the Brush Arbor," 229.

to Sallinger's Holden Caulfield, the silent perseverance of those in every generation from first to now who have chosen prison to blind obedience to the State, who have espoused the individualism of Thoreau and rejected submersion in the lonely crowd.[8]

Iconoclasm often carries a destructive meaning; a connotation of something being damaged, and destroyed. Some iconoclasts wreak retaliatory devastation, offering no constructive alternative. But not all iconoclasms are created equal. On one level, Campbell *has* sought to tear down the idols and unmask the powers, so he *is* an iconoclast. Yet Will deconstructs for the purpose of building (or rebuilding). His razing, in other words, is always a means to a creative, constructive, hopeful end—a freeing-up or removal of that which impedes and obstructs other, more desirable possibilities. For Campbell's redeeming, reconciling iconoclasm, the goal is a living embodiment or manifestation of the Beloved Community as envisioned in the Christian *kerygma,* where all individuals are respected, nurtured, sustained, and loved for being the image of God that they are. To incarnate such an alternative reconciling community requires an indefatigable opposition against—a subversive resistance of—the manipulative arrogance, condescending bigotry, the usurious chauvinism, and selfish activism that functions as political wisdom and science in our world. To be what God created and Christ redeemed us to be requires a contravention—a breaching—of the principalities and their powers that seduce us into oppressing and dehumanizing our sisters and brothers. Here we see Campbell at his prophetic and pastoral best. The thrust of his ministry is the good news that Christ has already provided the fix for what ails us. We can try to cover our pain and division by medicating ourselves with our own political nostrums, but these will not succeed. Thankfully we are left neither to our own devices, nor the disastrous history of our own making. God, through Christ, has set all aright. Enmity, anger, prejudice, hatred, elitism, greed, and fear are all defeated. Our task is to live the reality of God's reconciliation. Campbell, therefore, is not trying to sell us on a new progressive plan, so much as he is trying to communicate an alternative reality—an accomplished fact. Those who take the time to listen carefully will discern from Campbell how to pursue harmony in the midst of a discordant, fractious society. For Campbell, this reconciliation is the peculiar manifestation of the church, *sans* steeples and other institutional trappings.

8. Campbell, *Forty Acres and a Goat,* 225.

Campbell befuddles some, while scandalizing others, choosing to live according to this alternative, counter-intuitive reality. He simply will not conform to the way society—its institutions and power brokers—has arranged things. He will not live by its rules. The authorities are not his authority. Such a vocation can make for a lonely existence, but as Walker Percy encouraged Campbell, "If you make everybody mad at one time or another, me, [Les] Dunbar, [the Center for National Security Study's Robert] Borosage, [Physicians for Social Responsibility's Robert] Musil, [the TVA's] Frank E. Smith, George Wallace, Mrs. [Coretta Scott] King, the National Council of Churches, the Catholic bishop of Nashville, you must be doing something right."[9]

CAMPBELL AS RESTORATIONIST

If the Incarnation meant anything, Campbell believes, it was the accomplishment and annunciation in Jesus of the final closing of any divide between the divine and the temporal, between the holy and the profane, between the church and the street, between heaven and earth . . . But it is also Campbell's conviction that the organized church ever since has acted to resist and subvert that cosmic event by reasserting the old dichotomy between the divine and the earthly. And this failure of comprehension and of belief constitutes, to Campbell, the original and still single greatest betrayal of Jesus' meaning: when the sacred and the secular were resundered by the traditional church—when the gospel was reextracted out of the common daily dusty welter of humankind—that reopened gap then admitted all the grotesque discords [of history]. "Every time a group of believers has moved from a catacomb or a brush arbor to a steeple," says Campbell, "they have lost something they once knew about Jesus. And they never seem to get it back." Campbell seems, if nothing else, to be trying at least to realize that original implication of Jesus' appearance among men [and women] by observing, simply within the circumference of his own life and ministry, no real distinctions between the religious and the profane.

From Marshall Frady's *Billy Graham: A Parable of American Righteousness*

---

9. Percy, "Letter to Will Campbell," June 1975. Will D. Campbell Papers. McCain Library and Archives.

The Radical tradition in Christian history finds the norms of discipleship in passages like Luke 4, Matthew 25, Galatians 3, the Sermon on the Mount, and II Corinthians 5. Having no enemies, Christians have no need for weapons or other forms of coercion and punishment. They have no, to use Campbellian terminology, "gland-based" prohibitions or gendered responsibilities. Recognizing race as a social fiction, but a frightfully real political and economic power, Christians see their neighbors as equal siblings in God's human family. A word of warning, however: If too many Christians think and live like Will, refusing to worship the ideological, theological, political, social, racial, and gender idols, the church as we know it (aka, the "steeples") may cease to exist.

So, what does all this have to do with Cecelia Geronymus's epiphany, mentioned at the beginning of this book? Simply stated, on Good Friday and Easter morning, *God made history*—once and for all. Any quest on our part to prove that *we* have *made history* is to denigrate the sufficiency and supremacy of God's accomplishment. Striving to record how *we* have *made history* is the denial of God's sovereignty.

Few are more aware of Cecelia's temptation to allow the writing of the story to supplant *the* Story than Campbell himself.[10] He knows that the telling of *his* story is not *the* Story. As he once told a group at the Riverbend Maximum Security prison in Nashville, for example, he wished he were more worthy of the Anabaptists' tradition of martyrs, but doubted that he merited the gasoline needed to start a good executioner's pyre. Making history, however, is not his concern. He does not need the accolades and the notoriety. He need not be known by history as an icon of the civil rights movement, or a hero of social justice. The vocation of discipleship is not to make history, but to incarnate the reconciling history that God has already made.

Campbell reminds us that the moral of *our* ongoing, unpredictable story is that we relinquish control of history to seemingly inconsistent twists in the plot, despairing catastrophes, embarrassing failures, and frequently to some of the most uncooperative, outrageous characters

---

10. In *Forty Acres and a Goat*, Campbell writes that a Little Rock psychic once told him that in a previous life his name was Cecelia and in 1550 he was drowned in the Amstel River outside Amsterdam for being an Anabaptist. This, Campbell concludes, not only provided his Radical orientation, but also an irrepressible suspicion of Presbyterians. If, however, this fortune has any veracity, his suspicion should be directed at the Dutch Reformed and not the Presbyterians. He will have to find other reasons to distrust those descendants of John Knox.

imaginable. For those needing clear progress, definitive answers, and pure heroes in their stories, Campbell counsels that, of all people, *our* story—the Christian *kerygma*—has frustration at its center and disappointment as its recurring motif. In word and deed, Campbell reminds us that God had made the reconciled community. Precisely because that community lacks the imprimatur of any powerful institution, it can always be about the work of crashing the idols. As Will might say, "That's our story, and we're sticking to it."

Race and Renewal of the Church

Will D. Campbell

EDITORIAL INTRODUCTION

Perhaps the best entrée into Will Campbell's body of writing is his first major work, published in 1962. Here Campbell's iconoclasm is sharp and public. Heretofore he had immersed himself in events, becoming what Gayraud Wilmore called "a pioneer trouble shooter." By '62, for example, Campbell had intervened in situations throughout the South, (e.g., Oxford, MS; Clinton, TN; Little Rock, AR; Nashville, TN; and Montgomery, AL). With the publication of this book, however, Campbell reached out to readers who would seldom—if ever—find themselves in such civil rights hot spots. Most Christians, of course, would neither be an Elizabeth Eckford in Little Rock, nor stalk an Autherine Lucy seeking to integrate the University of Alabama. Instead of bombing schools, or having their churches burned, most Christians would live quietly as law-abiding citizens; well-adjusted lives according to the sociological and political conventions of society. Campbell suggests, however, that at the end of the day, this silent, all too compliant majority may be the most dangerous group of all.

What passes for "Christianity" in the U.S., Campbell asserts, is often little more than a compassionate humanitarianism or "good American citizenship"—values often taught in sixth-grade civics classes. Such confusion allows "Christians" to mistake courtesy, civility, and fidelity to the federal government for the scandalous proclamation of the gospel. Such a civil religion might make for a nice, more urbane and democratic America, but it hardly promotes God's good news.

In these chapters, Campbell indicts the so-called "right" and "left" for essentially working from the same assumptions. First, each in its own way operates from a "human point of view," classifying neighbors according to the prevailing sociological categories. Second, both the "right" and the "left" make humanity the measure of all things, which is, according to Campbell, blasphemy against the sovereignty of God. (Recall how politically charged the term "sovereignty" was in the early '60s.)

To fulfill our vocation and break down the walls of division, the church cannot degenerate into yet another political coalition, with our set of "good guys" pitted against their "bad guys." Our choice is neither to align with a principality, nor wield the power to eradicate racists and bigots. Rather, Campbell's call is for Christians to interpose God's accomplished reconciliation in the place of cunning "political realism" and manipulative legal coercion.

In the place of well-intentioned activism, saccharine tolerance, or legislated integration, therefore, Christians are to be what God through Christ has made us to be—an oddly redeemed and peculiarly beloved community. That reality of radical reconciliation is the message Christians are commissioned to tell, not only with our lips, but in our lives. "God has created this new humanity, this new creation—the church—'to preach good news to the poor, . . . to proclaim release to the captives and recovering of sight to the blind, to set at liberty those who are oppressed, to proclaim the acceptable year of the Lord' (Luke 4:18–19 from Isaiah 61:1–2)."

Perhaps the best endorsement of Campbell's *Race and the Renewal of the Church* came from his friend and college mentor, G. McLeod Bryan. Writing from Wake Forest on November 5, 1962, Bryan celebrates:

Dear Will,
Man, you're not a mere human relationist, you're a theologian! In the dirty word sense. Where did you learn all that stuff never before incorporated in literature of Protestant social action? Not from me. But what gets me is that I studied under Niebuhr too and was nowhere as bright as you! Who is your ghost-writer? Brenda [Campbell]? (Or Oscar Lee or some other liberal in the National Council [of Churches]!)

Naturally I'm talking about your *magnum opus* which I ordered as soon as I saw the by-line, received yesterday and read it before going to sleep. Will, it's powerful. Naturally my best compliment is that it is something I would have written myself, both thoughts and lines. I only wish I could have, but am happier that God has His man prepared and on the line to produce. Why, I thought you were lazy and wasting your time in either conferences or picket lines; instead you have produced one of the most penetrating theological analyses of the twentieth century. I apologize: for with all my regard for your relevance and courage and wittiness and piety (?) I had underestimated your theological awareness. (Why, you may get a doctorate from your alma mater before you know it—that is as soon as my present generation of students get thru reading and understanding your volume, establish their accommodated credentials in the world, and become members of our Board of Trustees. Then the only theological study produced by a Southern Baptist during my lifetime will get its proper prophetic monument. Bring your wheelchair.)

Will, I can't tell you how refreshing it is to wade through all the junk put out by all the mass media of the secular and religious world on this subject and suddenly come across your Word. It sounds like Barth at the rise of Hitler. And who but a sneaky dialectician like yourself would have slipped up on the successful church by saying its very success under God will be its specious success! I like those passages. They read like a twentieth-century Jonathan Edwards whose soul-passage has carried him through the mire of Southern Baptist piety and evangelism to the presidency of Yale and Princeton in an age when theology is the queen again. Man, if you keep saying these things, you will be crucified by the true church, not the spurious churches. Your enemies will come from all sides, not just the ones usually frowned upon. And just think that I had something to do with casting your bark upon the high seas. I never knew you would enjoy sailing so well, or be so good a pilot. Keep it up, man, and sometime just allow me a tow line.

Dig it, Man, dig it.
(signature of G. McLeod Bryan)

"ARE *WE* STILL THE CHURCH?"

IN MANY PARTS OF the world, our time has already been labeled "the post-Christian era." This is simply one measure of the fact that for many people the church has become irrelevant. It has waited too long to carry out its mandate, and to a large part of the world, what we Christians do from here on out really does not matter very much.

Christendom came very close to gaining the whole world. It is now, or so say its critics, dangerously close to losing its own soul. In no area more crucial to the future of the church is this more true than in the area of race relations.

In this context, to write a book on Christian race relations is not only presumptuous; it is downright ludicrous. And yet, if we believe the world will not find a better way, we must believe that someday it will turn back to the church. That day, however, has not yet arrived.

Let us begin by saying that our concern in this little book is not how to reform the world for freedom, justice, and democracy. If this was ever the responsibility of the church, the opportunity has passed us by. Exciting efforts are being made in this direction, but not within our ranks. The church has abdicated its position of leadership. If it ever was or should have been, it is no longer the initiator or prime mover of social reform.

In Africa and Asia the leadership is found today in the tidal wave of nationalism sweeping those two continents and carrying their peoples toward political and economic independence. In America, the most promising and exciting developments in human relations are taking place, not in the churches, but in government.

The church might have influenced these developments by being true to its own nature. It might have determined their success or failure, but it failed to act. It waited until government took the initiative to rescue human rights. And today when the church acts in the human relations field, it follows government or political authority. It imitates the action of the state or it confirms such action with a pious benediction. Moreover, when it has acted, the church has adopted largely a humanitarian approach. Its voice has been too often an echo of the cry for law and order, democracy, the rights of man, human dignity, constitutional process, the public schools.

These things are good, but are they the most basic, most distinctive, concern of the church? In these pages, we will try to determine whether our concern is not something far more basic and more radical than anything the state has said. In the process we will attempt to establish that the church's failure in the racial crisis has been not functional but organic, not sociological but theological. In effect, we have been asking the wrong questions. Instead of demanding, What can the Christian *do* to improve race relations? we should be asking, What must the Christian *be*? As the body of Christ, the church first of all must be the redeemed community. Then will it be empowered to redeem the world, and not before. The sin of the church is not that it has not reformed society, but that it has not realized self-renewal. Its sin is that it has not repented. Without repentance there cannot be renewal.

For the health of our own souls, it might have been better if the Supreme Court had not ruled favorably in 1954 on the subject of race. It might have been better if there had been no executive orders from the White House on fair employment, integration of the Armed Services, and open occupancy in public housing. Then we would have been forced to speak, if we spoke at all, from the vantage point of the Christian gospel. We would have been required to say, Thus saith the Lord! Not, Thus saith the law!

In South Africa, where the full force of law and government is on the side of segregation and discrimination, when churchmen speak they do not echo the state. They cannot fall back upon patriotic and legalistic arguments to urge their people to do what is right. Those Christians who have spoken as the voice of God have often been deposed, arrested for treason, subjected to continuing legal and political harassment. But their message has been strong and clear. They blow a lonely horn, but for them the church has real identity.

Within recent years some American churchmen have insisted that there is no such thing as *Christian* race relations, that our message on this subject is not in the least a particular and peculiar one, and that we are, therefore, justified in taking our cue from the social sciences or from the state. But is this really the case? And if there are indeed no *Christian* race relations, is it not because the Christian message on race is the same as the Christian message on every problem of human life? We shall develop this more fully in a later chapter.

Why is the church concerned about race? First, let us look at the usual reasons.

The church is *not* motivated by fear of reprisals by the nonwhite peoples of the world, although we must recognize that such reprisals are a distinct possibility. Both the Christian doctrine of sin and the most rudimentary acquaintance with man's nature make it sentimental and unrealistic to suppose that people who have been oppressed and exploited for centuries will reach independence and equality filled with love and forgiveness and free of any vindictiveness, prejudice, or animosity.

The Christian understanding of sin makes it highly probable that our generation will see white children marched into gas chambers by dark masters, clutching their little toys to their breasts in Auschwitz fashion. It could see senile whites forced to dig their own mass grave by a heavily pigmented Eichmann. Even a casual glance at history makes this just as probable as does the Christian understanding of human sin and the nature of man. Americans are not inclined to take this possibility seriously, for in this country the lack of superior, sophisticated Negro leadership is not acute. On a world scale it is serious, especially at a time when one miscalculation in Moscow or Washington, too much vodka in the Kremlin or too much bourbon beside the Potomac, could bring forth a day of blinding flashes and lethal explosions which would completely redraw the present power alignments. Great nations would be as nothing. New emerging nations would be great powers.

Alan Paton, in his poignant novel about life in South Africa, *Cry, the Beloved Country*, had the elderly native preacher comment: "My greatest fear is that by the time the whites have turned to loving, my people will have turned to hating." Recent developments in Paton's country, in the Congo, in the United States, and in other parts of the world, have already proved that his fear is not unfounded.

But this cannot be our concern. What may happen when black people rather than white people are "on top" is irrelevant to our task. Certainly the Christian is concerned any time brother is killing brother, but there is nothing distinctively Christian in being exercised about the fact that you may be the Abel rather than the Cain. As followers of Jesus

Christ we cannot say, "Let us be good to nonwhites; otherwise they may eliminate us."

Nor is our concern with international relations. There can be no question about the injurious effect of our policies and practices at home on our standing and prestige abroad. A riot in New Orleans, Little Rock, or Levittown is news throughout Africa, and the bombing of a Jewish temple in America may well be welcome propaganda material in Moscow. But this is still not a sufficient reason for concern by the church.

Nor can our concern be the salvaging of our overseas mission programs. One denomination that gives $18,500,000 a year to foreign missions and $30,000 for race relations (a ratio of 640 to 1) is beginning to take African nationals into local congregations because of what it may do for the missions program. But the African people will not be deceived, and it is doubtful whether our desire for better missionary statistics is any more pleasing to God than is the hue and cry of the real estate broker about depressing "property values."

Since none of these is reason enough for the church's concern, we must now say that this is really not a book on race. Nor can it accurately be described as a treatise on the church's position with respect to race, or an essay on the Bible and race. It is nothing more than an effort to discuss something about which the Bible said nothing, which the early church ignored, and which the historic church has never recognized as a valid concept within its own life, but which, nevertheless, has plagued the church for ages and is today the most serious issue it has to face.

Within orthodox Christianity, when race has been dealt with—even to the point of organizing segregated churches—it has generally been under the cloak of some other question: local autonomy, expediency, harmony within the fellowship. Seldom has it been under the bold banner of race per se. And where this has been the case in the historic church, the majority thinking has insisted that recognition of race to the point of segregation is not in accord with the true faith, but is at best a malignant dissidence or schism, and at worst a perilous heresy.

Because the Christian faith neither recognized nor tolerated the idea of race from its earliest beginning, a Christian in the field of race relations does not speak as a member of a racial group. Because the church did not begin as a racially segregated (or integrated) institution but rather as an institution in which race was irrelevant, the Christian does not speak as a white man, a Negro, an Oriental, or an Occidental.

Instead, the Christian speaks as a member of a community which has never asked any question save the one concerning redemption. What do you think of Jesus? The Christian, therefore, speaks as the offspring of a "peculiar family," so strange as to be called a *tertium genus*, a third race, a people neither Jew nor Greek, bond nor free, embracing master and slave alike, king and liege equally, asking only one question of each: Who, do you believe, is this man who is called the Christ? But despite the christening of the church as the third race, it has not been faithful to its name. Born above race, we have been attracted to the world of races. We have been a stubborn and stiff-necked people and again and again we have forgotten the name we bear.

To be sure, the church as an institution has made some progress in recent decades. When we compare the church of today with the church thirty or forty years ago, there is a clear line of advance. But as far as race relations are concerned, when we compare ourselves to such secular agencies as sports organizations, education, government, the Armed Forces, and even industry and the labor movement, we must ask ourselves whether we really are not even more backward now than we were three decades ago.

For example, in organized sports a few years ago Negroes were not allowed to participate, but they were permitted to be spectators, although the stands were segregated in some sections of the country. In the churches the same was true. Negroes could generally attend white congregations but usually could not join or participate in the full life of the church. Now, in industry, government, the Armed Services, and organized sports, Negroes are beginning to participate. This, however, has not come about in the churches, except on very rare occasions. True, there are a few more interracial congregations than previously, and some denominations on the national level have begun to employ a few Negroes in executive positions. But for the most part, there is still a white church and a Negro church, just as there once was white baseball and Negro baseball. Relatively speaking, the church is farther behind than ever.

We have now come to the whole point of this rather painful disclosure. We must ask ourselves, earnestly and prayerfully, whether we are still the church. If we discover that God has turned to other vehicles, it will not be because he has left his people, but because the people have left God. The Temple of Israel was finally brought low, not because God had ceased to be the God of the people, but because the people had ceased to be the people of God; the Temple had become a market place and a symbol of national idolatry.

The church is not the church because of what man is and has done but because of what God is and has done through Christ. The first mark of the church is that it belongs to Christ. Yet we find ourselves speaking of "our church" and "their church," and of how "*they* seem to want to come to *our* church." As members of the body, we are clearly usurping the power that belongs only to the head of the body. These things are not ours to decide.

The Christian message on race relations is, "God was in Christ reconciling the world to himself" (2 Cor 5:19). Throughout the New Testament, Christ's work of reconciliation reestablishes not only the father-son relationship but the brother-brother relationship. These are not two separate truths somehow related and requiring proper balance. Nor are they mutually related; they are one and the same truth. The New Testament writer who said "God was in Christ," said a few sentences earlier (v. 16), "From now on, therefore, we regard no one from a human point of view." This was to insist that those who are received into this fellowship, into the community of the redeemed, the church, are to be seen, not as they once were—Asians, Africans, Jews, Greeks, slave, free, male, female, not in any of these human categories or classifications—but in a new category or a new classification.

"Therefore, if any one is in Christ, he is a new creation; the old has passed away, behold, the new has come" (2 Cor 5:17). Thus for the Christian to continue to place his brothers and sisters in Christ into the old classifications is for him to deny the faith he claims. It is precisely at this point—the denial of the faith in the name of the faith—that the church is most in danger of losing its life. For the apostle Paul, whose words we have just cited, continued: ". . . and entrusting to us the message of reconciliation" (2 Cor 5:19). But how can we preach the message of reconciliation if we are a living denial of it? If we deny that message of reconciliation entrusted to us, are we in fact still the church?

This question has many hazards. John Calvin said: "We have no right lightly to abandon the church because it is not perfect." Certainly all branches of the holy catholic church are subject to error and do err. Certainly all individual members of the corporate body are subject to sin and do sin. The church does not cease to be the church because it errs or because its members continue in sin. The institution may be able to neglect its mission and remain the church. But there is real doubt that it can both neglect its mission *and* deny its very nature and yet remain the church.

When the church excludes those who come crying for inclusion, confessing their sins, professing belief in the Lordship of Christ; when it views fellow believers through human categories and classifications, it is denying its nature. For the church, by nature, is inclusive and corporate. One cannot say, "I will live in fellowship with all who believe in the same Lord as I, provided they do not come from Philadelphia." Being from Philadelphia, being a white man or a Negro, is a human category, and, following the apostle Paul, "from now on . . . we regard no one from a human point of view" (2 Cor 5:16). There is now only one category for those who are Christ's, and we cannot arbitrarily rule otherwise. Race is a human category and is not one of the questions the church asks. Therefore, when we ask about the race of a fellow Christian, explicitly or implicitly, we are not being true to our nature as Christ's people.

The same truth holds when we evangelize according to racial neighborhoods or racial households. This is to neglect the true purpose of our mission. God has entrusted to us his message of reconciliation. When we withhold it, when we pass over a geographical locale because "they are not our people," we are neglecting or betraying our mission. God has created this new humanity, this new creation—the church—"to preach good news to the poor, . . . to proclaim release to the captives and recovering of sight to the blind, to set at liberty those who are oppressed, to proclaim the acceptable year of the Lord" (Luke 4:18-19, from Isa 61:1-2). If the church regards people from a human point of view in the pursuit of this mission, it neglects the calling and the charge that its Lord has laid upon it.

Of course, the segregationist will say: "But I can love the member of a minority group, I can have his welfare at heart, I can do all the good things one Christian might be expected to do for another and *still insist that he stay in a separate neighborhood, school, and church.*"

Two things must be said in answer to this. First of all, Christ left us no such freedom. The nature of the church denies us such a privilege. As members of the corporate body of Christ, we may not classify or categorize. "The eye cannot say to the hand, I have no need of you. . . . On the contrary, the parts of the body which seem to be weaker are indispensable" (1 Cor 12:21-22). Thus, even if one could prove that a racial group or any other human category is inferior, low in morals, lazy, shiftless, lower in intelligence, given to various weaknesses of character, the New Testament tells us that these are all excellent reasons for that group to be included.

The second thing that must be said to the segregationist who insists that he can love his brother and still restrict his freedom through a system of segregation is that this simply is not true. Who, having two children, can claim to love them equally if he puts one in a room—which he himself selects—gives that child the same toys, clothes, food, and medical care as the other child whom he has not restricted to an assigned room but has given the freedom of the house and grounds, including even the room assigned to the first child? The segregationist is often honest and sincere in his belief that he loves the minority person whom he restricts, but we may well question whether he really knows the meaning of love.

We must say, then, frankly recognizing the danger of such a position, that at some point, some very fine but very real point, it is possible for the church to cease to be the church, and that at that point it should identify itself by some other name.

During World War II, because of the extreme shortage of coffee in Europe, authorities began putting small amounts of parched barley in the brew. Since no one could tell the difference, the amount was gradually increased. Eventually the people were drinking nothing but parched barley. But the change had come so gradually that many thought they were drinking the finest coffee.

There are two remarkable things about this story. The first is that so few people knew the difference. The second is that those who were responsible for it and who did know the difference insisted that this was indeed coffee their people were drinking and that it was a superior coffee to that of other countries. It did not contain caffeine, the aroma was more pleasant, it was easier on the digestive system.

Despite the fact that these things were true and perhaps desirably so, the true lover of coffee would have to differ with this reasoning and say that the people were drinking something other than coffee. The question is: How much barley can be put into coffee and still have coffee? When should it begin to be called by some other name? Or, with respect to the question now before us: How far can the church wander from its mission and nature and still remain the church?

The Christian faith certainly can be changed at many points so as to make it conform more to my personal preferences, more palatable, more easily acceptable, more in keeping with my culture and my way of life. But the question is: Will it be a Christian church when we have finished with this adjustment to human desires, needs, prides, and prejudices?

An adherent of the free church tradition always hesitates to use the term "heresy." But what we have been saying is that racism has negated so much of the mission and nature of the church in America that there is no other name for it except that opprobrious term—heresy. It is the question that was raised for us by the parable of the "barley-coffee" that made heresy extremely serious and dangerous throughout the history of the church. It is not that the heretics wished to oppose the true faith. On the contrary, they argued that they alone held the true faith.

The task of the church would be considerably less arduous and difficult if the racist would denounce the church. He seldom does this. Far more often he will claim to be defending the faith when he expounds his racial theories. He may denounce the clergy, or certain boards or bishops, but always the racist insists that the Christian faith does not really mean what that clergy or that board or that bishop says it means. It is the bishop, the minister, or the priest who is apostate. The racist is orthodox. It is he who loves the church and must protect it from those who preach false doctrines and would deceive the people.

Here the failure of the church today becomes patent—not because the church today spawns heresy. That has always been so. There is no reason to believe that Christian doctrine will ever be free of misunderstanding and willful distortion. The contemporary church has failed because it has not learned how to prevent racism from poisoning its life and mission. When one, within the church and in the church's name, justifies and presents a wholly un-Biblical doctrine of creation, redemption, and life in the Spirit, founded on racist presuppositions and prejudices, he is living in serious heresy; and the church, if it is to save its own life, must somehow learn to deal with him. In so doing, it does not tremble for its physical, institutional life; but it remembers that it has not been called to great numbers or great wealth, but to wholeness and health.

QUESTIONS FOR STUDY AND DISCUSSION

A. Was the Supreme Court decision on segregation in the schools essentially a legal and sociological decision or essentially a religious decision? Is it possible to say that this decision was based on moral law to which the churches have borne a constant witness?

B. Is it true, as the author suggests on page 75, that it is the nature of man to be vindictive as a consequence of oppression and exploitation?

C. It has been said, and the author gives supporting biblical evidence, that "Christianity creates its own culture." How would you evaluate this contention?

D. Many people, not all expressly segregationist, have argued that people prefer to go to churches of their own color. To what degree is this true or false?

E. Does the church cease being the church when it refuses to admit persons of a minority group? What are the marks of a true church or the requisite factor which makes a church false?

THE NATURE OF THE PROBLEM

THE TERM "SEGREGATIONIST" MEANS many things. It means the Ku Klux Klan and a large part of the White Citizens' Councils who support the strict separation of racial groups without reference to any other values.

It means the session member who says he would not object to having his children attend Sunday school with members of another race or living in an integrated neighborhood, but will not allow it because he fears it will lead to intermarriage.

It means the rapidly increasing Black Muslim movement among urban Negroes. This movement, whose membership lists are estimated to contain between 100,000 and 250,000 persons, advocates violence similar to that of the Klan. Unlike the "Uncle Toms" among Negroes who favored segregation because they derived some personal benefit from it, the Black Muslims oppose integration on the grounds that the white man is inferior and unfit for full citizenship in the coming black society. Not integration, but separation and the founding of a black nation on American soil, is their cry. Theirs is the voice of the disillusioned Negro masses.

The term "segregationist" means the Montgomery woman who held her small child in her arms during a mob attack on bus riders, and clung to the hair of a Negro girl in an effort to pull her close enough for the lad to strike her in the face with his little fists.

It means the Governor of Alabama whose repeated vitriolic outbursts inflamed the passions of the mob and by innuendo invited violence. It means state legislators who use every conceivable device to evade the law of the land. It means the gentle dowager, or, as reported by the Attorney General of California, "little old ladies in tennis shoes" who dearly love their maids, their cooks, and their cocker spaniels, but believe that the term "civil rights" is a communist slogan.

"Segregationist" means restricted neighborhoods in Westchester County, New York, or hooded night riders in Mississippi. It is the Tennessee Society for the Maintenance of Segregation or the New England congregation that generously builds a mission for the colored people because "they will be happier with their own people."

The truth is that "segregationist" means most of us in one form or to one degree. It does not mean only the rabid and lunatic fringe that expends all of its energy in race hatred. For the Christian, it must also mean anyone who regards people "from a human point of view," and who classifies and categorizes members within the body of Christ.

Anyone who believes that discrimination and prejudice are peculiar to the southern region of America has only to look at the list of hate groups that have been active over the past decade. Although most of the new organizations that have sprung up since the Supreme Court's 1954 decision are located in the South, older and more established groups with headquarters in other regions have published the major portion of hate literature in this country.

Such organizations as the Christian Nationalist Crusade, headed by Gerald L. K. Smith, of Los Angeles, the American Nationalists of Inglewood, California, and the group that publishes *Common Sense* in Union, New Jersey, have blanketed areas of unrest. They have served as catalysts of violence in community after community, North and South.

Notwithstanding the fact that anti-Semitism has been the chief stock in trade of these organizations, they have more recently adopted the racial crisis as the chief vehicle by which to peddle their wares of suspicion and rancor. This has served more to stir anti-Negro feeling in the North than it has to arouse anti-Semitism in the South. Generally speaking, a dormant form of racial prejudice is more prevalent in the North than is religious bigotry (especially anti-Semitism) in the South.

While the Southern resistance groups have far more respectability than their Northern counterparts, both couch their purposes in lofty, culturally approved, and generalized terms. For example, the White Citizens' Council of Mississippi has as its slogan: "Dedicated to the maintenance of peace, good order, and domestic tranquility in our communities and in our state and to the preservation of our state's rights."

Such high-sounding phrases create an aura of respectability about the movement and permit the central organization to be free of responsibility for the often drastic pronouncements and actions of local units. However, the organizations themselves make no attempt to conceal their belief in white supremacy, biologically, socially, ethically, and politically.

They are categorically opposed to desegregation in schools, churches, and public accommodations, and frequently object to Negroes' registering and voting. The political strength of these groups is impressive. At the beginning, most of them disclaimed any political ambitions. This is no longer the case. Such groups now have virtually absolute power in one state in the South and are a significant political factor in several others. It is evident that they are not concerned only with race. In 1955, W. J. Simmons, executive secretary of the Mississippi Citizens' Council, had this to say:

> I think... [the White Citizens' Council] is much more than a white supremacist group, and I think it is much more than a protectionist group. I think it is fundamentally the first real stirrings of a conservative revolt in this country, judging by the responses we've gotten from other states.... Some of the people who are attracted to this movement may not be concerned about the Negro.

Developments since Simmons' statement was voiced have proved his observation to be an accurate appraisal of the situation. Many politically conservative and reactionary organizations, among them the John Birch Society, have become working allies with the White Citizens' Councils. While the councils are most concerned with the preservation of segregation, they will gladly co-operate with other groups whose diverse aims may be, for example, to abolish the income tax or prevent the fluoridation of water. Put them all together, and in some sections of the country and on some issues you have a powerful political movement.

What does all this have to do with the renewal of the church? A great deal. First of all because these groups have succeeded in creating the image of a holy crusade. Some of them deliberately and with astute calculation see the churches as a convenient "front" for their activities. For example, Robert B. Patterson, secretary of the Citizens' Councils of America, told a group in New Orleans that they should infiltrate the churches and there take the offensive against "the mixing of the races."

"By organizing within churches," said Patterson, "foes of integration could bring pressure on ministers to support segregation and change the position of state and national church organizations which have endorsed mixing of races." He added with solemnity: "We love our churches just like we love our schools, and we want to preserve them." Protestant Patterson's advice seems to have been followed by a number of well-known Roman Catholics, and it appears that it was this kind of "creeping Protestantism" that disturbed the Archbishop to the point of exercising the seldom used but powerful weapon of excommunication.

But while the ultimate allegiance of spokesmen such as Patterson is to racial hate and while their manipulation of the churches is coldly calculated, by far the greatest number of these people are convinced that their cause is just and righteous. They are convinced that God is on their side. In seeking to maintain segregation they are doing nothing less than his will. Indeed, one of the greatest dangers we face is that the racial doctrine of white supremacy, which has always been an element of secular culture in America, will become a part of the church's body of dogma, an unwritten article of faith.

Perhaps the following story will illustrate how this gloomy prospect can actually be realized. One of my earliest recollections is of sitting one evening in a rural church in a Deep South county and watching the Ku Klux Klan file solemnly into the little frame building. In the ceremony that followed, a large pulpit Bible was presented by the Klansmen to the congregation and was accepted by the revival preacher. On the back cover of the book was stamped in brazen letters: K.K.K.

Several years ago I was preaching in that same pulpit and as I held the back cover of the Bible while reading the Scripture, my fingers moved across those large, embossed letters. Later in the afternoon, talking with several members of the congregation, I asked them what they thought about having a pulpit Bible in their church that had been given by the Klan and bore its symbol. Although these were people who had lived their entire lives in that community and who had been present at that original Klan ceremony, each one stated that he had quite forgotten the incident and had never known that the letters K.K.K. were raised on the back cover of the Bible on their pulpit.

The greatest test and danger facing the Christian church in America is not racism as such, but that racism has become, consciously or unconsciously, a part of the faith. The Klan no longer exists in that rural community, but it has left its stamp not only on the cover of the Bible but on the minds and hearts of the present generation and those yet unborn. The groups which now have the prestige and power that formerly was the Klan's—the White Citizens' Councils and the John Birch Society—will also pass away. But the seedlings they are planting today will grow and thrive for a long, long time. And these seedlings are essentially religious in character. Most of what is written and distributed by groups seeking to subvert the law of church and nation has a basically religious theme. Religious meaning is increasingly being written into the race literature of the hate groups and no subject arouses more religious support in America today than the subject of race. The segregationists in pew and pulpit who appeal to such authority are not simply resorting to rationalization. The stamp of racism has become a part of their religious heritage, and for them the integrationists are those who are apostate. In the eyes of the segregationist, the man who believes in racial justice denies the faith. The true defender of Christianity is he who would keep the races forever separate in the church and in the society.

As indicated earlier, the task of the churches would be less difficult if the segregationist would say: "I like segregation in my church and neighborhood and school, and I am going to keep it that way no matter what Christ or the Bible or the church say to the contrary." If that were the situation we faced, the churches could simply put their numerous mission boards and departments of evangelism to work converting the heathen. But instead, the segregationist defends white supremacy in God's name. With Bible in his hand, and chapter and verse on his lips, he presents and documents his arguments. In the name of God he denies the love, mercy, justice, and judgment of God, and it is virtually impossible to break through and reach him.

The attempt must be made, however, and sometimes it is effectively accomplished on the level of Scripture. One of the biblical passages most often quoted by the racists is the Genesis story of creation. (Indeed, a critic once remarked, somewhat unjustly, of a Nashville segregationist minister: "His trouble is that he never got any farther in the Bible than Genesis.") Let us now examine that well-known but much misused account of Creation.

"The blue birds and the red birds don't fly together," say the segregationists. It's true. They don't. And the Genesis account tells why:

"And God said, 'Let the earth put forth vegetation, plants yielding seed, and fruit trees bearing fruit . . . *each according to its kind.*' . . . And it was so. The earth brought forth vegetation, plants yielding seed *according to their own kinds*, and trees bearing fruit in which is their seed, *each according to its kind.* . . . God created the great sea monsters and every living creature that moves . . . *according to their kinds*, and every winged bird *according to its kind.* . . .

"And God said, 'Let the earth bring forth living creatures *according to their kinds*: cattle and creeping things and beasts of the earth *according to their kinds*.' And it was so. And God made the beasts of the earth *according to their kinds* and the cattle *according to their kinds*, and everything that creeps upon the ground *according to its kind*" (Gen 1:11–12, 21, 24–25; italics added).

". . . Each according to its kind." This is probably the most important passage of Scripture in any treatment of race. The phrase, or a slight variation of it, appears no fewer than ten times in this account. But suddenly a dramatic change takes place: "Then God said, '*Let us make man in our image after our likeness*'" (Gen 1:26; italics added).

All the other creatures had been made "each according to its kind," but man was made in the image and likeness of God! Thus man became the highest of God's creatures—not some men, but *man*! But there is still another significant note in this story. God made man in his own image. Certainly that alone makes man of considerable importance. But he also made him out of dirt! Man is at once made after the image of God and created out of that lowly commodity—dirt!

Various doctrines have sprung from these two facets of the Creation story. Some have emphasized the idea of man being a little lower than the angels and in the image of God and have insisted that he is therefore the very heart and center of the universe. Others have insisted that being made from dirt, man is precisely that—dirt, with all the connotation which that humble substance brings to mind. At this point it is not important which is the correct emphasis or interpretation. What is important is that whatever is true of a man, he is God's creature and he is one and inseparable from every other human creature.

The account of Creation, of course, does not really have to do with race. It has to do with grace; with what we could not do for ourselves because we were not. It is something unearned, undeserved, something we could not even ask for, because we were without existence and without power until God performed his creative act. For the segregationist to question creation is to question God's grace, for creation *is* grace—nothing less nor more. "It is he that made us and we are his" (Ps 100:3). And whether we are a little lower than the angels or as lowly as dirt, God made us, and neither the color of the angels above us nor the color of the dirt beneath our feet is important.

Interestingly enough, if the color of the dirt of which we are made is important, it really adds credence to the Black Muslim argument for black supremacy. For so-called white man isn't white at all but is about the color of hill clay, and anyone who has ever been a farmer knows hill clay won't grow much of anything except crowder peas and pine trees, while dark soil is always at a premium! But whatever we men are made of, one thing is certain—we are all of the same stuff. All of us are in the same boat and the boat is captained, not by ourselves, but by God. It is the captain above who has the right to rank and place the passengers, and God has given no indication that this is done on the basis of race.

The church must be concerned with the segregationist not only because he is within the institution, but especially and above all because he too is a child of God. He too is a brother. The church cannot force the racist out of its fellowship by any arbitrary or highhanded discipline. The church must understand him, but at the same time it must not permit understanding him to mean that its own policy becomes silence or inaction. There is no one in America more troubled, more distressed, than the pastor who truly understands, who looks out over his congregation and his city and understands that his people are, at least in part, victims of the bitter crop of the seeds of time and the inexplicable forces of modernity which they did not plant, whose furrows they did not cultivate, but whose harvest is imposed upon them. At the same time such a pastor will know that he has no choice but to preach the uncompromising and scandalizing imperatives of the gospel. Jesus understood the real condition of the people of Jerusalem, but the knowledge that certain social and political factors played a role in the popular customs and ethos of the city did not keep him from entering Jerusalem and turning it upside down.

The racist is the greatest challenge the church faces today in both the North and the South. One might say that he is the true adolescent of adult Christianity; the most unlovely and the most in need of love. Certainly the church must not tolerate what he stands for, but it must not abandon him in its attempt to force him to maturity. Those of us who consider ourselves the children of light with respect to our attitudes and practices in race relations must ask ourselves what happened in our lives to make us so different from the racist. What combination of genes, what freak of historical circumstance and personal association, gave us vision to see the truth? Even if God laid his hands on us, even if some are chosen, to what credit can we claim, what reason have we to boast, and what right to condemn? Somehow we cannot hate the racist, for most of us do not know how or when we left his ranks, if we have left them at all.

I have seen and known the resentment of the racist, his hostility, his frustration, his need for someone upon whom to lay blame and to punish. I know he is mistaken, misguided, and willfully disobedient, but somehow I am not able to distinguish between him and myself. My sins may not be his, but they are no less real and no less heinous. Perhaps I have been too close to this man. Perhaps if I had not heard his anguished cry when the rains didn't come in time to save his cotton, if I had not felt the severity of his economic deprivation, if I had not looked upon his agony on Christmas Eve while I, his six-year-old child, feigning sleep, waited for a Santa who would never come; if I had not been one of him through these gales of tragedy, I would be able to condemn him without hesitation. If I had not shared his plight; if I had not lived with him in an atmosphere of suspicion, distrust, ignorance, misinformation, and nefarious political leadership, surely my heart would break less when I see him fomenting mob violence in front of *his* schoolhouse and *his* church house. Perhaps I would not pity him as much if I were not from his loins. But pity him I do.

But the church must not pity the racist. It must love and redeem him. It must somehow set him free. With the same love that it is commanded to shower upon the innocent victim of his frustration and hostility, the church must love the racist. Moreover, the church is called to love those who use and exploit both the racists and their victims for personal wealth and political gain. The church must stand in love and judgment upon the victim, the victimized, and those, both black and white, who exploit both, for they are all the children of God.

QUESTIONS FOR STUDY AND DISCUSSION

A. To what extent must one differentiate between the Black Muslim movement and the National Association for the Advancement of Colored People? Can they be lumped together as racist? Further, are there significant differences between the NAACP and the White Citizens' Councils?

B. The author speaks of dormant racial prejudice in the North. Is this accurate, or would this be better designated as class or economic group prejudice?

C. What is, if any, the linkage between political conservatism and the doctrine of racial segregation? What does the John Birch Society stand for, and what should be the attitude of the church toward it?

D. What do you think of the author's refutation of the segregationist's argument from Genesis? Does the account of Creation really support a doctrine of racial assimilation?

E. What is our responsibility as Christians to friends who say that they cannot, in good conscience, acknowledge the rightness of racial integration?

THE GODS OF LAW AND ORDER

Prior to 1954, most of the Protestant denominations in the United States were relatively silent on the question of race. Since that year innumerable statements, resolutions, and pronouncements on segregation and discrimination have come from virtually all the major Protestant groups. Many of them begin by endorsing the Supreme Court decision of May 17, 1954, on segregation in public education. Most of them call for harmonious relations and a calm acceptance of what the court has decreed. Almost all deplore violence, but few choose to vex themselves with the thought of what their position would be if the court's decision and Christian doctrine were not in agreement. Indeed, it would almost appear that the court had made a decision binding upon Christians that the churches had no competence to make for themselves.

Before 1954, most liberal churches and churchmen were not insistent upon a doctrinaire position of strict obedience to the law. Today the American churches argue that segregation must be abolished because it is illegal. It is interesting to note, however, that for some years, at least a few churches and churchmen occasionally admonished their people to join in disobedience to law if such law was patently contrary to the will of God.

For example, delivering the Knapp Lecture at the University of Wisconsin on March 19, 1952, Chancellor B. Harvie Branscomb, of Vanderbilt University, said:

> The second contribution which religion has made to American life has been the insistence upon a law of God which is supreme above all human institutions and man-made legislation. To this divine law man owes final obedience. If the laws of state or government deviate from this standard, they have no moral authority and, in fact, should be disregarded or rejected.[1]

---

1. Branscomb, *The Contribution of Moral and Spiritual Ideas*, 11.

Eight years later, one of Chancellor Branscomb's students, the Rev. James M. Lawson Jr., had this to say about the breaking of law:

> Defiant violation of the law is a contradiction of my entire understanding of and loyalty to Christian nonviolence. When the Christian considers the concept of civil disobedience as an aspect of nonviolence, it is only within the context of a law or a law enforcement agency which has in reality ceased to be the law, and then the Christian does so only in fear and trembling before God.[2]

Even a cursory glance at these two statements will show that Chancellor Branscomb's words are considerably more emphatic and uncompromising than those of the student. Yet Mr. Lawson was expelled from Vanderbilt by the chancellor on the allegation that he "advocated a planned campaign of civil disobedience."

There is no evidence to suggest that Chancellor Branscomb was insincere either in 1952 or in 1960. It seems more likely that the events of the past eight years brought a change in his position. Dr. Branscomb has never favored racial segregation in his public policies and has worked diligently to effect desegregation on his own campus. Prior to 1954 he had insisted that if the laws of the state were in conflict with the laws of God, the laws of the state should be disregarded or rejected. In fact, he did disregard them when he desegregated Vanderbilt University, for the law of Tennessee holds that private schools may not have Negroes and whites in the same classrooms. As late as 1960 he was still speaking in behalf of racial justice, but now he maintained that this must be accomplished within the framework of man-made, not God-ordained, legislation.

There seems to have been a similar change in the position of many of the churches. The churches with dispatch adopted the dictum that the clear duty of the Christian is always to obey the law when, in 1954, the law became what the churches wanted it to be. Advising their people to desegregate because the law said to do so seemed less risky than taking a bold position based on the Christian doctrine of man, the biblical imperative of justice, and the doctrine of the sovereignty of God.

But the worship of law proved quickly to be a two-edged sword. For the integrationist Christian it was pleasant to be able to say, "The law is on our side!" But the segregationist Christian was able to argue on the same basis. Particularly in the South, he had clear and unequivocal

---

2. Quoted in *Nashville Banner*, March 3, 1960.

legislation at the state and local levels which explicitly forbade any form of racial mixing. He could argue convincingly that there is nothing in the Christian body of doctrine which holds that federal laws are any more sacred than state or local laws.

The legal argument within the churches made for further confusion when those favoring desegregation began arguing for disobedience to law in the sit-in movement during 1959–1960. The General Assembly of The United Presbyterian Church in the U.S.A., meeting in May, 1960, went on record as advocating a degree of civil disobedience when it said among other things: "Affirming that some laws and customs requiring racial discrimination are, in our judgment, such serious violations of the law of God as to justify peaceable and orderly disobedience or disregard of these laws . . ." The National Council of the Protestant Episcopal Church and several other groups took similar positions. One could assume that this was a swing away from the "let us obey the law" position which developed immediately following the Supreme Court decision of 1954 and a stronger ground upon which to fight. But one week after the United Presbyterian General Assembly took its action in Cleveland, a spokesman for the White Citizens' Council in New Orleans strongly recommended and called for a campaign of civil disobedience (as a matter of conscience) to combat desegregation of the New Orleans public schools! On the other hand, in Montgomery, Alabama, when Negro demonstrators were rudely handled by state and city police and a group of citizens who had been quickly deputized as a mounted force to assist in the brutal dispersion of the demonstrators, the local ministerial alliance had the following to say:

> Let us continue to depend upon law and order administered with a concern for all citizens to stabilize our society.

The appeal to law is at best a confused picture within the churches. We must say quite frankly that it appears that the churches have often used it to evade their deeper responsibility. It has been the easy way. But the church has not always appealed to law for the rightness of its action. Here is another kind of statement regarding this problem:

> We believe it is sinful to have two congregations in the same community for persons of separate and distinct races. That race prejudice would cause trouble in the churches we know. It did this in apostolic days. Not once did the apostles suggest that they

should form separate congregations for the different races. But they always admonished them to unity, forbearance, love, and brotherhood in Christ Jesus.

Upon first glance this would appear to be just another statement among the reams of resolutions and pronouncements that have heated the presses for the past seven years. And it would surely be assumed that such a statement represents the view of the more liberal church bodies, for it moves far beyond schools, parks, and lunch counters; and it affirms without equivocation that if there are two congregations in one town because of race, one of them should be abandoned. Actually the statement comes from one of the most conservative groups in Protestantism. The man who wrote it was far from notorious for his social liberalism. He was David Lipscomb, a Church of Christ evangelist. He made the statement in an article on "Race Prejudice," in the February 1878 issue of *Gospel Advocate,* when a Texas Church of Christ congregation objected to a Negro who sought to affiliate with the local church.[3] David Lipscomb was one of the foremost leaders of that denomination, and one of its colleges (still segregated [at the time of original publication, 1962]) bears his name today.

Lipscomb's statement is important for several reasons. In the first place it is generally thought that we have come a long way in race relations since 1878 and that if given time, patience, and understanding we will "work this thing out" in our churches. Yet in 1878 a spokesman for the most conservative group called it a sin to have separate congregations because of race, while almost a hundred years later in the most liberal groups we still have, not only racial congregations, but racial synods in the Presbyterian Church, the Central Jurisdiction for Negroes in the Methodist, separate judicatories in almost every communion, and a racial ministry in all.

But an even more remarkable feature of this statement, in the light of which we might re-examine our own positions, is that it made no appeal to harmony *or* to the law. Many church appeals and pronouncements today are based on one or the other of these prime values. Lipscomb's was not. With respect to harmony within the fellowship, he did not try to avoid conflict but seemed to think that harmony or its absence was irrelevant to the question at hand. In an almost casual manner he

---

3. Lipscomb, "Race Prejudice," 120–21.

moved on to state what was for him the heart of the matter. Apparently to this spokesman of a group sometimes referred to as a "fringe sect," the problem of Christian behavior had nothing to do with what people *wanted* to do, or were *ready* to do, or with what did or did not violate the local mores. Like many before his time and since, Lipscomb recognized the test that the church faced by its double concern for conformity and loyalty to God. Implicit in his statement was what social scientists have indicated in our own time: there is a difference between prejudice and discrimination, between feeling and behavior. In effect, Lipscomb said: Surely there is such a thing as race prejudice in all of us who are in the churches, and it will cause trouble. So what? His was the strange notion that Christian behavior had to do only with the uncompromising demands of Almighty God as revealed through the life and teachings of Jesus Christ.

Contrast this to our day when cardinal virtues are harmony within the fellowship, peace, good will, "tact" on the part of the preacher, dignity and respectability of approach, law and order, constitutions, status, preservation of public schools and property values. All these values are important to us and doubtless were to the group for whom Mr. Lipscomb spoke, but they did not seem primary. Lipscomb made no appeal to law, to the courts, to democracy, or to any political ideology. His was a simple proclamation: "Thus saith the Lord." This despite the fact that the Emancipation Proclamation and the tumult of Reconstruction were as close to him and fully as controversial as recent Supreme Court decisions on civil rights are to us.

If arguments for law and order, peace and harmony, are irrelevant to the church's concern on race, so are appeals to the social sciences and humanitarianism. These are all valuable and valid approaches, but they are not the distinctive approaches of the church. Law and order is the business of government, social science is the concern of the sociologists and anthropologists, and humanitarianism is the inspiration of thousands of dedicated men and women who spend their lives alleviating human suffering. All of these have a place in the church; and the church, which has learned much from these sources, cannot ignore them. But the church must not be distracted by them. Its concern is more profound and more radical than any of these.

The advocate of racial justice often loses the argument because he permits his antagonist to choose the weapon and field of battle. The racist usually meets us on sociological grounds, and we become social scientists because it is so simple to refute his arguments one by one, and we are deluded into believing that thereby we have won the day. He says the minority group is dirt, is low in intelligence and lax in morals, is less ambitious, doesn't pay his just share of the taxes, is shiftless, lazy, and uncouth. Such arguments are easy to answer on sociological grounds. We can explain to him that he really means achievement and not intelligence, and we can point out why this is true. It is no difficult matter to show that morality is a relative matter. The double standard and the success of the majority group in keeping its questionable morals under wraps will document the case. We can say that a group which is the last to be hired and the first to be fired would understandably have less ambition, for what is the use of trying under such circumstances? We can say that taxes are paid on income, and if we give the minority jobs with higher income, they would then pay more taxes. We can skillfully puncture the racist's stereotypes one by one. But generally he remains unconvinced.

The real question takes us in another direction. Why should we rely upon our knowledge of the social sciences when there is a Christian answer? If we use *that* answer, if we pick the field of battle, the segregationist has less advantage. The Christian answer is that whether or not his analysis is correct, God has not called us into the body of Christ, into the fellowship of the redeemed, the church, because we are clean or have superior intelligence or high morals. He has called us into a fellowship in which we are all unclean, lazy, uncouth, lax in morality, low in ambition; in which we are all undeserving yet loved and accepted of God, our common Father. In our present state of sophistication in the churches we might find it difficult to give this answer, but it is nearer the truth than the attempt to refute racial stereotypes. Race is not a rational matter. The consciousness of race, ethnocentrism, as even some social scientists admit, is largely a state of mind and it is difficult to combat a state of mind by logical refutation. God made no such approach when he brought man into being and when he stooped to save him. His move was irrational, foolishness, a stumbling block. A king was born amidst sheep manure and murdered as an enemy of the people and a subverter of the state. What possible rational argument can we devise from the story of Creation and redemption. And yet this is all we have to offer. This is the distinctive Christian apologia.

Why should we not grant the segregationist his facts? They are not always accurate. But what if they are? Let others boast of *facts!* Ours is a faith that transcends facts to lay hold upon truth. Our task is not to refute by facts, but to lead the racist to see that when he confronts the Christ he claims to serve, his facts are irrelevant.

From a rational point of view, the segregationist sometimes has sound arguments. And the churches themselves have sometimes used the same arguments. In several places, for example, the churches have established schools when public facilities have been closed. History has already recorded the fact that, when the secular culture failed to preserve segregation, the churches took up the fight and held on for yet a little while. Why did we do it? We did it for the sake of good, for the advancement of knowledge, for the increase of wisdom, for the sake of our children. No one will question these motives. It cannot be denied that we have a responsibility to our children. Who would be prepared to argue that Christians ought to suffer their children, black or white, to grow up in ignorance?

These are rational values. They appeal to the common sense of ordinary men and women. But what is their real validity within the fellowship of believers? In the final analysis, when our most rational arguments and common sense appeals fail to fill the yawning void of unfaith, when we stand nakedly under the command of God, we know that these values we have worshiped are creatures of the false gods of race and culture.

A young white Christian mother once said to me in Little Rock that she could never again send her child to one of the schools established to evade the law as long as they accept her child but refuse the child of another mother because of some degree of skin pigmentation. She could not permit herself this privilege, she said, and maintain her integrity as a member of a church which in its public posture stood for equality and brotherhood. She reported with some emotion how it felt deliberately to sacrifice her son when by one stroke of the pen she could save him. She was in good company.

"Take your son, your only son Isaac, . . . and go to the land of Moriah, and offer him there as a burnt offering upon one of the mountains of which I shall tell you. . . . And Abraham took the wood of the burnt offering and laid it on Isaac his son; and he took in his hand the fire and the knife. So they went both of them together. . . . Then Abraham put forth his hand, and took the knife to slay his son" (Gen 22:2, 6, 10).

Compared with this radical faithfulness, how puny and petty our rationalizations about our property values, our children's future, our neighborhood pride, must be to the Creator. We cannot obey the teachings of our church and our nation, we say, because it will injure our little children! Whether this prediction of the tragedy that will befall our children is true or untrue is not yet clear. It is true, by the mind and spirit of Christ, that this is not the first question we must answer. Is it even worthy of debate? This Little Rock mother (she and others like her have been the salvation of that city) was right. It was that kind of obedience that made the faith of Abraham a great religion and his righteousness imputed to the New Israel of Christ.

"He who loves son or daughter more than me is not worthy of me" (Matt 10:37), said a man whom most racists, North and South, still call Lord. This is the question before the church in America: Do we believe in the God of Abraham, Isaac, and Jacob, the God and Father of our Lord Jesus Christ, or do we worship at the shrine of state sovereignty, restricted neighborhoods, white schools, and racial supremacy? Today it is white supremacy; there is a good chance that tomorrow it will be black supremacy. Either is contrary to the will and purpose of God, and no amount of rationalization will be able to obscure that truth.

QUESTIONS FOR STUDY AND DISCUSSION

A. The question of civil disobedience has come to the fore again in this country through the campaigns in the South of the sit-in movements. Is the Christian justified in disobeying the law when he believes such laws conflict with his religious convictions?

B. The author admits that the social sciences, law, and humanitarianism "have a place in the church ... but ..." Do you agree with his understanding of their role? To what extent does the gospel transcend these "human agencies"?

C. Should Christian parents be willing to sacrifice the peaceful social adjustment of their child in school for the "radical faithfulness" of Abraham by enrolling the child in a school seething with racial tension? What does God expect from us in such moments of decision? What is the responsibility of the whole church, rather than individual parents, in such situations?

THE HUMANISTIC DETOUR

THE SEGREGATIONIST CHRISTIAN is playing a most significant role in the life of the church. He is constantly forcing those who consider themselves the children of light to defend and define the Christian message. If when we begin to define and defend what we think is the Christian message, we discover that it is little more than a sentimental veil of humanism, it is because we have not met the segregationist on the field upon which the Christian must fight. When we speak, it is most often of law and order, of human dignity, of man's rights, of democracy, of constitution, and, at best, of the principle of the brotherhood of man and the fatherhood of God. More and more this has become the most unfavorable terrain for battle. The humanist has done a great service to mankind by supporting the egalitarian line. But for the Christian church to assume this role is to court failure. We fail for two reasons. First, we cannot do well what the secular and humanist organizations can do. Our churches can become adjuncts to human relations councils and civil rights organizations, but this is to sell what we have much too short. For what we have to say is far more radical, far more demanding, far more inclusive of all of society than anything the humanistically oriented groups have said. If race is not a valid concept in Christian doctrine, there is no room to debate such irrelevancies as who sits where on a bus, who lives in which neighborhood, and who marries whom on the basis of propriety, law and order, and egalitarian philosophy.

As we have championed the humanistic arguments, we have also tended to become more and more humanitarian in our action programming. When a church organization needs personnel in the field of human relations it is inclined to look for effective, skilled social reformers or human engineers, but rarely preachers and prophets. There is a considerable difference. Doubtless the church historically has made use of both, and will continue to do so; but in our effort to find renewal for the church in the area of race relations, it is necessary to say more than that all men are brothers and ought to act brotherly. For we know that all men are not going to act like brothers and that the Christian faith has a great deal to say beyond that point. Moreover, our critics raise valid questions as to whether or not the church has any concern or right to be concerned with the desegregation of society so long as its own record is so dismal. If all church institutions, colleges and universities, hospitals, medical schools, secondary and primary schools, camps, assembly grounds, congregations, homes for aged and orphanages were open to all, there would not be very much remaining for society to do.

It is often said that we have this concern for justice as citizens of our nation; that as Christian citizens we must exercise this responsibility within structures of law and order which also have their influence upon the church. There is truth here. Action in society has often influenced the pattern of church life. But are we not also, and foremost, citizens of the Kingdom of God? What right have I to indict a real estate agent for restricting residential developments when my own church will not admit anyone other than white Protestants to its home for the retired? The admonition, "Physician, heal yourself" (Luke 4:23), is appropriate. To ignore it or even to offer rebuttal to what it implies is to add to our already abundant hypocrisy.

The second and more important reason we fail is that the Christian message on race does not depend upon egalitarian premises and arguments. Ours is not a message of law and order, of man's rights, of constitutions. The Christian view of race is not limited to the principle of the fatherhood of God and the brotherhood of man. When we tell the segregationist that the gospel is to obey the law and accept the Supreme Court decision, he can see no gospel, no "good news" here. This, for him, is only bad news, and he is not wrong to ridicule the church and tell it to mind its own business.

Of course, the segregationist is wrong if he means that the church should steer clear of controversy, but he is right when he says that purely humanistic values are not our basic concern. He is likewise right when he insists that the gospel is not a proclamation of what we ought to do.

But if he is told, as he *must* be told, that the Christian gospel was and is a message of grace and redemption, then it is an entirely different matter. Tell the segregationist that by this grace God became flesh—flesh meaning "like one of us." Tell him God was in this flesh. Tell him the *Christian* message on race relations and all human relations: God was in Christ reconciling the world to himself. God was in Christ reconciling his children to one another and thus to himself. God was in Christ breaking down the walls of hostility that separate man from man and all men from God. God, furthermore, was in Christ loving him—the segregationist himself; loving him, accepting him, forgiving him, even if he cannot yet love and accept and forgive his brother. This is what we have to say to the segregationist, whether he belongs to a Black Nationalist movement in Harlem, a White Property Owners' Association in Chicago, or a Citizens' Council in Birmingham. If he hears this and accepts it, there is more likelihood of achieving an integrated church in an integrated society than if we simply tell him that he should go home and be good, or that he ought to obey the law.

Those who take the position that there is no specific program of Christian race relations—that we must take our cue from economics, politics, and sociology—are mistaken. That is simply to say that there is no Christian message. It is well that the racist forces us to hear that message anew, and in the hearing will be our true renewal. The Christian message on race is nothing more nor less than the Christian message. It has to do with grace, not law, not order. That something has been done for us, something free, something with which we had nothing to do, something undeserved and unearned. It is the mercy and grace of God which has given us newness of life. In this "new creation" (2 Cor 5:17), we are neither Caucasian, African, Asian, male nor female, bond nor free. We are a third race. All our human engineering is vain if we miss the unambiguous point that, in the message of grace, race is irrelevant. The only relevant point has to do with redemption, not race class or caste. This is not an invitation to complacency by the preacher. This is no license to mumble, "God was in Christ, let us pray." This is not pious quietism. The relevance of this grace, this creative act of God, must ever be spelled out and applied over and over again in the rough and tumble of daily life.

Of course, we are reminded that this message of grace has been preached for two thousand years and that little has changed. Preaching just does not seem to achieve for us the goal of an inclusive church and society. The world goes merrily on its segregated way, and churches go on being exclusive. Businessmen from our ranks go on discriminating in hiring, in placement, and in promotions. Inevitably we feel that we must devise gimmicks, develop techniques. We are overwhelmed by the drive to be *effective*. It is at this point that we call upon the social scientists, the human engineers, the race relations specialists. We adopt uncritically the sophisticated methods of our secular colleagues. If we tell the cultured despisers among them that "God was in Christ" (2 Cor 5:19), so that "you are all one" (Gal 3:28), they are apt to wink slyly and chuckle. "A bunch of squares." Unrealistic, utopian. And so we compete with each other in the "do it yourself" market of the latest methods, techniques, and gimmicks. What we seem to have difficulty remembering is that we are a bunch of squares—we Christians.

The message we have is not the "latest word" or the most intellectually respectable; it is the same scandal, the same stumbling block it has always been. It does not reject method or spurn success, but it does not depend upon either for its ultimate validity. Our task is not to be successful—as if success proved validity. Our task is to proclaim the gospel. Proclamation means more than verbalizing from the pulpit, to be sure, and yet we can find no substitute for the sacrament of the Word. The world may not hear us. It never really has. But the message has not lost its power, and when it seems not to be heard, not to be *effective*, that is the time to proclaim it with greater resolve.

Crash programs and grand strategies may make us more acceptable to the public, the press, and the secular agencies in the field of race relations; but our "crash program" was initiated and has been accomplished; our "grand strategy" was designed and fulfilled centuries ago. And indeed not in a court of law, not within a political document, but in a tragic scene of bloody sweat and agonizing death on a scarred hillside outside the city of Jerusalem. If the world cannot see the error and folly of racism, if it cannot see that racial consciousness and prejudice is in conflict with the program and strategy of redemption, if it does not repent of the dreadful sin of racial exclusiveness as a result of our practice and proclamation of the gospel, then God has judged us and we are his impotent people. But, if as his servants we will not preach the gospel and will not demonstrate in our own ranks the oneness of all men as creatures of God, we will have sat in judgment upon God, and there will be nothing but frustration and failure for such a church. When that day comes, and God forbid that it has already arrived, we will have long since ceased to be the people of God.

The oneness of all men to which we are alluding does not have to do with man. It is possible that we are ineffective in race relations because we begin at the wrong place—with both the wrong subject and the wrong object. Churches frequently begin their Christian social concern programming by pointing out the suffering and deprivation of the minority group—photographs of undernourished children without shoes, standing outside of tar-paper shacks or in slum ghettos, their brown faces reflecting the confusion and sadness of heart of those who have too soon come to understand that the world holds for them few of its privileges. Anyone who cannot empathize with these victims of a ruthless and selfish society is far gone. Yet is there anything peculiarly Christian about such empathy? Does this express the authentic response of the church?

As one who has spent the last five years trying to minister in the numerous racial crises of the South, I know how easy it is to be motivated by feelings of pity and sympathy. Watching a mother stumble feebly along behind the casket of her son, murdered by a mob; going with a pastor into what is left of his church after a sack of dynamite has been thrown into it in the dark of Christmas Eve; seeing the bewilderment and pain of children whose presents, carefully concealed by Santa, are now broken and scattered throughout the debris of the manse; seeing a mother struck with a bottle as she takes her little girl to school; watching a pastor kicked and spat upon as he walks holding the trusting little hand of a six-year-old parishioner who is not yet old enough to be told that the screaming, unruly mob is there because she is going inside, that seven hundred grown men and women are terrified and frightened of her, one little six-year-old child—these are scenes which tear out the heart. Christian concern to correct such injustices as these is not just effusive sentimentality.

But the reactions that such scenes stir within us are not necessarily Christian reactions. At any rate this is not where we begin. To do so is surely to confuse subject and object; to be falsely oriented for Christian action. This is the starting point of the humanist. Certainly we must admit that from this point he has borne a most creditable witness. But the concern of the Christian is more basic. It is at least a different concern.

The Christian must first of all be concerned with souls. He will leap to the side of those who are being harmed, but his anguish at the suffering of the victims of racism will not blind him to the dangers facing the souls of the oppressors. The suffering of the minority group does not separate it from God, but the sin of the majority group does separate it from God. Thus, the soul of the dispossessor must concern us as much as the suffering of the dispossessed, and when this is not the case, our concern and action is something less than Christian concern and action. Even in terms of strategy, one-sided emphasis on the suffering is not very effective. For the suffering of the minority group does not greatly impress the dispossessor. He has grown callous to it and does not really see, much less is he shamed, by the tar-paper shack, the bare feet, the exclusion from jobs, the residential restrictions. For him, it has always been this way. These are realities of the normal white world in which he lives. He is surprised and angered that anyone would suppose that they should be otherwise. Let me illustrate.

In Fayette County, Tennessee, Negro farmers have been evicted from the land because they dared register to vote. A blacklist was circulated throughout the county through a long cold winter, with the naked ground for a floor. One man was shot with a high-powered rifle while asleep in his tent. His wife and children fled in terror into the darkness of a December night. Crop loans were denied tenant farmers even when a Federal court enjoined the owners from turning them off the land. A baby was born in one of the shabby, mud-splattered tents. An elderly woman had pneumonia. Local doctors reportedly denied medical aid to any Negro person who had registered to vote. A blacklist was circulated throughout the country with names of those who had registered, as a convenience for merchants who agreed to refuse to sell them groceries and supplies.

These conditions stimulated a rash of material aid from denominational groups throughout the country. One church agency sent volunteers to put floors in the tents. Others provided money for relief. Another purchased a four-hundred-acre farm and relocated several families from the tents. This was action that should have been taken, and it was taken with the purest motivation. No one could deny the responsibility of the churches to provide assistance to people without clothing, shelter, and food. Yet we failed to minister to the majority group, the dispossessors. There is some question, therefore, whether the whole gospel of redemption was heard and heeded by the people of Fayette County.

This pattern is repeated in virtually every case. And consequently the segregationist has been able to see a major weakness in our social action. He has seen our marked similarity to the purely secular and humanistic groups. He has seen that we have generally made the deprived the subject and him the object. In terms of simple strategy—a word that requires reinterpretation in the Christian vocabulary—the dispossessors might well have been more influenced, and the injustices corrected more quickly, if *they* had been the subject of church concern; if, at the same time there had been a ministry to them. If the segregationist had been told that what was happening to the suffering and the disinherited was not as dangerous as what was happening to him, he might have listened. If he had been warned that the judgment of God was upon him, not upon the victims, that he was separated from God because of his deeds, such a witness would, at least, have had strategic significance in terms of the church's objectives.

None of this is to deny the obligation of the Christian to relieve the suffering of the oppressed. It is rather to say that when this is all we do, we are stopping short of the Christian imperative. Jesus showed concern and pain when he saw people suffer, and he relieved them. But in a moment of great emotion, he looked out over his own people and cried: "O Jerusalem, Jerusalem, killing the prophets, and stoning those who are sent to you! How often would I have gathered your children together as a hen gathers her brood under her wings, and you would not!" (Matt 23:37). Here was real tragedy. This was not merely sympathy for the suffering of the prophets. This was a cry of despair over the alienation and sin of the people. To be sure, their hardness of heart, their stubbornness, their refusal to recognize truth, resulted in human misery, but this was not primary. The suffering was merely a symptom of a functional and basic sickness. And it was for this that he went to his death.

If there is something missing in most denominational approaches to the problem of race in America today, it is that which the secularist rightly espies as our weakness—feeling, emotion, a maudlin sense of tragedy. Christian compassion is not the cheap sentimentality of the junior choir performing "I'd Rather Have Jesus," but the white-hot emotion and indignation of the prophets, the piercing experience of the pathos and stark tragedy of man's condition, the brokenheartedness of the truly penitent, the groaning of man under his burden of guilt. A woman once explained to me how she had been indifferent about the problem of race in her city until she became a Christian. (And the term "became a Christian" had special meaning for this person who had been "born and reared" in the church.) When I asked her how she behaved differently after becoming a Christian, what difference it had made in her behavior toward other races and groups, her response was instant. "Only one difference," she replied. "One difference. Now my heart is broken."

Religion still involves *feeling*, and of God it can still be said: "The sacrifice acceptable to God is a broken spirit; a broken and contrite heart, O God, thou wilt not despise" (Ps 51:17). Too much of our programming in the field of race relations has been of the coldly objective, human engineering variety which precludes a broken heart. It is a bringing of the Thanksgiving baskets, the counting of noses for the poor children's Christmas party; the coins thrown into the special collection; programs of manipulation; designs for maneuvering, *handling* people into the Kingdom. We talk much about reconciliation. But too often we understand by the word something that can be accomplished by getting people together in buzz groups or by some other clever technique of group dynamics. There can be no questioning the value of providing opportunities for people to communicate. But communication is no substitute for reconciliation, and there can be no reconciliation without repentance. Nor can there be renewal of the church without repentance. And repentance comes with suffering, with a broken spirit and a contrite heart. No other possibility is available for the Christian. None of the steps can be skipped. It is a broken heart-repentance-forgiveness-reconciliation-renewal sequence that expresses the order of salvation.

In moving toward a starting point in Christian race relations, we should not forget that grace, redemption, and judgment are words the segregationists will hear. He may not understand them in the finest orthodox sense, but the sound of them is not unfamiliar even out of the "Bible belt." For many people there is not yet in these terms the emotional block there may be for other words. If, for instance, a Southern segregationist is told that it is the United States Constitution that is supreme and he is just beginning to regard seriously his own state constitution of 1890, he may find it difficult to understand why a constitution with which he feels he had nothing to do should be more sacred than one much closer to home. If he is told that the gospel is a message of law and order, he is apt to ask, whose law and what order? Or if he is told that the Christian view on race is the universal principle of the fatherhood of God and the brotherhood of man, he can make a rather convincing case to the contrary by a quick recitation of Scripture. "But to all who received him, who believed in his name, he gave power to become children of God" (John 1:12). But if he is told that the acute problem of race has to do with the judgment of God upon his people, that it is a symptom of man's estrangement from God and a symbol of the brokenness of the body of

Christ; if he is told that we are liars when we say we are in the light but hate our brothers (1 John 2:9); if he is warned that it is the last hour (1 John 2:18–29) for the Christian and for the church, this is language he may be able to understand. This is the profound and prophetic Word of the church which is the bearer of the judgment of God that pins a man's back to the wall.

It is true that we have outgrown the scorched flesh policy of Jonathan Edwards' evangelism, but few Americans are so secularized as to have no sense of the meaning of the judgment of God upon his people. Whatever that meaning may be in New York, or Atlanta, or Biloxi, we should remember (and this is especially true in the South) that the racist is seldom an atheist. Usually, in so far as he is able, he is a godly man. The message of Christianity still suggests to him that "in Christ," he can overcome his culture and his glands—in short, his prejudice. He may not have found this to be true, but he still has an uneasy feeling that it may be true nevertheless.

The redemptive purpose of Jesus Christ and the judgment of God upon his people are more than distantly related to race relations. They are at the very heart and core of the solution. Though this is not quite the starting point, it is close. Moreover, this is not a message for the majority group alone. The disease exists just as acutely in the minority group as it does in the majority. It is no startling discovery to say that original sin is not peculiar to white people. And it would sound defensive and commonplace to say it, if those of us active in the broad field of race relations did not so often realize that we were bringing one message to the prejudiced and another to the victims of prejudice. The message is not divided. There may be differences of degree and manifestation, but the sins are the same in both groups. About this we will say more in a later chapter. At the moment it is sufficient to point out that while the church did not go to the majority group in Fayette County, Tennessee, with the Christian message of judgment and redemption, neither was this its ministry to the minority group.

Despite the fact of infighting within the protest movement, the jockeying for power and position, the brokenness here, the disharmony there, the shattered fellowship within the Negro group in some ways more serious than the relationship between the two races, the churches had nothing to say. Should we not have spoken to the sharp division within the Negro groups, to the bitterness of their lawsuits, to their litigation tying up funds and relief supplies while people were hungry, to the enjoining of one another from administering relief and claiming mail, to the factionalism which found each group breaking off and announcing to the public that it alone was legitimate and true guardian of the welfare of the people? Most of our religious agencies were aware of this situation but, for the most part, the position was taken that we could not involve ourselves in the internal affairs of the movement, but would relieve the suffering of the innocent as best we could. Certainly the suffering had to be relieved, but there were no innocent. All were guilty, all were sinners and stood in desperate need of the message of judgment and redemption. Somehow, the churches have not yet learned to be critical of the new and dramatic protest movements. But they too must hear the gospel of the Lord who burns and heals. Whenever the church has been exclusively concerned with symptoms, with obvious, surface problems, choosing wrong subjects and wrong objects, it has brought forth fallacious answers. We have asked inappropriate questions and have moved into Christian social action from the wrong point of departure and with a superficial understanding of the depth of man's involvement in sin.

QUESTIONS FOR STUDY AND DISCUSSION

A. Do you agree that the church has no right to criticize segregation and discrimination in secular society until it has desegregated its own local congregations and church agencies?

B. What do you think of the author's approach to the segregationist Christian? If you grant its theological validity, would you also grant its realism and effectiveness? Should the two be considered mutually exclusive? Are we concerned with "success" in the struggle for racial justice and the racially inclusive church?

C. The author insists that compassion in race relations is the wrong attitude with which to begin. Do you agree? Did Jesus regard men first with compassion or was he first concerned with their sin and alienation from God? What should be the basic motivation of the church today?

D. How should the church respond to economic reprisals like those imposed upon the Negro farmers of Fayette County, Tennessee? In some areas Negro Christians have retaliated with economic boycott of white merchants. Is the boycott a legitimate means of Christian action?

E. Do you think that pronouncement of the judgment of God is an effective means of making the modern American become aware of his sin? How is it received by people who are not members of the church? How can it be communicated with contemporary relevance?

THE CHRISTIAN CONCERN AND STARTING POINT

WE CAN NOW BEGIN to probe more deeply into the reasons for the church's failure in race relations. Part of the answer has already been hinted—the preoccupation with law and order, the emphasis on humanistic arguments for desegregation, and the often uncritical reliance on sociological approaches. But an important question remains: Why has the church chosen this path? At least a partial explanation lies in the organizational structure of American Protestantism. Here sociological analysis can be useful without being permitted to define the form the church should take in its mission.

From the point of view of social effectiveness, Protestantism has had difficulty making a witness in the crisis of American race relations, partly because it has had no widely recognized spokesmen, no clearly defined lines of authority for policy and action, and no strong lay support. Generally speaking, when the Roman Catholic Church has been attacked, all three of these factors have been used to support the church and sustain its decisions. Its laity consistently rally to its defense. Societies and action groups are organized to engage in energetic campaigns of propaganda and moral support. Authoritative spokesmen make declarations of policy, and lines of implementation are cleared and effectively utilized.

When the positions of the Protestant churches or of the individual clergymen are attacked, on the other hand, frequently it is our own laymen who gather the faggots. An example is seen in the fact that in several states of the Southeast, laymen of Protestant denominations have organized to oppose actively the official position of their churches on race relations. They have organized within the churches themselves and have used church machinery to launch attacks against those very churches.

Such groups as the Methodist Laymen's League of Alabama have done much to prevent the local parishes from putting into action—or even discussing—the position of the national church. They have been successful in eliminating from the conference ministers whom they deem "undesirable," and they exert considerable influence from the local congregation to the General Conference. In other regions of the country, laymen join such organizations as the John Birch Society and actively participate in propaganda diametrically opposed to that for which their churches stand.

I am not pleading here for a monolithic ecclesiastical structure, nor for an infallible clergy. My point is simply that American pulpits do not have the authority requisite for leadership in social change. Our elected officials and professional staffs charged with the social witness of the denominations do not possess sufficient authority to represent the church in such a way as to help it become an effective influence for change in society. I am also saying that pulpits must be free or there is no hope for the churches in a crisis as filled with emotional intensity as the race issue. Unless the Word of God is heard, how will it be able to combat the pressures of culture upon the thinking of the people? "Woe to me if I do not preach the gospel!" (1 Cor 9:16). But woe to a people who will not tolerate the preaching of the gospel in their own sanctuaries. And woe to the church that will not permit its officials to implement its policies.

Two permanent elements constitute the means of grace in Protestantism. The first of these is the preaching of the Word; the second is the sacrament of Holy Communion. Both declare the gospel—equally and indispensably. It is a curious fact that, despite the gag that has been applied against preaching, it has been only rarely that a clergyman has been physically barred from God's altar to administer the holy mysteries. Yet this sacred service speaks more eloquently of the unity of all God's people, of the redemptive purpose and message of Jesus Christ, and of the sin of segregation, than do all the words that a pastor may be forbidden to speak during a long tenure.

It would be a mistake, however, to push too far the argument that the blame for the church's inadequacy lies principally in its organizational structure. If the lack of a strong hierarchy were the sole or even the chief reason for the weakness of Protestantism in race relations, we should have expected a much better record from the Roman Catholics, for that communion is not burdened with such organizational deficiencies.

In fact, however, this has not been the case. Catholicism's record in race relations, like Protestantism's, has been spotty—good in some places, poor in others. On the whole there is probably little to choose between the two. Two years after the desegregation of public schools in New Orleans, for example, the city's parochial schools are just beginning to desegregate, despite promises to the contrary from the Archbishop several years ago. In the fall of 1961, when the Atlanta public schools were desegregated with great appreciation in Washington and nationwide attention, the color bar remained in full force at the parochial schools.

In Nashville, on the other hand, the desegregation of the parochial schools preceded that of the public schools by two years. Yet in Memphis, a city in the same diocese with a far larger Catholic population than Nashville, the parochial schools are still segregated. The fact remains, however, that where Catholicism has been most effective in this struggle, its obvious advantage has been unity and organizational structure geared for action. But there must be another, more basic reason for the church's failure, and not only for the failure of the church, both Protestant and Catholic, but for failure of American society as a whole.

In the last chapter we saw that when Christians choose the dispossessed minority as their only subject of concern they will usually meet with failure. There the emphasis was that as Christians we have a clear and unmistakable responsibility and mandate to lighten the burden of our brothers whoever they are and wherever we find them. We cannot escape our obligation to aid and console the brokenhearted, whenever God places them in our path. But the frustration, the brokenheartedness, the suffering, the dispossession are all symptoms of something more basic. More important than relieving the symptoms, we have to treat the malady itself. As it is so often said, one does not have a cold because he sneezes but sneezes because he has a cold. Similarly we can say of the society in which we live that it is not sinful because it segregates; rather it segregates because it is sinful. Segregation and discrimination is the sneeze, the symptom of the condition of a sick and sinful society.

And what is the sin? To force fellow citizens, because of the color of their skins or any other reason, to live in ghettos which breed hostility, bitterness, and crime is wrong. But this is symptomatic. To refuse to employ people on the basis of race can hardly be justified by any Christian standard, but this is not the real threat to Christian doctrine. To threaten, taunt, and jeer mothers who take their children to the schools to which they have been assigned by law is to demonstrate less than Christian love, and yet the segregationist can debate you to a standoff if you make this your starting point. These are all humanitarian and egalitarian concerns that certainly lie within the province of Christian witness but which, taken alone, are not enough. The segregationist who is honest and who wants to remain loyal to the church has very clearly seen this point and has taken clever advantage of its weakness.

There is, however, something that neither the segregationist nor the integrationist has seen. In a real sense man is *not* the subject, the point of reference for his own well-being and happiness upon the earth. Neither the racist nor the person upon whom he casts indignity, the disinherited, Negro or white, the builder of houses or the rejected from houses, the employer or the one deprived of employment, the passer of legislation or the victim of repressive legislation, the murderer or the murdered—none of these is the true referent, the true subject. The only point of reference is God.

The sin, therefore, is that the whole issue of race is an effort to deny the sovereignty of God, to negate the absolute supremacy of God. Once a man has truly seen this truth he can no longer be a racist, nor can he any longer grovel in the agonies of self-pity. From that point on, the racist logic and desire for self-justification terrify him. As for the racist, he is now afraid to call any man unclean, to discriminate against any man, to stand in judgment over any group or individual or to set himself above any of God's human creatures. From the moment either the segregationist or the integrationist really accepts the absolute sovereignty of God, he is forever thereafter terrified to usurp that authority or claim any part of it for himself. And that is precisely what one does when he determines his pattern of behavior by classifications of race and class or thinks that God is obliged to conform reality to his notion of what ought to be.

Now, of course, many people who hold the segregationist position claim also to accept the doctrine of the sovereignty of God. Most of those within the church have certainly been exposed to it. It has been dinned into the church and Christian society for two thousand years through the theologians from Paul to Augustine, Calvin, Barth, Niebuhr, and others. It is obvious, however, that the segregationists have not understood, for if they had, they would acknowledge that God, being truly supreme, could create as he saw fit, and that he did not create a hierarchy of man. The segregationist who uses Scripture to buttress segregation convicts himself at this very point. In not one of the passages he uses is there any record of the alteration of creation subsequent to the time God made man in his image. God did not intervene to alter creation until the appearance of the new creation in Jesus Christ and in the Kingdom of Christ categories and classification by color and race do not exist. It is worth noting that over most of the generations of Christians this truth was clearly perceived. Racism, as we know it today, is a modern development. C. Vann Woodward traces the development of Jim Crow legislation in his book *The Strange Career of Jim Crow* to show that restrictive statutes that are taken for granted today would have been considered completely unwarranted in the United States before 1900. Racism as a doctrine and a way of life was little known before the rise of the modern nation-state on the continent of Europe. In this country, the historical and sociological developments that helped make Jim Crow possible were preceded by a theological development that really evolved in the matrix of the whole history of Christianity in America.

The theological aspect of racism has its roots in the shift from incarnation to deification in Christian belief—the shift in emphasis from God become man to man become God. F. O. Matthiessen has pointed out this inversion in his treatment of the American renaissance when he writes, "Anyone concerned with orthodoxy holds that the spiritual decadence of the nineteenth century can be measured according to the alteration in the object of its belief from God-Man to Man-God."[1] Matthiessen understands this as a shift from belief in the salvation of man through the mercy and grace of a sovereign God, to belief in the potential divinity in every man. In no country was this theological development more rapid than in Protestant, democratic America. The preaching of the early church concerned a God who had become man, a Christ whose birth was unique and whose nature was divine; who was crucified and who died back into eternal life. Theological liberalism, particularly second-generation liberalism, within Protestantism interpreted Jesus as a rebel prophet who was murdered by a society that was unable to abide the horror of truth. Accordingly, man *became* God. Thus God was no longer incarnate in the person of Christ. He did not become man by being 'in Christ'; rather, the man Jesus became God.[2] In this formulation Christ did not descend from the right hand of God to be born of a virgin, to suffer under Pontius Pilate, to be crucified for us men and for our salvation. In fact, this position does not really admit of the incarnation. Jesus

---

1. Matthiesson, *American Renaissance*, 446.
2. Ibid.

was thrust by man to the right hand of God as a reward for the life he had lived and the deeds he had performed. This was, in short, deification.

It is evident that the meaning of the crucifixion and death of Christ is completely changed by this theology. One of its most serious consequences is the rejection of the doctrine of the absolute sovereignty of God, and it is precisely this that has had far-reaching implications in the whole field of Christian social relations. It is not difficult to see why this is so. The deification of Jesus was the celebration of man's triumph, whereas God "in Christ" (incarnation) had to do only with the sovereignty of God. It has to do with what God had done by his sovereign power. Protestant, democratic America could move easily from this man-centered religion to the belief that nothing was more important than the individual. It would be expected, therefore, that Protestant leaders, under this theological influence and bound by the spell of the American creed of individual rights, would tackle the problem of racial prejudice from this vantage point. With the diminution of the idea that man might find completion in something greater than himself, what could follow more naturally than for Protestantism to make man the subject of racial and social justice? With man rather than God as the subject, the motivation for human brotherhood was lodged firmly in humanitarianism and man's need. What now impels the seeker for justice? Often it is that drive, that urge to "go about doing good" in order that the spark of divinity in every man might shine forth.

With God as sovereign (subject), the basis for human brotherhood is, as Matthiessen suggested, "in men's common aspiration and fallibility, in their humility before God."[3] When man is the subject of social action and when humanitarianism is its motivation, we are all too likely to badger people into loving each other, to tell them that men are good and worthy and, accordingly, there should be no discrimination among them. The segregationist counters with facts and figures about some men, the behavior of whom deserves, by our standards of goodness and worthiness, only a second-class citizenship. It is not sufficient to question his facts. Although he may not, for the most part, take into account basic causes for the behavior he describes, his facts are often quite accurate. But our argument does not rest upon factuality. If God is sovereign, if the basis of our brotherhood is in our common frailty and humility before the One who "has made everything for its purpose, even

---

3. Ibid., 72.

the wicked for the day of trouble" (Prov 16:4), then the statistical data of the segregationist, accurate or not, are of no account. They must be rejected as the basis of Christian decision.

The second generation of theological liberalism in the social gospel movement probably did more to impede progress in race relations in America by keeping man at the center of thought and action than did even fundamentalism, which, though often a caricature of orthodoxy, contained more incarnation and less deification than liberalism. This is not to "beat a dead horse to death." A discussion of the social gospel movement is appropriate at this point in history only because the ethics of that movement persist (where race relations is concerned) even though the ghost of its theology has for the most part disappeared. How familiar at Christian race relations conferences are words of law and order, constitutional process, democracy, human dignity, and the rights of man! And how strange and out of place seems talk of "God in Christ," of incarnation, and of the mystical body when applied to social problems! And the person who is known for his biblical preaching, who takes seriously the creeds and has a reputation for being "a good churchman," is not expected to involve himself in the social crises of his day, and if he does, his "churchmanship" becomes just a bit suspect.

Racist logic is primarily concerned with what man thinks about man. Sometimes, either as a technique to influence those who *must* have God on their side, or as a result of his own misguided piety, his doctrine speaks of that which man, usually himself thinks about God. The biblical writers, on the other hand, as Karl Barth has so often pointed out, were concerned with what God thinks about man. Their account makes God the subject and man the object. Their point of reference was God. When one is able and willing to confess that sovereignty belongs to God alone he is no longer able to be at ease in the camp of the racist. He ceases to be excessively preoccupied with man or with any particular man or group of men.

"It is he who sits above the circle of the earth.... who brings princes to nought, and makes the rulers of the earth as nothing.... He blows upon them, and they wither, and the tempest carries them off like stubble" (Isa 40:22–24). Isaiah's words now define the true center of human thought.

The Christian can now see that all his stereotypes about groups, even when true, have no real significance, for, again with Isaiah, he perceives that the inhabitants of the earth are as grasshoppers, and the folly of a quarrel between the Acridiidae family and the Locustidae family. The fact of having a Negro neighbor or shop foreman fades in importance when God becomes the center of thought and life and one acknowledges his absolute rule, authority, and government. There is no exception from this theological principle. The sovereignty of God means simply: "Know therefore this day, and lay it to your heart, that the Lord is God in heaven above and on the earth beneath; there is no other.... See now that I, even I, am he, and there is no god beside me; I kill and I make alive; I wound and I heal; and there is none that can deliver out of my hand" (Deut 4:39; 32:39).

This, then, is the sovereignty of God. It is the beginning and the end of Christian race relations. It is only by beginning with God that we get a true perspective for the understanding of man. It is precisely this understanding of the nature of man that comprises the content of Christian race relations. Are some men different? Did God have intrinsic differences in mind when he created some men white and some colored? The priority of God's sovereignty is what Calvin is driving at when he explains that when we begin with ourselves rather than with God, we see ourselves in a more powerful, glamorous, and impressive light than we actually are. To see ourselves as we really are, we must begin with God. Otherwise the picture is distorted and what is presented to us is the image of a creature who has the right to dispose of his fellow men as he sees fit.

One cannot look God in the face without getting a painful exposure to man's frailty and finiteness. We cannot look at God without "the shock of cemeteries." And a casual glance at these ubiquitous abodes of those gone before reminds us of the simple truth with which both the Bible and secular history are filled—that life is suffering and sorrow and the beginning of death; that we all come forth like a flower and are cut down; that we are all of a few days and full of trouble; that all flesh is grass and we are all here dying together. What man can face this truth and continue to see the relevance of human classifications of people into colors and races? What man can continue to prate such "Bible belt" absurdities as "God was the original segregationist." When we confess God as Creator and Sovereign who not only brought the world into being but continues to be its sole sustainer and judge, we see that no matter how high man may rise, no matter what legislation he may engineer, no matter how loudly he screams "nigger, jew, dago, kike," his final outcome will be that of the mighty kings of Judah, in the books of the Chronicles and the Kings—Jehoahaz, Joash, Jeroboam. Each died and slept with his fathers and another reigned in his stead until he too died and slept with his fathers and another took his vacant throne. To recognize God as Sovereign, Creator, Judge, and Ruler of the universe is to see how weak is the hand of men who must die and sleep with their fathers and go down into the great sepulcher of the earth together with "all sorts and conditions of men" only to be raised and judged by that one Sovereign who is Lord of all.

So it is that the sin of the children of light has not been their failure to tell the world that "red and yellow, black or white, they are precious in his sight." That has been said sweetly and often enough. Our problem is that we have spoken too much of man's worth and dignity and not often enough of his insignificance in God's scheme of things. Sermons on race relations like to use the text from The Acts: "He made from one . . ." The favorite rejoinder of the segregationist has been the rest of the verse: ". . . having determined . . . the boundaries of their habitation" (Acts 17:26). Perhaps a more appropriate text for both would be from 2 Sam 1:19: "How are the mighty fallen!" Here is a grim reminder for the potential self-righteousness of the integrationist and the vanity of the segregationist. "How are the mighty fallen!"

Thus far we have said little of the Lordship of Jesus Christ, which is the way the Christian must ultimately speak of God's sovereignty in this "time between," this "era of the church." It would appear, however, that today when the comfortable life of Americans deludes them into thinking that they have already achieved redemption one must speak more forcefully of creation, of finitude, and of sin. The doctrine of the sovereignty of God needs to fall afresh upon the ears of this generation. The God who is Sovereign has made Jesus "both Lord and Christ" (Acts 2:36). But before we can really understand what this means—before we can give up the illusions of the theology of everyman's deification, we must read again the Old Testament and stand under the judgment of Creation and Fall.

This is the note that must now be reintroduced into Christian race relations. It is found in both the Old Covenant and the New. "Thou art the God, thou alone, of all the kingdoms of the earth; thou hast made heaven and earth" (2 Kings 19:15). "I am the Alpha and the Omega, says the Lord God, who is and who was and who is to come, the Almighty" (Rev 1:8).

The Sovereign God who is our Lord Jesus Christ—he is the only subject, the sole referent of human relations and the social action of the church. What can be said of us, whatever our race or class, except that we and all our fortunes and destinies belong to him? And this is enough to know.

QUESTIONS FOR STUDY AND DISCUSSION

A. What are the dangers of a "monolithic ecclesiastical structure" in the Protestant churches today? Is the loss of some democratic privileges in the church a reasonable and necessary price to pay for an effective social witness?

B. How is the doctrine of God's sovereignty related to human brotherhood? Campbell contends that Christian race relations begins with this emphasis. Do you agree? What teaching of the church seems to you more basic?

C. Is the dignity and worth of the human personality a Christian doctrine? What are the dangers of an excessive emphasis upon man, his needs, his rights and privileges? Is it too much to assume that oppressed groups will understand the idolatry of basing the struggle for justice upon anything other than God's sovereign will to turn men from their own needs to his judgment and mercy?

ACCOMPLISHMENTS AND NEW DANGERS

THE PICTURE WE HAVE painted of the behavior of the churches during the long, dark night of American racism has not been a pretty and optimistic one. We do not propose at this point to put it in a pastel frame. It is, however, only fair to point out that although the churches do not do the good they want, but the evil they do not want is what they do (see Rom 7:19), they are, nevertheless, doing more that is of long-lasting significance in the field of race relations than any other institution of our society. The churches can still be a decisive influence in this struggle.

Robert Hutchins is reported to have said of the University of Chicago when he was its Chancellor: "It isn't a very good school. It's just the best there is." The record of the churches, as disappointing as it is, is not so bleak when it is compared with the record of secular groups.

Before we can talk about what the church can do we must look briefly at some of our limitations and at some of the achievements of Protestant Christianity despite those limitations. Of course, the term "Protestant Christianity" is so broad that anything claimed in its favor can be refuted with numerous exceptions. One might ask: "Which Protestants are you talking about? There are sixty million Protestants in this country." And if we could answer satisfactorily the question, "What are Protestants called to do?" we would have made a contribution which four hundred years of Protestant history has been unable to provide. For Protestantism has seldom been able to define clearly its role in society on any critical social issue, and in any given social crisis it is usually divided into warring factions.

The reasons for this have been suggested by various students of the relation of the Protestant churches to American culture. It has been pointed out that a major limitation the churches face is the manner in which Protestantism has divorced religious faith from institutionalized authority. The result has been that Protestantism does not recognize leaders who are authorized to speak the mind and will of the group. For example, all the major denominations have passed strong resolutions regarding racial segregation. Even though these statements have been approved by some authoritative body, there is no clearly delineated line of authority for implementation, for seldom is any person invested with sufficient power to act with anything like the immediacy necessary to make the church's declared policy effective in a crisis situation.

A second factor stressed by those in the field of the sociology of religion is that the excessive individualism of Protestantism gives every church member the right to interpret doctrine or Scripture as he sees fit. The consequence of such freedom is often conformity to values, prejudices, and attitudes acquired outside the church. Certainly there has been no dearth of positive statements by Protestant groups on the subject of race, but they are not taken seriously by legislatures and policy makers because it is well known that these statements only reflect the thinking being done at the highest level. At the grass roots, attitudes are apt to reflect that prevailing regional or community sentiment. Thus such denominational statements never quite comprise a clear threat to any individual or group of officials who retain power by election.

The painful awareness of this weakness is evident in the various ministerial statements and resolutions that have come out of communities in racial tension. There is always the preface that these clergymen, the signers, are speaking as individuals and not representing anyone particularly. This is not intended as a criticism of the individual minister who signs such statements. In a sense this is in his defense, for it is often to his peril that he signs antisegregation resolutions at all. But while the minister cannot speak for his constituency, other organizations with ideologies at variance with the Christian faith have developed, in a short time, clear channels of authority to speak convincingly to elected officials. Frequently these organizations speak for the same people for whom ministers or other church leaders are unable to speak, and they speak for those who would strongly object if the church or their councils sought to enunciate policy. A good example is the White Citizens' Councils or the John Birch Society. Christians within these groups generally resist any effort of their churches to represent them but strangely enough do not seem to object to having a small and powerful clique speak for them as members of those bodies. It is safe to say that people generally do not resent being represented if they share the adopted position. One can only conclude that while the official positions taken by Protestant bodies in various social crises may reflect a summation of the Law and the prophets, they are not a summation of the wishes of the majority of Protestant church members!

The point is that while Protestantism can and does plant seeds of revolution, it cannot see them through to fruition. To continue the struggle, its prophets and actionists often must turn to other vehicles. While it is true, however, that Protestant churches are not providing a leadership in race relations commensurate with the ideals and principles of Protestantism, it is equally true that they have produced many of the persons who *are* providing such leadership. Take a careful look at the reformers in the present crisis in race relations. Ask them where they got their start. Most of them will reply that it all began when they started to take seriously that which they had learned in religious training. We can be critical that Protestant polity has not provided the kind of organization necessary to influence social change, but we cannot ignore the fact that its doctrines and teachings, when taken seriously, have provided leaders for the groups that are organized for effective action.

Clarence Jordon is a Baptist minister who was one of the founders of Koinonia Farm in South Georgia. He holds a degree in agriculture and a PhD in Greek from a theological seminary. Jordon organized the interracial farm from the coercion of a Christian conscience. Koinonia Farm has done much for Sumter County. It has introduced new agricultural techniques into the community and it has been a constant reminder to the world of the meaning of the word by which it is named. Because of his views and practices in race relations, Clarence Jordon was excluded from the Baptist church in which he held membership. We may be critical of that church for excluding such a good man from its fellowship, but we ought not to forget that it was that same institution which produced the good man in the first place. Like an eagle teaching its young to fly but deserting them once they begin to exercise what they have learned, so Protestantism is often capable of inspiring its own to action but almost as often rejects them when action occurs, especially if such action is taken in the name of the church. It is nothing new for Protestants who apply their faith to social, economic, and political problems to be told to mind their altar fires and tea parties. This restrictive policy is partly a consequence of the Reformation polity and doctrine of the church which left little room for institutionalized authority in its almost total rejection of Roman Catholicism.

Despite the fact that Protestant churches are not geared for action, some of the ablest leaders who *are* exerting the pressure for social change were nurtured by Protestant churches, even if they now deny the mother who gave them birth. Few of the people who are presently active in the struggle for racial justice have escaped the influence of the Judaeo-Christian ethic in one way or another. Indeed many of them have come disillusioned from the ranks of the Christian church itself—both Protestant and Catholic.

Much of what we have said in this book concerning the behavior of Protestantism in the racial crisis does not apply to Negro churchmen and Negro congregations. What follows here is not an attempt to exempt any group from its share of guilt. Rather, it is to single out some of the accomplishments of this particular wing of the church and suggest certain hazards that challenge the Negro churches.

No one can seriously question the role played thus far in the racial crisis by Negro clergymen and congregations. From Birmingham to Buffalo, Negro church buildings have served for years as centers of operation for groups working for racial justice, and ministers have usually served as their leaders. In part this has been redemptive. For, in view of this fact, no one can say categorically that Protestantism is making no worth-while contribution to the desegregation process. In Montgomery, Nashville, Atlanta, Detroit, Chicago, New York, Los Angeles, Negro Protestants have kept the pressure on, brought into being organized protest movements and undergone suffering and sacrifice to effect social change. Although it has been groups such as the National Association for the Advancement of Colored People which have played the major organizational role and have taken the giant legal steps, much of their leadership has come from within the churches. But in situations such as the Montgomery boycott and in many of the recent sit-in movements, it has been the institutional church itself that has made the greater contribution. Not only were the meetings held in church houses, but these meetings were essentially religious meetings in which religious values were dominant. The prayers, the refusal to return evil with evil, the agreement of ministers and laymen to accept imprisonment, the acceptance by entire communities of legal harassment and economic deprivation—these are things familiar to these people and it must be said that this was and is the church playing a vital role in the achievement of justice for all people.

It has often been said that the real key to the solution of our current problem of racism in America rests in the hands of the enlightened, liberal Negro churchmen, and not in the hands of white people—not even white people of good will. Actually it is strange that there should ever have been expected that white churchmen *could* be the real leaders of racial integration. Anyone even remotely familiar with community structure and organization, and, as we have seen, anyone acquainted with the Christian doctrine of man, would not have entertained such a hope.

The role of Negro churchmen in keeping the pressure constantly upon the status quo is a vital one. In every case desegregation has not come when a group of whites of good will gathered and said discrimination was wrong and should be stopped. Rather, it has come when a group of Negroes gathered and said: "We have been discriminated against long enough. Let's stop it." This has been true in the schools of the South, and it has been equally true of housing, employment, and church membership in the North. There can be no minimizing the action-oriented witness of Negro churchmen. They have a distinct and unique role to play, and there is no denying that thus far they have played it more than well. But the point we shall now try to make has nothing to do with all that, as significant as it well may be.

What we need to see is that when God chooses people to do his work, it has nothing to do with the intrinsic merit of those he has called. The fact that God has summoned Negro churchmen to do his work in this crisis is not to their credit in the least. It has only to do with the Caller. It has nothing to do with the suffering of the chosen, the injustices wrought against them, the humiliation of being segregated as an inferior people, the inconvenience of discrimination. There is a clear parallel in the history of Israel. All these problems were also their problems. They too were for a time slaves, maltreated and humiliated. They too were chosen. But the choice had nothing to do with Israel. When the Children of Israel asserted their rights, as if rights gave them special merit and justification, there was nothing but trouble and violence from that moment. It was difficult to see what good could come from their struggles. The more they strove to be free, the more Pharaoh and the Egyptian majority caused them to suffer, and the more were arguments advanced against their freedom. But Moses, an outside agitator with no obvious business in Egypt but to make trouble, persisted. The "Uncle Toms" of Israel grumbled throughout it all. "Would that we had died . . . in the land of Egypt, when we sat by the fleshpots and ate bread to the full" (Exod 16:3). Pharaoh persisted in his policy through plagues of blood, frogs, gnats, flies, boils, ferocious weather, locusts, and darkness at noon—Little Rock hanging on through a plague of no much-needed new industry for two spiteful years; New Orleans with its loss of Mardi Gras revenues—refusing to give in.

The objective observer doubtless could see nothing but continued bitterness resulting from this kind of extreme recalcitrance. Certainly there were many moderates in the land who cautioned against the radical methods of the Jews. Israel won. Then lost. It won as long as the Israelites could see that they were chosen by a God whose aid in all their struggles proved nothing about themselves but only proved something about God—his supremacy, his sovereignty. Israel lost when the Israelites began to assume that all their afflictions and the favorable issue from them had to do with themselves. They lost whenever they believed that their being chosen had been for their own glory. The sin of the Children of Israel was not that they caused trouble for Egypt. This was inevitable. And what could have been more natural than to believe that as a people they were somehow favored because of their successes? But God had called them to establish his supremacy and not their own. The sin of Israel was their assumption that their calling had to do with their cause rather than with God's purposes.

If God has chosen Negro churchmen in this crisis, it is for the purpose of establishing to them, and to America, something about himself. The fact that Negroes are in the vanguard of the fight for justice must not lead anyone to think that they are less guilty of sin than any other group. Whenever people assert their rights, whether in this country or anywhere in the world, there is trouble. There are riots in Montgomery, arrests in Jackson, and panic in Leopoldville. The Negro, like Israel, is called to destroy the idols, to smash the images which we have erected and which have become more important to us than God himself. And when idols fall, there is always trouble and violence. It is foolish to derogate those who seek redress and to blame them for ensuing violence and trouble. It is, however, the better part of wisdom to sound a warning. In the struggle for righteousness, God's righteousness and God's purposes are the true meaning of the struggle. Here again it is not a matter of democracy, a man's rights, of constitution, of the Supreme Court. It is what God is able to do with sinful people and with sinful instruments to draw attention to himself and his purposes of redemption that matters.

In the various movements led by the Negro churches there is serious need for theological depth. Many of these efforts being made by churchmen and presumably in the name of Christ are more humanistic than Christocentric. It is interesting, for example, to note the degree to which the name of Mahatma Gandhi is invoked in the literature of the desegregation campaigns. The entire nonviolent movement is built much more around the teachings of the great Indian leader than around the teachings of Jesus Christ. This despite the fact that Negro Americans, like all other Americans, have been more exposed to Christian doctrine than to the Gandhian philosophy and despite the fact that a rationale for nonviolence has traditionally been derived from the life and teachings of Jesus Christ.

That Gandhi has been so widely used in this movement may reflect the Negro's subconscious rejection of Christianity as the white man's religion. The rapidly growing Black Muslim movement states this in unequivocal terms as a major reason for repudiation of Christianity. It is certainly understandable that the Negro has begun to look to other religions for spiritual substance to undergird his struggle for freedom. The danger is that the Christian church seems to offer nothing more than its institutional form as a vehicle to accomplish ends motivated by an alien philosophy.

It is nonetheless true that if there is to be real renewal of the church in our century it is possible that it will be achieved through the predominantly Negro communions, especially if there is no drastic change from their comfort-loving, status-ridden complacencies by white Protestantism. It has always been that a suffering people seem to respond more readily to the call of God.

But again the danger is that the response to the call will not be a true "covenanting" with God. It is a false idea of covenant to say to God: "If you will deliver us out of our afflictions we will be your people." This is not what a covenant relationship means. If Negro churchmen in America can see the covenant only as the privilege of serving God and living in communion with him, aware all the while of the dangerous condition of being a special agent of his holy concern, if they see man's role in the covenant as the acknowledgment of the unconditional sovereignty of the

Ruler of the nations, then there is hope that Christianity will survive this period of testing. But if Negro churchmen begin to assume that on the basis of the covenant they are entitled to claim selfish rights before God and to be dealt with in some favored manner that accords with their own notion of what is good for them, there will not be a renewal of the church through them. The word "covenant" does not mean a bilateral contract between two equal parties. This was precisely Israel's sin. It is cause for alarm to hear repeatedly at freedom rallies: "*We* are going to win because God is on *our* side!" This is assumed in every revolution. It was assumed in the American Revolution, but what happened? "Jeshurun waxed fat, and kicked; . . . then he forsook God who made him, and scoffed at the Rock of his salvation" (Deut 32:15).

The freedom movements working within the churches are, to some extent, the victims of the same theological shift mentioned earlier. They have tended to forget that there is something more at stake than the satisfaction of the individual, that man must find completion in One who is greater than himself, that the real basis for brotherhood is not humanitarianism but our common fallibility before God. The indignities the Negro has known, the injustices he has endured, are a sin against God on the part of the majority, and the sour grapes we have eaten will set our children's teeth on edge for generations to come. The struggle for freedom should not, must not, and will not be stopped. But let us not permit the successes that are now evident to tempt us to be prideful. Let the warning be sounded that the victors, to their despair, often come to accept the gods of the vanquished. In so far as that god is not the God and Father of Jesus Christ, let the Freedom Movement and the rising Negro middle class that will gain momentum by its victory test the spirits which impel their forward march. God has called and is yet calling the Negro churches to be the source of renewal for the whole church of Christ. Upon their understanding of the true meaning of the struggle for racial justice hangs the possibility of the church seizing or missing the opportunity God holds out to it in this generation.

QUESTIONS FOR STUDY AND DISCUSSION

A. How much should a pastor undertake an active witness in race relations without the official support of his congregation? Is it feasible for the General Assembly of the church to move out in race relations and other social questions beyond the attitude and commitment of the churches?

B. Is it enough for the church to send leaders in the struggle for justice into secular organizations to carry on the fight or should the church itself enter the struggle at the level of politics and direct action? Will this blunt the religious effectiveness of its ministry?

C. What should be the role of the Negro churches? Should the white churches encourage them to carry on the effort for racial justice and play a strong supporting role rather than pre-empt their right of initiation and leadership?

D. Do you consider the use of Gandhian philosophy a dangerous trend in the desegregation movements? Can Christianity use this philosophy and method for social change without losing its distinctive Christian orientation?

THE CHURCH: PROPHET AND CONSERVATOR

THERE ARE MANY THINGS the church might have done in the racial crisis. Modern prophets could have thundered from thousands of pulpits against the sin of segregation and injustice. The church could have given more time to the proclamation that in the sight of God there is no difference between black and white. The church could have led the attack on racism, first of all, by throwing wide its own doors to the Negro. These things a truly prophetic church would have done, but there is little to be gained by weeping for what might have been. There is still time for faithfulness. There is yet a chance for the church, if indeed we are still the church, to find its life, to be renewed. But if it happens, it will be God's doing and not ours.

We have said that many religiously motivated people cannot find a channel within the institutional church to express the social implications of their faith. But Protestantism does not hold that the Sunday morning expression of the church is the only type of the beloved community. Protestantism is free to encourage a congregation to find expression in groups geared to accomplish their own purposes in mission. In a sense it is tragic that Christians seem obliged today to go outside the framework of the church to bear witness. Nevertheless, such a witness is valid and efforts to relate faith to secular action groups cannot be dismissed as outside the pale of Christian social action. It should, however, be acknowledged that more and more Protestants are finding it possible to work within the structure of the church. In one city, a congregation rejected the gift of a valuable building site rather than compromise its conviction on man's unity in God. In another community, an entire congregation endorsed a nonchurch committee that had been formed to try to reopen the public schools. Such instances are still exceptional, however. More often it will be found that *individuals* are doing something, but that there is no concerted action by a congregation. One man is not a church. At the same time, we must not underestimate the significance of the statements condemning segregation that have been released by the major denominations. While such pronouncements do not ordinarily impress political leaders, they often give leverage to the local minister who faces congregational opposition in his efforts to be faithful to the gospel.

Another obligation that many Protestants are beginning to accept is the correction of the flagrant misuse of Scripture by segregationists. For some years Protestant leaders assumed that people were not being influenced by the spurious use of certain Bible passages which appear to support racial prejudice. Some leaders considered it boorish and unsophisticated to fight over proof texts and certainly not at the level that many of the segregationists had pitched the battle. It has now become obvious that the segregationist Protestant is neither rationalizing nor deliberately deceiving when he cites what he thinks is Scriptural authority for his convictions. God became the original segregationist, he argues, when he turned some of Noah's children black. And did not Jesus teach in the Golden Rule that we were not to do unto others what we would not want them to do to us? "Therefore," continues the segregationist, "since I don't want others to force me to integrate, it is my Christian duty to see that no one else is forced to integrate."

To point out that these arguments are illogical and false is not enough. This man is usually incapable of grasping the meaning of mythic context of some of the biblical literature and often he may be unable even to read the text correctly. We must remember the educational level of those who are the most ardent antagonists and keep in mind the constant flow of low-grade emotionally inflammatory literature that goes into the R.F.D. mailboxes. The only answer that will have meaning for these people is a steady refutation of segregation by citing chapter and verse. Even this may not succeed, but it appears to hold out the best promise for the present.

Still another role that Protestants are assuming is the support of those clergy and laymen who have dared to put their faith into action whatever the cost. Several denominations and groups as the National Council of Churches, American Friends Service Committee, United Presbyterian Church, the American Baptist Convention, and the United Church of Christ social action units have provided financial and other assistance to numerous individuals who have been displaced or have suffered in bringing the imperatives of their faith to bear upon the racial crisis. Certain congregations that have experienced financial loss because of their witness have also been aided by these agencies. We cannot, however, overlook the possibility of a grave danger in this policy. Consider the case of the local pastor who is warned by his denominational executive not to move too fast in the face of controversy lest there be a decline in membership or giving. When the pastor heeds the warning and his ministry flourishes in measurable terms, his ecclesiastical superior is apt to point out to him that God has blessed his cautious efforts and that it pays to serve Jesus in this way.

But let us suppose the pastor is troubled by this and seeks to prove to his superior that one can be daring in his witness and still meet his denominational quotas. Unfortunately it is true that this cannot always be done, and when a minister launches out into the deep of controversy he may discover that it does *not* pay to serve his Lord. Quotas are not met, the number of tithers decline, and the institutional structure *does* sag. It is at this point that we are tempted to come to the pastor's support to prove to the bishop or the presbytery that God will in a material way bless a strong witness in social relations. We try to protect the man from suffering and to shield his church from organizational failure. But is this consistent with the Christian understanding of evil and the necessities of faithful obedience? The Christian who does battle with the devil, the powers, the world rulers of this present darkness, will undoubtedly suffer. But often such suffering is redemptive. When we try to mitigate the suffering, to prop up the faltering institution, and to insist that one can fight the world and the devil without suffering, we are denying a fundamental truth of Christian history and moral experience.

In any case, the denominations, even though the prophetic voice at the congregational level has been disappearing from long disuse, have begun, however haltingly, to act with effect. And it is high time, for the issue of racial injustice is nationwide and must be fought on a wide front by the national denominations as well as local congregations. Apart from schools and places of public accommodation, it is difficult to distinguish between the treatment of Negroes in Dothan, Alabama, and Montpelier, Vermont. A Negro looking for a house might easily have more trouble in suburban Philadelphia than in suburban Birmingham. A Jewish doctor might well be better received by the community in Vicksburg, Mississippi, than in Aberdeen, South Dakota.

The Church: Prophet and Conservator

Throughout the world racial bitterness, suspicion, and mistrust is poisoning community life. The Black Muslims flourish among Negro Americans and represent much more than the impulsive passions of a few hotheads. The resurgence of the Klan and the rapid growth of the White Citizens' Councils are not merely a manifestation of Southern die-hardism. This feeling shows up all over the land—in Levittown, Dearborn, Deerfield Park, Little Rock, Sylacauga, Fayette County. Everywhere man in his sin thinks more highly of himself than he ought and finds it convenient to regard himself different from and superior to his fellows. Everywhere men categorize and classify one another. Everywhere race, color, class, religion, nationality tear men asunder. One cannot read a major daily paper anywhere in the world without finding at least one front-page story with racial and ethnic overtones— from South Africa to the Soviet Union, from England to the Congo, from Little Rock to Westchester County. Apart from the contest between communism and democracy, the struggle between the races, between the white and the colored peoples of the world, is the most deep-seated and perplexing problem of our time. We are in the midst of a revolution. Make no mistake about that. People of color will not halt in their drive for freedom. You can hear their song throughout the world, and it will not be silenced. It is the plainsong of the oppressed, the chant of the disinherited. "Free-dum. Free-dum." The passive and gentle bus rider in Alabama sings it as an anthem of praise; the restless and turbulent Congolese shouts it as a marching song. Neither will be stopped. Nor will the overarching seriousness of the East-West struggle and its eventual outcome silence the challenge that has been thrown down to the white man all over the world.

These people will be frustrated again and again by the Verwoerds, the Eastlands, the Kaspers, and the Levitts, but they will not be stopped. Man, by nature, does not give up privilege and comfort, status and security, without a struggle. At the same time, man does not cease to yearn for freedom. All of us are caught between these forces, whether we are innocent victims or calculating participants. It is evident that we will experience an extended social convulsion—a generation, perhaps more, of racial disharmony.

But the church has in the past found spiritual renewal in just such a day as this. It has found renewal because it rediscovered its purpose, or perhaps because God, in such a day, chooses to exert his purpose. This can be a time of greatness for the church, its hour of faithful obedience to the Word of God. And yet even without the full measure of obedience God can use the church to serve his purpose. This truth should not make us lessen our effort, but it has always been so. It may be that in our day God will use the church in quite a different way than those of us who have been on the battle line have hoped.

The church has always had two edges—a prophetic or pioneering edge and a stabilizing or conserving edge. Critics of the church usually see its conservative nature as the church's greatest weakness. In the present crisis in race relations this side of the church may become its strength and the source of the only important contribution the church may make.

Where civil disorder and commotion hold sway, where there is violence and strife, there is one role which the church has played well and may play with real effect in the future. This is what we may call by the rather unlovely term "cleaning up the mess." There is no better way to put what must, in all events, be done, and what the church perhaps is able to do best. Generally speaking, white Protestantism cannot be expected to play an active role in getting Negro children into all-white schools, in breaking up ghettos and admitting Negroes and Jews to previously restricted neighborhoods, in carrying the full brunt of the fight for employment on a fair and non-discriminatory basis. White Protestantism could do these things, but it will not. It will not engage in the rough-and-tumble of politics to force civil rights cases through the courts. It has usually and it may be expected to continue to act in the interest of peace, harmony, good will, and order within the fellowship of its members. As social institutions, white Protestant churches are by nature conservative.

Moreover, based on past performance, there is little likelihood that white Protestantism will play any significant role in preparing communities for true integration or even desegregation. This is not to minimize the good work that has been done in some situations. It is simply to say once again that Protestantism is not geared for this kind of action and will not seek to exert the influence necessary for such preparation. We are *not* saying that is the way it should be and that we are happy about it. As the thrust for freedom becomes more radical in method with freedom rides, sit-ins, jail-ins, the action of the churches becomes more irrelevant. The Protestant social action professional was considered a radical by the end of 1959. Today he is hardly considered a liberal by the new movements for desegregation. If Protestant social action does not shift its tactics for any other reason, it needs a new strategy to justify calling itself by that name.

The task of "cleaning up the mess," if it comes to this, will be done well by the largely conservative Protestant denominations. For example, the churches in Clinton, Tennessee, played virtually no part in pressing for justice to admit Negro children to the public schools, and when they were admitted by court order they did little to prepare the community for an orderly transition. This was true to their conservative nature. A conservative institution seldom threatens another conservative institution. But when the whole structure of the community was falling apart, when cultural values even more sacred than racial views were threatened, that same conservative nature compelled the churches of Clinton to become involved. It was a "cleaning up," stabilizing, restoring job. For the churches to press for justice in court or community would be to jeopardize the success of revivals, membership drives, building funds, every member canvasses, and the whole life of the institution. But mob rule, riots, general hysteria, and bad publicity were an even greater threat. Decency had to be restored, and with it came some modicum of justice.

While a conservative institution will seldom threaten another conservative institution, it will almost always defend one. Thus, it was not that the Baptist church in Clinton had moved to a more liberal position when it supported its minister who walked to school with the Negro children and was attacked by the mob. Instead, this was a clear demonstration and re-emphasis of its continued conservatism. If their pastor had been beaten while circulating a petition to admit Negro children to the schools, he probably would have been dismissed from his pulpit. Agitation by petition would have been a betrayal of the peace-loving nature of the church. But when he was beaten in what amounted to the defense of a still more important community value—peace and stability—he became something of a Christian hero. The conservative nature of the institution had not changed. The identification of the enemy had.

Thus, white Protestant churches can be counted upon to play a vital role when the walls of civilization are caving in around them. In view of events, it must be admitted that this "caving in" is one phase of the process that we are observing today in most communities and nations where the race problem exists. Whether it takes the violent form of the crisis in the Congo or the one in Southern United States, or the more subtle—though always potentially violent—developments in Harlem, Dearborn, or Chicago, the result is largely the same. There are prophets within the Protestant fold who would like to see the church plug the dike with its right arm. Most of Protestantism is not willing to do this, but it is at least willing to rescue the drowning victims. And this much is not lightly to be dismissed.

Most Protestants will agree that the judgment and justice of God must precede any real reconciliation. They can avoid any doctrinal inconsistency by acknowledging that judgment and justice must come through channels other than the church—the NAACP, the courts, the President's Committee on Employment Opportunity—accepting as the church's role the mending of a broken and shattered society, the putting of the pieces back together in some kind of order, the cleaning up of the mess. Some of us will doubtless argue that this falls far short of the ideals for which the church should stand and that such a "let John do it" attitude can be given no room in the faith. Both of these things are true. But we are a selfish people and God has used selfish motivations before, and he may use again our selfishness for his own glory. This is precisely the point I wish to make. The church may be renewed in spite of man. God may take our greed and ambition, our fondness for the status quo, our desire for bigness and success, our concern for membership statistics, and use them in a manner we could never have imagined.

If God permits the church to play the role of putting the pieces back together because we love harmony and order, that does not mean that he has removed from his church the responsibility for bearing a prophetic and pioneering witness. It is only to say that this is the last chance. And if we are *content* with this, if it does not trouble us, we are in real trouble. But it is only recognizing what God can do with our faithfulness, our fears, and our weak motivation.

If the church does well this task of putting the pieces back together, it will have served its Lord despite itself; and it may even find its life. But let us be quite clear. Even so, the church must become, or allow itself to become, something it now is not. If we are looking for something the church can do and still hold on to the success and glamour of the institution, even the conserving, restoring role must be rejected. This role can be performed only at great risk and sacrifice. This is a skin graft; the operation is painful and hazardous to both patients. I am not suggesting this task as a way for the church to salve its conscience and still maintain the status quo. The church must be a haven for those weary of the battle. It cannot be just another pot in which to stew and boil. It must be the third race, the people of God, not the stiff-necked people of the culture.

When the church was young and yet without a name, a descriptive title given to it by some outsiders was "the people who love one another." Whether or not this was a derisive cognomen is not clear. But the world today uses it in jest and has turned it into an epithet. It asks, "Where are the people who *claim* to love one another?"

The church began as the people of God. The measuring rod by which Christians tested themselves in the "new creation" was whether or not they had love one for the other. "We know that we have passed out of death into life, because we love the brethren" (1 John 3:14). These people loved one another because they knew the tragedy of human existence and in their common frailty they saw the greatness and sovereignty of God. And the only *raison d'etre* of the people of God was and is the service of God. Therefore, before we can begin the task of mending the broken bits of society, our own humpty-dumptiness must be considered and remedied. We can deceive neither God nor ourselves. We cannot for long make ourselves believe that there are certain rights and privileges which he has ordained for some of us and denied to others because of race. But as long as we languish in this sin we can only hope that God will take our selfish motives and enlarge his love for the world by using us to mend its wounds.

Already there are signs of an ill wind blowing some good. One of the highlights of my experience during the past five years in a ministry that has taken me into every major racial crisis in the nation was to be a part of an interracial conference held in the Deep South for the purpose of discussing race relations. At the conclusion of the conference we knelt at the Lord's Table in a Methodist chapel in a Communion service following the order of the Presbyterian Church. The service was conducted by a white Congregationalist and a Negro Baptist minister. Kneeling together were Baptists, Episcopalians, Methodists, Presbyterians, and members of other communions, without thought of race.

This was no meeting for general fellowship. There were problems that had to be settled, but I know of no other occasion that would have brought the group to partake of those holy mysteries in the spirit that prevailed in that chapel. When Christians are caught in a serious crisis they will sometimes transcend ecclesiastical structures and barriers. True ecumenicity at the grass roots might well be accomplished in a crisis long before it is achieved at the top level. This conference was held in the midst of a crisis—a crisis brought about by the weakness and ineptitude of institutionalized religion.

Another example of unity born, not out of the strength, but out of the weakness, of the church in this crisis is now being seen throughout the country. Its symbol is a little lapel pin worn by members of various Christian bodies who have committed themselves to an informal fellowship of penitence called simply "Brothers." There are no dues, no membership roll, no officers. A group of individuals wear the pin and carry in their pocket a card which pledges them to remember at Mass, Holy Communion, quiet hours, worship services, and in their private devotions the brokenness of Christ's body because of racial divisions.

If one inquires what the pin means, the "Brother" shows his card which explains the fellowship. If someone expresses an interest, he is given the pin and card and the Brother writes for another. He may secure another set from one of four addresses, all of them the offices of men who give their time and effort to the healing of racial division. One of these addresses is that of a Roman Catholic organization. Another is the address of an unofficial denominational office. A third is the location of a Protestant Council field office. The last is a local church. No one anticipates in this an early union of Rome, Canterbury, and the rest of Christendom, but at least members of the separate branches of the holy catholic church at the unofficial and local level are being brought by the racial crisis to a recognition of the existence of each other.

Still another case of ecumenicity that is a result of the racial crisis (really the crisis of the church) is a group of theological students who call themselves "The Student Interracial Ministry." These young men and women come from all over the country and are attending seminaries in New York, Atlanta, Washington, Nashville, and other cities. White students spend one or more summers as assistant pastors in Negro congregations. Negro seminarians do the same in white congregations. Denomination is not a factor. Race is, but only in order that race may someday cease to be a factor in the church of Christ. The broken body of our Lord may yet be healed because God is moving us to heal our own racial divisions in such movements as these.

The churches are discovering many practical ways of helping their fellow Christians who are caught in the throes of racial upheaval. But we must be willing to use no gimmicks, no program kits. The only way we can minister to a man is to go with him. In the words of Barak to Deborah when he was assigned an almost impossible task: "If you will go with me I will go; but if you will not go with me I will not go" (Judges 4:8). More and more we see Christians, clergy and lay, "going with" fellow Christians, minority and majority alike. If he must suffer, we must suffer with him. If after our Gethsemane together there must still be Calvary, we must go as far as we can go together. And many are finding in this crisis that though Gethsemane preceded Golgotha, it did not take its place.

The early church did not exist in utopia. Neither did it have the notion we seem to have today, that if it could somehow change the society in which it existed into a sea of tolerance and brotherly love then it could truly be the church. It is dishonest and cowardly to assume that if we can make culture into what the church wishes it to be but isn't, the church can then be what it ought to be. The church will not regain its health when it is able to influence society to desegregate the many aspects of its life. Originally it was *because* of the brokenness, the misery of society, that the church could have any identification, any existence at all. We may be living in such a time.

As significant as the prophetic edge of the church is, and as much as most of us regret the present dearth of prophets in the land, it may well be that heroic deeds will come, not by the appearance of more and greater prophets, but as God uses the conserving edge which is, from our point of view, the weakness of the church. Making the conscious decision to play the conserving role and put our house in order is far from what the church might fairly have been expected to do. And if even this much is done it is not something of which we can boast, for it will have been that which God has done through us and often despite ourselves. And if it is done, the Kingdom will not have come, only the starting point will have been reached—that which was established at Pentecost concerning race will have been realized.

If we must despair of man, let us not despair of God. If God accepts the church with its selfishness, its fears, its obsession with peace and prosperity, and uses it once again as the channel of his grace, then we can at least know that this beleaguered church still belongs to him and he has not despaired of man.

QUESTIONS FOR STUDY AND DISCUSSION

A. What is the value of church public pronouncements in the area of race relations? Should local churches make them?

B. Should economic assistance be provided for clergymen who are under economic duress because of their stand on the race problem?

C. Is it too pessimistic a view of the contemporary church to assume that only its "conservative role" will be relevant to the present crisis in race relations? How would you modify this point of view as stated by Campbell?

D. What are the encouraging signs of the prophetic role and the renewal of the church in the movement for justice and human rights in your community? What can be done to strengthen this aspect of the church's witness? Is the "Brothers movement" a prophetic or conservative response?

E. Should the main burden of the church's witness be upon changing society or changing people in the church and healing denominational fragmentation in America?

Incarnating Radical Christianity in the American South

THE IMPORTANCE OF WILL D. CAMPBELL

Richard C. Goode

In his biography of Will Campbell, Thomas Connelly effectively portrays Campbell's distinctly Southern identity.[1] Campbell's life and writing bears distinctive Southern trademarks, an elucidating wit and wisdom reminiscent of such Southern luminaries as Flannery O'Connor, Walker Percy, and Willie Morris. Moreover, Connelly depicts Campbell as a "troubadour" or "balladeer" of the South's alienation, estrangement, and insecurity, and Campbell as the high priest of a Southern civil religion. Like the region's country music, Campbell simultaneously articulates the region's self-loathing and despair, while also providing a message of hope and redemption. For Connelly, Campbell fulfills this priestly function by confessing the South's sinfulness and dejection, while speaking the words of absolution that provide the downtrodden with hope. The South may have a history of unspeakable transgressions and appalling injustices, but Campbell assures his fellow Southerners that those failures are not insurmountable barriers to hope and healing.

Connelly rightly appreciated the region's influence on Campbell, yet Campbell is more than a functionary of a Southern civil religion. Born a son of the South, the grinding poverty and social disenfranchisement that prompted so many white Southerners to wrap themselves up in a flag of bigotry and resist authentic community did not form Campbell in like manner. Campbell may sound

---

1. Connelly, *Will Campbell and the Soul of the South*. Over the years Campbell and Connelly shared an unusually personal journey. Not only did Connelly write Campbell's biography, Campbell baptized Connelly and later performed his funeral.

quintessentially Southern, but his story transcends any geographical, cultural region.² Several writers explain the larger world of Christian Radicalism into which Campbell fits—for brevity's sake let us consider two. First, Campbell's colleague and *Katallagete* contributor, John H. Yoder describes Radicalism's "free church syndrome" throughout history. Yoder traces that tradition from the Donatists, Bogomils, and Waldenses, through the radical Zwinglians and the Anabaptists, to The Church of the Savior's Gordon Cosby, and Kononia's Clarence Jordan. Campbell may not have exhibited all the trademarks of this decentralized, often underground, tradition, yet his anti-institutionalism, rejection of state violence, and "subgroup solidarity" bears the marks of this "free church" history.³ Second, Robert Inchausti has described a cadre of "orthodox avant-garde" Christians over the last few centuries, from William Blake and Nikolai Berdyaev, to Walker Percy, Thomas Merton, Dorothy Day, and Jacques Ellul. Noteworthy for their ability "to 'say' what the world looks like as seen through eyes transformed by an encounter with the living God," individuals in this tradition are "orthodox" because they see a world utterly transformed by the ancient incarnation of Christ. They are "avant-garde" in their incessant proclamation that "we haven't yet grasped the full implications of this revelation because our imaginations are dominated by superficial 'differences'" (i.e., cultural delusions and political fictions). Working from a reality that most of society misses, the orthodox avant-garde "desires to *live in the truth* even more than they desire *to be effective in the world*, and this puts them on the far side of a very important and a very deep intellectual divide: it puts them in the camp of the stoic poor, the moral outcasts, and the political and literary pariahs."⁴ When considering communities in which Will Campbell might fit best, "free church syndrome" and "orthodox avant-garde" are better candidates than "Southern civil religion."⁵ More than a Southern radical, Will Campbell incarnates Radical Christianity in the American South.

2. The claim that Campbell is a "paradoxical figure in Southern religious and literary life" makes sense—insofar as one views him from a cultural perspective. Campbell is quite consistent, however, when viewed from a theological perspective. (See Ramsey, *Preachers and Misfits, Prophets and Thieves*, 88–93).

3. Yoder, "The Free Church Syndrome."

4. Inchausti, *Subversive Orthodoxy*, 181–88.

5. Connelly, *Will Campbell and the Soul of the South*, 138.

We find Campbell's importance, therefore, not in his mediation between American optimism and Southern pessimism. Rather Campbell's importance becomes manifest in his irrepressible conflict against the principalities and powers of the world. He has embodied the peculiar, scandalous, culturally objectionable, politics of Jesus—offering an alternative ethic that historically transcends civil religions. Although Campbell is forthrightly, even proudly, Southern, he is quintessentially a Radical Christian. Campbell is an important expression of that Radical minority tradition throughout Christian history, committed to the command "Thou shalt have no other [social, national, regional, ideological, political, military, racial] gods before me."[6] Certainly Southern sins have fueled his iconoclastic fervor, but the source of the prophetic fire shut up in Campbell's bones has less to do with the American South, and more about the Radical tradition's 2000-year history—perhaps most clearly manifest in the Anabaptists, or Radical Reformation, of the sixteenth century.[7] Thus, Campbell is not so much a Southern symbol, as he is an embodiment, in the American South, of Christian Radicalism's

---

6. For a quick appreciation of Christian Radicalism's long history, see Bradstock and Rowland, *Radical Christian Writings: A Reader.*

7. As Tom Yoder Neufeld has illustrated, the term "Anabaptist" is better appreciated in terms of tradition*s* rather than a singular Anabaptist tradition. Radicals can range from passive nonresistance to resistant activism, with Will Campbell arguably fitting the latter Anabaptist subset insofar as "this paradigm [has] a certain separatism. But it is a separatism not of ethnicity, nor even always of church/world, but more often a separatism of assumptions and lifestyle. There is a commitment to attempt already to live the way the world should function if it were fully subject to the reign of God." (See Yoder Neufeld, "Contemporary Mennonite Peace Witness," 255.) Elsewhere Yoder Neufeld explains that this Anabaptist activism has a vein of "suspicion" and "subversion" running through it. Such Radicals are suspicious of all establishments and their proclivity to "disenfranchise and marginalize on the basis of gender, race, education, and wealth." In response, these Radicals look to subvert—to "undo the establishment from within and underneath, at both practical and ideological levels." (See Yoder Neufeld, "Christian Counterculture: *Ecclesia* and Establishment," 207.) More recently Yoder Neufeld concluded, "We must take courage to acknowledge that the Bible not only unabashedly depicts God as a powerful resister to evil, but just as unabashedly implicates the people of God in that resistance. *Not to resist is to betray the high calling of the 'sons and daughters of God.'*" (See Yoder Neufeld, "Resistance and Nonresistance: The Two Legs of a Biblical Peace Stance," 62, emphasis in original.) Campbell's Anabaptism, in other words, represents a tradition of resistance to, and subversion of, the principalities and powers. For further discussion of Anabaptist diversity see, Yoder, *Nevertheless: Varieties of Religious Pacifism*; Burkholder and Gingerich, "Mennonite Peace Theology: A Panorama of Types"; and Koontz, "Peace Theology in Transition: North American Mennonite Peace Studies and Theology, 1906–2006," 77–96.

alternative ethic. One might say that Campbell has illustrated how to "Theologize globally, and incarnate locally."[8] If the significance of Campbell is found more in Christian than in Southern history, how might we develop an appreciation for this larger, longer Radical Christian tradition?

---

8. Because this chapter seeks to define both Will Campbell and the Radical Christian tradition, the discussion will broaden the conversation to illustrate the larger historic community into which Campbell fits.

BEYOND H. RICHARD NIEBUHR'S *CHRIST AND CULTURE*

For the better part of the last sixty years, H. Richard Niebuhr's *Christ and Culture* has served as a standard text for placing competing Christian ethics and political theologies in some meaningful order and arrangement. *Christ and Culture* has so dominated thinking that it often provides the starting point, if not a *lingua franca*, for the common consideration and deliberation of, what Niebuhr called, the "enduring problem" of the Christian being "in the world," but not "of it." Jesus taught his disciples, for example, to pray for God's kingdom to come "*on earth*," yet Jesus told Pilate his kingdom was not "*of this world*." Properly navigating such prepositional phrases ("in" or "on" but not "of") has proven quite the dilemma for disciples of all times and places. In terms of Niebuhr's *Christ and Culture* typologies, where might Campbell's claim that "Christianity creates its own culture" fit?[1]

In five broad categories Niebuhr charted what he saw as the political theologies Christians have historically used to engage the cultures in which they find themselves. "Culture," as Niebuhr defined it, stands for the human-centered systems (political, philosophical, economic, artistic, and scientific) that societies craft in order to arrange, value, and prioritize their aspirations and commitments. Culture communicates, "This is how '*we*' do things," or narrates "This is what '*we*' value." "If you are going to be one of '*us*,'" culture announces, "these are parameters for rightly reasoning, appropriately acting, or aptly expressing yourself." Ideally, "Christ" is a more constant, enduring, unified, and transcendent ethic than "culture." While the latter (often synonymous with the biblical phrase "the world") changes from generation to generation and from context to context, Hebrews 13:8 portrays Christ as the same yesterday, today, and forever.

---

1. Campbell, *Race and the Renewal of the Church*, 82.

Given the differences, how can "Christ" relate to "culture"? Should "Christ" be its own culture, separate and apart from those cultures crafted by "the world"? If Christianity is too aloof and reticent, will it resonate with anyone? Can this "Christ" be approachable, accessible to individuals already formed in the ways and logics of "the world"? To what extent might "Christ" (seeking to "be all things to all people") appropriate cultural forms and expressions from the world, without sacrificing its own genius and uncritically succumbing to "the world"? If "Christ" makes concessions and accommodations to transient, inconstant cultures in order to communicate with the people of a given culture, might "Christ" enter into a process whereby it is forever chasing a legion of "cultures"? What would happen to a once-for-all *kerygma* then? Niebuhr proposed that over the course of millennia Christians have responded to this "enduring problem" in essentially five ways.

On one end of the spectrum Niebuhr placed the "*Christ against Culture*" typology. As the name suggests, this position finds "Christ" and "culture" locked in irreconcilable conflict. God's order and ethics are incomparable and superior, with the exclusive economy of "Christ" guiding and governing the historic communion of saints—the body of Christ on earth that abides no cultural distinctions. Tertullian illustrated this Niebuhrian typology when he asked in the third century, "What has Athens ['culture'] to do with Jerusalem ['Christ']?" The correct answer according to Tertullian was, "Nothing." Like the charge to the Israelites in Joshua 24, individuals must choose the system by which they will operate, i.e., either "Christ" or "culture." Disciples must cast their lot, or pledge their allegiance *to* the normative system of Christ, and thus *against* all others. No cooperation or synthesis is possible.

For Niebuhr, the Anabaptists and Leo Tolstoy provide two of the historic examples for this "Against" typology. They are Radicals because they strive to return to the *radix*, or root, of the original, peculiar norms of Jesus, "The Mennonites have come to represent the attitude most purely," Niebuhr declared, "since they not only renounce all participation in politics and refuse to be drawn into military service, but follow their own distinctive customs and regulations in economics and education."[2]

On the other end of the spectrum, Niebuhr placed the "*Christ of Culture*" typology. Far from incommensurability, disciples here believe that "Christ" and "culture" are in such fundamental agreement that

---

2. Niebuhr, *Christ and Culture*, 56.

believers can, and should, find ways to accommodate both "Christ" and "culture." Jesus, therefore, was not a deviant, subversive, extremist proclaiming an anti-cultural message, but one of the great (if not the greatest) champions of human history and culture. Jesus was the great enlightened moral philosopher in the tradition of Socrates or Plato. His reasonable and tolerant ethics of forgiveness and service illustrated what all humans, at all times, and in all places can and should aspire to. Temporal distinctions will certainly exist, but at the end of the day faith and culture are striving to achieve the same humanitarian goal. In Western civilization, individuals like John Locke, Thomas Jefferson, and Albrecht Ritschl celebrated Jesus as this paragon of ethical civilization. Successful citizens in any enlightened society, therefore, would tend to look a lot like Christ (or vice versa).

Between these two polar extremes of "Christ Against" and "Christ Of" culture, Niebuhr charted three moderating typologies. The *"Christ above Culture"* position—similar to the "Christ of Culture" model—finds considerable congruence between "Christ" and "culture." Nevertheless, instead of the two being synonymous and interchangeable, in the "Above" position—in an almost Hegelian fashion—"Christ" synthesizes what is contradictory in culture into a higher truth or reality. "Culture" is right and good, insofar as it goes, yet insufficient or incomplete in itself. Perhaps best represented by Thomas Aquinas and the medieval synthesis, "Christ" helps "culture" take the necessary qualitative leap forward (or above) to a holy level, which is a leap culture could never make on its own (e.g., via culture's own logic or reasoning).

The second mediating position Niebuhr offered between the extremes of "Christ Against" and "Christ Of" culture is *"Christ and Culture in Paradox."* This dualist typology acknowledges that the norms of "Christ" and "culture" may often be, in fact, incommensurate, but Christians ought not be lured into the false dilemma of choosing either "Christ" or "culture." Instead, Christians often have dual allegiances. Those with a strong sense of moral responsibility will respond wisely and judiciously to *both* their "Christ" and their "cultural" contexts. Instead of choosing between ethics (culture v. Christ), the mature and sensible political strategy is to balance the irreconcilable, *especially* when the commitments of "Christ" and "culture" seem most antithetical, antagonistic, and inconsistent. As Martin Luther argued, humans often find themselves living simultaneously in "two kingdoms" (e.g., "Christ" and "culture"), and must hold these two politics and their ethics in creative polarity and tension, honoring both as best they can, given the realities and the circumstances. The art of discipleship, therefore, is successfully living the irreconcilable paradox of "Christ" and "culture." Typically this means that instead of resisting or subverting culture, Christians honor social convention as best they can, being a good citizens by conscientiously "playing the hand" culture has dealt them.

The third mediating position between the extremes of "Christ Against" and "Christ Of" culture, was H. Richard Niebuhr's personal preference, "*Christ Transforming Culture.*" This typology also recognizes the inherent tension posed by the unique ethical and moral demands of "Christ." Moreover, transformationists confess "culture's" often lamentable habits and practices. Nevertheless, transformationists reject the notion that "culture" is inherently evil. Instead culture is better appreciated as misguided and astray. Although undeniably flawed, "culture" is nonetheless *redeemable*. Like all of God's gifts, culture was created good, but sinful humans have misused and sullied culture's original purity and beauty. Instead of giving up on culture and writing it off as the "Against" types seem to, the goal for Christians is to take over, convert, or transform culture—redeeming culture back from its fallen state and making it all that God had originally envisioned and enabled culture to be. Stated differently, the goal or mission for disciples is to coax a Christian culture out of the society that one happens to inherit. Historic examples include Augustine's conversion of the Roman Empire (or at least remnants of it) into medieval Christendom, and John Calvin's attempt to transform sixteenth-century Geneva into a Bible commonwealth.

For three generations Niebuhr's *Christ and Culture* has arranged the political theologies of Christian history into a meaningful order. Any tool providing such comprehensive service is to be applauded. Like any map, however, such arrangements operate from an agenda, with its own story to tell, e.g., codifying winners and losers.

Although Niebuhr was a theological ethicist, his *Christ and Culture* was more of a historical narrative—and one with a strong thesis at that. As Craig Carter avers,

> Niebuhr did not simply write a sociological study of the various ways in which Christians, at various times and places, have sought to relate Christ and culture; he told a story that made sense as a connected narrative and in which many diverse readers could see

themselves. The story began in the first century with a few small bands of zealous, deeply committed, but somewhat naïve believers huddled together in their little enclaves waiting for Jesus to return at any moment. Of course they did not try to transform culture; they could not conceive of such a thing. In their zeal for holiness, readiness for martyrdom, and heroic anticultural stance, we see sincerity, faithfulness, and a reduplication of Jesus' own lifestyle. But we do not see an adequate model for discipleship today. Our Lord did not return in the second or third century, and Christian history did not come to an end. Instead, a Roman emperor embraced the faith, and Christianity became the official religion of the most powerful empire on earth. As that empire crumbled over the next few centuries, the church inherited great civil and social responsibility for society in the face of potential chaos and violence. Did not Christians have a duty to their fellow human beings to step into the gap and even get their hands dirty stemming the tide of lawlessness and barbarism?[3]

John Howard Yoder believed the "entire presentation" of *Christ and Culture* was "set up to predispose the reader to see that the superiority of the fifth position [i.e., 'Christ transforming culture'] is the response of readers who have borrowed the scheme for all kinds of applications." More significantly for the purposes here, Yoder maintained that it was not only clear which "of the five types of thought Richard Niebuhr is himself inclined; it also becomes increasingly evident that only one of the other positions needs radically to be challenged. It is the first position, the 'radical' one, which Niebuhr makes the object of serious negative arguments."[4]

Admittedly, Niebuhr confessed his sincere respect for the early church's discipline and fortitude as it struggled—even to the point of martyrdom—against the dominant power of Roman culture. Early Christians distinguished themselves from the cultural superpower of the moment, for example, by shunning military service and allegiance to the emperor, pledging to live out such countercultural ethics as nonviolence and voluntary poverty. In that historical moment (i.e., when the nascent church faced a mature Roman culture), Niebuhr admitted that the "Christ against Culture" political theology may have been an acceptable, even laudable, option, but as the church matured and Roman

---

3. Carter, *Rethinking Christ and Culture: A Post-Christendom Perspective*, 59.
4. Yoder, "How H. Richard Niebuhr Reasoned: A Critique of Christ and Culture," 52–53, and 42.

culture declined Niebuhr believed it became socially irresponsible—even immoral—for Christians to continue their "sectarian" resistance to culture.[5] The moral of H. Richard Niebuhr's *Christ and Culture* story, therefore, is that no matter how tempting the "Against" political theology may seem, and despite the fact that it may have been the example of the early church, Christians who are attuned to the needs of their culture today must foreswear the Radical approach. At least since the advent of Constantine, Christians have had little need to resist or subvert culture. To the contrary, for the last 1600 years of Western history, "culture" has embraced "Christ," and "Christ" should wisely and responsibly return the favor.

Simply stated, according to Niebuhr, the problem with the "Against" typology is twofold. First, society (and some in the church) perceives the "sectarian" position as little more than angry condemnation and fatalistic abandonment.[6] Thus Christians who foreswear cultural practices and strategies sacrifice their social influence and lose the ability to accomplish what the world needs done.[7] Second, the "sectarian" project is bad logic. No Christians, even the most devout, introspective, and committed, Niebuhr noted, can actually extricate themselves from culture.

---

5. The supposed immorality of imitating the early church sounds close to Reinhold Niebuhr's critique of Christian pacifism. As Michael Baxter has presented, the term "sectarian" is a term of derision in the "lexicon" of the Ernst Troeltsch-H. Richard Niebuhr-James Gustafson "lineage." Sectarianism refers to a way of living ethics and politics that is "embedded in the beliefs and practices of the Church and therefore cannot serve as the basis for universal, supra-ecclesiastical ethical principles that are then applied in making public policy." In other words, so-called sectarians believe that "gospel ideals pertain to politics," and that both the ends and the means of politics and public policy must be congruent with the ethics of Jesus. Pragmatic policy making is beyond the pale for disciples. (Baxter, "'Blowing the Dynamite of the Church': Catholic Radicalism from a Catholic Radicalist Perspective," 205.) This issue will be developed further below.

6. Universally dismissing the "Against" types as "haughty" and "caustic," Jean Bethke Elshtain reviles the position with an *ad hominem* attack announcing, "People quite reasonably resist the ministrations of those whose proclamations are all negation. Confronted with such jeremiads, we tend to focus on what's eating such people, why their lives are all bitterness and rue, rather than on what may be vital and true about the message." See her "With or Against Culture," 30ff. Do Radicals, however, merely offer "negation," or might they envision a lively alternative?

7. Although the Niebuhr brothers, H. Richard and Reinhold, were often on different theological pages, when it came to their views of the Radicals, Yoder found them remarkably consistent. Whether speaking of Reinhold or H. Richard, both could have used the "backhanded complement" that the Radicals are "consistent but irrelevant." (See Yoder, *Christian Attitudes to War, Peace and Revolution*, 296–98.)

Radicals denounce all culture, but then "cherry pick" its preferred parts. Niebuhr's point, therefore, is that the "sectarians" really lack the choice they think they are making. No matter how contrary to culture one professes to be, everyone is *unavoidably immersed* in a culture, and will *inevitably use* some cultural components to function in the world. Even the most die-hard sectarians, like Tertullian, Tolstoy, and the Amish, unwittingly and inescapably draw from culture. With such inconsistencies established, the "Against" typology logically collapses like a house built on sand, Niebuhr suggested. Although Niebuhr may have applauded the well-intentioned enthusiasm and rigorous commitment of the "Against" types, he found so-called "sectarians" like the Anabaptists misguided and negligent. Given Will Campbell's Anabaptist orientation, Niebuhr's critique is a serious indictment.

Despite its long-term popularity, Niebuhr's book-length attack on the Radical tradition is often misguided and unhelpful. First, Niebuhr condemns the Radicals' dream to extract themselves from the taint of culture. As John Howard Yoder effectively illustrates, however, Radicals have never professed to deny every last vestige of culture, as Niebuhr charged. Just because Radicals accept the counter-cultural nonviolent ethic of Jesus, it does not necessarily follow that the same Radicals *must* reject modern medicine, agricultural science, or meteorology. Yoder illustrates how historically the Radicals have been cultural discerners, conscientiously discriminating the acceptable from the unacceptable. Radicals have never argued that everything concocted by culture is inherently anti-Christ. Not even the Old Order Amish make such an argument. Second, Niebuhr mistakenly equated the "Against" position with escapist "withdrawal and renunciation," as if these Radical Christians conveniently abandon the difficult challenges of responsible social leadership. He echoed, in other words, the cliché "The only thing necessary for evil to triumph is for good people to do nothing." Such a platitude presumes that to be on the side of "good," one must "do."

Here, however, is the rub. According to Niebuhr, *responsible* Christians choose their acceptable action from a predetermined list, proscribed by the dominant culture of the moment. In the modern context, the dominant culture privileges the government as the most efficient and effective means for *realistically* getting things done.[8] Doing

---

8. Yoder, "How H. Richard Niebuhr Reasoned," 66. As Craig Carter notes, the "amorphous Christ transforming culture position justifies the Christendom project of

good and defeating evil, in this scenario, is a political science in which culture defines our options. Or, described differently, Niebuhr depicts the enduring "Christ and culture" dilemma as the proverbial "fight or flight" syndrome. If one is not fighting according to one of the culturally defined and proscribed ways, then one is irresponsibly fleeing—and arguably perpetuating—the problem. Read from this perspective, we should not be surprised that Campbell's "do nothing" manifesto scandalizes so many. "Doing nothing" is effete, embarrassing, irresponsible, and entirely un-American. "Doing nothing" will never carry the day, get things done, or, for God's sake, *win*.

As Campbell and Yoder announce, however, choosing to live counter to, or against, popular convention is something far different than seeking to withdraw from, dodge, or escape social problems. "Some elements of culture the church categorically rejects (e.g., pornography, tyranny, cultural idolatry)," Yoder explains.

> Other dimensions of culture it accepts within clear limits (economic production, commerce, the graphic arts, paying taxes for peacetime civil government). To still other dimensions of culture, Christians give a new motivation and coherence (agriculture, family life, literacy, conflict resolution, empowerment). Still other forms of culture are *created* by Christian churches (hospitals, service of the poor, generalized education, egalitarianism, abolitionism, feminism). Some have been created with special effectiveness by the Peace Churches (prison reform, war sufferers' relief, international conciliation).[9]

In their life and work, therefore, Radicals proclaim the preeminence of a competing culture (politic, convention, logic, grammar). This contravening culture of "Christ" supersedes and impoverishes all others. A self-professed Christian anarchist, Campbell's Radicalism envisions an alternative or counter culture.[10] Radical discipleship, in other words, rec-

---

Christians compromising the teachings of Jesus Christ in an effort to be realistic and responsible by *managing* society and making it a bit less violent and cruel than it might otherwise be." (*Rethinking Christ and Culture*, 63–64. Emphasis added.)

9. Yoder, "How H. Richard Niebuhr Reasoned," 69. Later Yoder will point to colonial Pennsylvania as an example. Instead of a form of withdrawal, William Penn Jr. and the Quakers launched the colony as their "Holy Experiment" incarnating their countercultural political theology vis-à-vis English political convention.

10. In his biography of Will Campbell, Merrill Hawkins acknowledges that Campbell's "belief system is similar to the worldview of Christian anarchy. Moreover, Christian

ognizes the contest of competing narratives (or contesting conventions) at work in the world, but instead of yielding to the dominant narrative or predominant social convention as the only live option (the only right answer on our multiple choice test of responsible social leadership), these disciples choose to live according to an alternative, objectionable narrative. "Christ" is more than alien to culture. "Christ" is an alternative culture; a counterculture maintaining its autonomy distinct from "the principalities and powers."

The incomparable Christian *kerygma* is, in other words, a convention unto itself. "Jesus was a particular kind of politically committed poor Palestinian preacher of a coming Kingdom," proclaiming ethics and constitutions for his movement.[11] Radicals choose this counter or anti-cultural approach as their fully engaged, theologically responsible way of unmasking and disarming the principalities, rather than allowing the powers to continue to proscribe and form their thinking. Instead of withdrawal, or escape, the so-called "Against" political theology can be a most intentional form of iconoclastic resistance and conflict. "The believing community's assignment is to represent *within* society, through and in spite of withdrawal from certain of its activities," Yoder avers, "as well as through and in spite of involvement in others, a real judgment upon the rebelliousness of culture and a real possibility of reconciliation for all." This gift of "Christ's" counterculture, "constitutes a [or *the*] new cultural option."[12] Instead of merely playing the hand dealt by the dominant culture, or working to take over and convert culture into something

---

anarchy has influenced him and captures much of what Campbell believes about the relationship of God and humanity, as well as his present sentiments about religiously-oriented social activism. . . . While he did not use the term 'Christian anarchy,' Campbell's reflections on the 1960s activism of the churches nonetheless reveal an anarchist perspective. That is, Campbell believed that the churches had placed too much emphasis on political solutions." (Hawkins, 76 and 80.) Unpacking that claim, Hawkins connects the writings of Jacques Ellul and Vernard Eller—both frequent contributors to *Katallagete* as well as authors of books on Christian anarchism—to Campbell. In the same way that the Romans condemned Christianity as atheistic because it exclusively worshipped Yahweh, so radical Christianity is "anarchistic" insofar as it purports to be a politics unto itself—rejecting the competing political systems as authoritative. (See Goode, "The Political Scandal of Christian Anarchism." Christian anarchism will be discussed in more detail below.)

11. Yoder, "How H. Richard Niebuhr Reasoned," 83. For specific details one might start with Matthew, chapters 5–7, and 25, or Luke 4.

12. Ibid., 70–71, and 75. Emphasis added.

other than society created it to be, Radicals understand that "Each event, each relationship will open for us a set of options or challenges, where we shall need to decide how to love our enemies, how to feed the hungry, how to keep our promises, how to make the earth be fruitful, how to celebrate our community, how to remember our heritage."[13] This so-called "anti-cultural" stance, therefore, can be one of the most culturally creative contributors to human history.

As Will Campbell frequently counsels, we must query ourselves concerning our gods and icons. Who is defining *our* terms, establishing *our* norms, and proscribing *our* options? If we surrender that responsibility to society's powerbrokers, where might we be led? What happens to our ministry of reconciliation? What might we do to the vulnerable "least ones"? Moreover, as Campbell's life makes manifest, the practical difficulties of living according to a minority, alternative, contrasting narrative hardly makes the so-called "Against" choice the easy dodge or convenient escape, as Niebuhr portrayed it. Campbell's history of conscientious cultural discernment proves the creative capacity of Radicalism's iconoclasm. Because H. Richard Niebuhr's *Christ and Culture* typologies obscure Campbell's Radical contribution, we need better ways of thinking about ethics and political theology.

---

13. Ibid., 89.

BEYOND MARK TOULOUSE'S
GOD IN PUBLIC

WITH A MORE INTENSIVE focus on U.S. religious history, Mark Toulouse's *God in Public: Four Ways American Christianity and Public Life Relate* investigates this enduring "Christ" and "culture" dilemma. Instead of replacing or refuting Niebuhr's typologies, Toulouse offers another schematic for understanding the major political theologies at work in American history.

Toulouse designates the first type as *"Iconic Faith,"* a strategy where "culture" (rather than "Christ") holds most of the initiative. In this approach, cultural leaders both appropriate Christian symbols and language for political use, and impose society's secular icons onto the church. Advocates of this political theology, for example, might zealously place copies of the Ten Commandments in the secular public arena, use the Bible as a visual prop in ceremonial events, or celebrate the flag as a sacred image invested with divine meaning and holy purpose. Oddly enough, these "Iconic Faith" types might have limited knowledge of the actual content of the Ten Commandments or Scripture,[1] but fidelity to the historical content of the symbol is not the principal concern. The desire is to expropriate the power of these religious symbols, utilizing the prestige for their own purposes. Those who successfully wrap themselves and their agenda in the mystique of the sacred can hope to earn a hearing and/or following they might not gain otherwise. Fortifying their speeches with God-talk and religious imagery, national leaders like Presidents Ronald Reagan and George W. Bush have extolled the work of the United States as a righteous cause or holy crusade, investing themselves and their policies with divine endorsement.[2] In this vein, the

   1. Congressman Lynn Westmoreland (GA) sponsored a bill to have the Ten Commandments placed in government buildings because such postings would support good citizenship, yet when asked in 2006, he could not recite the Commandments.

   2. David Dark's *The Gospel According to America* effectively explores some of the more recent expressions of this practice in American culture and politics.

church becomes a civic institution that, like other good civic institutions, assures the stability and well-being of the nation-state. Although the political leaders who use the "Iconic Faith" strategy are neither working for the church, nor engaging in Christian evangelism per se, resistance to their homilies and leadership earns denunciations for being unpatriotic—Iconic Faith's unforgivable sin.

Second, Toulouse describes the *"Priestly Faith"* model. Although "Iconic" and "Priestly" Faiths may appear similar, the difference is largely one of initiative. Where "Iconic Faith" uses the church for the purposes of the nation-state, "Priestly Faith" flips the balance of power so that the church uses the nation-state. Beyond conveniently employing the symbols and language of faith, these nationalist-minded Christians combine and confuse the United States and the Christian tradition, asserting that the two are inextricably linked—and have been from the nation's inception. God, in other words, formed the United States as a nation separate and apart from all others, uniquely commissioned to lead all other nations toward a greater practice of God's will. Although recently associated with organizations like the Moral Majority and the Christian Coalition, "Priestly Faith" goes back centuries. Some eighteenth-century proponents of a Christian nation, for example, drafted an alternative, Christian preamble for the U.S. Constitution, because the founding document avoided God entirely.

Toulouse's juxtaposition of "Iconic" and "Priestly" Faith helpfully moves beyond simplistic "right" and "left," "conservative" versus "liberal" labeling. Looking back into America's religious history, examples of "Priestly Faith" emerge on both the so-called "right" and "left." Conservatives and progressives may differ over their enemies, or God's supposedly perspicuous plan on a given issue, but their reasoning is largely similar. Whether "liberal" or "conservative," this American form of Constantinianism emboldens the "Priestly Faith" advocates of the "Christian America" thesis to use the power of legislation and enforcement to promote their faith-informed causes.[3] Having absolutized

---

3. As Stanley Hauerwas has noted, one of the presumptions of Constantinian thinking is the belief, on the part of Christians, that "the meaning of history lies outside the church." Because the so-called "real world" is so complex, nasty, and brutish, the church (i.e., its ethics, resources, and story) is incapable of achieving God's outcome for the world. Christians must learn and use the state—the principalities and their powers—to accomplish the church's mission and calling (e.g., peace, justice, and reconciliation). As Christians study "history, political science, English literature, economics,

"good" as simultaneously Christian and American, "evil" is no longer merely a mistake or a misdeed in need of correction. "Evil" is an unambiguous enemy of God and the United States, awaiting divinely sanctioned eradication.

Third, Toulouse outlines the "*Public Christian*" model. In contrast to the "Iconic" and "Priestly" political theologies, the "Public Christian" believes that the *church* should focus on its distinctive work of salvation, rather than partisan politics. Churches, in other words, should remain outside and beyond the political fray. Nevertheless, *individual* Christians may get deeply involved in the public life of the nation as outspoken activists. Disciples might, for example, work as operatives in political parties, or seek elected office themselves, but, because of the inherent and historic dangers of political practice, the collective church body must remain aloof, dispassionate, and non-participatory when it comes to public policy. The temporal "city of humanity" will never become the eternal "city of God." Consequently, Christians should never confuse the two—operating in the former to promote the latter. Individual disciples might serve the temporal city as executioners, soldiers, or elected officials because in doing so they might help advance the cause of justice in the secular public arena. Nevertheless, these same disciples ought never justify their activism by proclaiming that their political service is God's commission for the secular state. Admittedly, this is a tricky dance.

Such intentional activism was a change for many fundamentalist and Evangelical types, who, since the early twentieth century, had expressed reticence toward culture. By mid-century, however, Carl F. H. Henry, editor of *Christianity Today*, was frequently appealing to his Evangelical readers to get involved, as responsible members of their public square, in domestic and international concerns of justice and peace. More recently Jim Wallis and *Sojourners*, according to Toulouse, has also carried the "Public Christian" banner. Despite their principled, theologically-informed activism, Christians must always remember their overriding commitment to the sacred, transcendent work of bringing others to a

---

[and] the various sciences," however, they not only serve and perpetuate the secular state, but simultaneously undermine the distinctive, peculiar Christian *kerygma*. "They [Christians] reproduce the practices of the secular and in the process make invisible the alternative that we should be in a world that denies there is any other world." Christians, seeking to be relevant and effective in the world, deny the scandalous genius of their faith. (See, Hauerwas, "The State of the Secular: Theology, Prayer, and the University," in *The State of the University*, 165–86.)

saving knowledge/experience of Christ. Again, "Public Christians" can be involved in the temporal, secular, political work of charity and social justice (e.g., feeding the hungry, housing the homeless, health care for the sick), but always as a penultimate duty, or secondary vocation to saving souls.

Like Niebuhr, in due course Toulouse builds toward his final and preferred model—in this schematic, the "*Public Church*." This political theology rejects the idea of sacred-secular/eternal-temporal/body-soul dichotomies that seem to limit "Public Christians." The fullness of the kingdom of God may be yet to come, but the work of the church is not focused on some separate sacred sphere in some otherworldly hereafter. The work of the church is to move the here-and-now ever closer to the ethics of the kingdom, so that God's will is in fact triumphant on earth as it is in heaven. To fulfill that task, *churches* must prophetically use the collective power at their disposal.

How, therefore, is "Public Church" different from "Priestly Faith" on the one hand, and "Public Christian" on the other? The "Public Church" may sound like another form of "Priestly Faith," with the church conflating "Christ" and "culture" and embarking on an evangelistic conquest of culture. The difference between "Public Church" and "Priestly Faith," however, is that the former never expects the pluralist American public to live by the exclusive dictates of biblical revelation. Where "Priestly Faith" absolutizes good and evil, the "Public Church" has a healthy appreciation for the ironic. Throughout history the most self-assured have often been the most likely to trip up, fall, and make a mess of things. Learning from history, the "Public Church" seeks to participate in the public square, but not to monopolize it. Instead of trying to impose some "Priestly" version of "*the* Christian good" on all, the "Public Church" goal is to help the public arena become more *just*, which does not require making the public square exclusively *Christian*. The "Public Church" is humbly aware that "the ethics and values of the Kingdom are not easily translated into blueprint plans for civil governments and society," and the Christian *kerygma* is always subject to misuse and abuse—especially by the most devout. To achieve progress, or some proximate justice in society, therefore, the "Public Church" makes thoughtful, careful, relative compromises with culture, seeking common or middle ground with fellow citizens—whether they be of different, or no faith. "Priestly Faith" types, of course, would find such compromises with non-Christians anathema and heretical.

The distinction between the "Public Church" and the "Public Christian" is of much more significance for the discussion here. On one level, Toulouse contends, the individualistic "Public Christian" strategy might be the correct political theology if evil only resided in individuals. Sin, however, often reigns through vicious systems and principalities. In fact, the evil collected in social organizations (e.g., capitalist corporations, militaristic governments, and racist fraternities) far exceeds anything an individual could acquire or affect. To confront such systemic sin, the "Public Church" insists that Christians need their own concerted, collective response, i.e., the voice and witness of the church militant. Stated otherwise, to the extent that political, social, and economic systems exploit and disenfranchise humans, the church must employ its collective political wisdom and clout to accomplish a greater degree of relative justice in public life. Committed to social transformation as well as individual redemption, the "Public Church" is a political theology that, according to Toulouse, better enables the church to win a voice for the silenced, respect for the oppressed, and a seat at the political table of power for the marginalized. Toulouse extols the Social Gospel of Walter Rauschenbusch and the Black Church tradition as historic illustrations of those who have properly implemented the "Public Church" political theology in America's religious history.

The distinction between "Public Christian" and "Public Church" is yet more substantial. At the heart of the "Public Church" critique of the "Public Christian" is the persistent question whether humans—irrespective of our differences—have some innate consciousness or common knowledge that enables peoples of diverse intellectual, political, and religious backgrounds to reason morally and make right moral judgments together. Can peoples and communities outside the Christian church make right political decisions? If so, how do Christians function and reason in this heterogeneous public environment? These questions become all the more important as our cultural world becomes smaller, and the public square becomes evermore varied. "Public Christians," according to Toulouse, tend to believe that correct political reasoning is achieved via distinctively (or peculiarly) Christian means. "Public Christians" like George Lindbeck, John Milbank, and Stanley Hauerwas, for instance, might live and move in the public square, but they strive to think and act according to their patently Christian concepts and commitments. "Public Church" types, like James Gustafson, David Tracy, and Richard McCormick,[4] on the other hand, believe that humans do have common intellectual ground. Thus in the public square Christians can utilize what is common rather than what is unique to their faith tradition. To be fair and responsible, "Christians must address non-Christians on grounds acceptable to non-Christians."[5]

The discussion between "Public Christian" and "Public Church" types becomes really interesting when the latter accuses the former of being sectarians, who isolate themselves from the world and fail to provide any responsible leadership in civic and public life (i.e., the indictment Niebuhr leveled at the "Against" types). "Sectarianism," according to Gustafson, is the assertion that because one's beliefs are incommensurate with others, one's beliefs need no testing or external confirmation, verification, or corroboration. Sectarianism is "idolatrously maintaining a historic social identity" while dogmatically rejecting the veracity of all others.[6] Historically sects, presuming to have *the* Truth, strive to live apart, retired from the rest of the culture that fails to appreciate the sect's Truth. Because humans can, however, no more live apart from culture than they can breathe without air, in moments of intellectual clarity and honesty everyone knows that "the destiny of life in the world is determined by secular centers of power,"[7] and not from small isolated self-righteous enclaves.

Applying this critique to political theology, Gustafson warns against tribal "Public Christians" who presume to have the Truth, and use their Truth as normative for public policy. Bluntly stated, imposing in the public square "conformity to the stories of Jesus" is, to Gustafson, sectarian. The stories of Jesus are simply "unintelligible," and unpersuasive to many in society. Even for many rational theists, "Jesus is not God." Thus Christians cannot use "the faithful witness to Jesus" as a "basis for addressing the moral and social problems" or informing public

---

4. Toulouse draws upon the work of James Gustafson, David Tracy, and Linell Cady in developing his "Public Church" model (see pages xxii, and 180–91).

5. D'Costa, *Theology in the Public Square: Church, Academy, and Nation*, 85.

6. Gustafson, "The Sectarian Temptation: Reflections on Theology, the Church, and the University," 153. This essay is a reprint of the original published in the 1985 *Catholic Theological Society of America Proceedings*.

7. Ibid., 151.

life and drafting policy.⁸ Referring specifically to the Anabaptist Radical tradition, Gustafson notes, "Christians, whether they choose to or not, are members of, and make choices in, other social communities." All appeals for social justice in a pluralist public square must use reasons, knowledges, truths that are intelligible and credible to the diverse community; a society "more comfortable construing reality from multiple perspectives than from one."⁹

To summarize, therefore, Toulouse acknowledges that "Public Christian" Radicals have a public consciousness and involve themselves in the public square, a fact that Niebuhr often missed. Nevertheless, Toulouse and Gustafson, critique these "Public Christian" Radicals for entering the public square on their own terms and with their own ways of knowing; speaking their own "unintelligible" language, rather than operating according to more publicly accessible grammar (i.e., epistemologies and rationalities). "Public Church" types challenge the benefit of the "Public Christian" Radicals who enter the public square thinking and speaking in ways that other public participants cannot fathom. Ultimately, what good are "Public Christians" for society, for justice, and for reconciliation?

At the end of the day, Toulouse's critique of the Radical tradition is not substantively different from Niebuhr's. Niebuhr condemned Radicals for being withdraw-minded sectarians, hiving off from the larger public, striving to live their peculiar, largely irrelevant private existence. Toulouse and Gustafson acknowledge that some "Public Christian" Radicals are in fact concerned to show up in the public square. Nevertheless, these Radicals remain self-marginalizing, ghetto-dwelling, tribalistic sectarians. Even if Radicals *could* consistently live out their ideas, which, according to Toulouse is implausible, the political theology of Radicals makes them powerless to benefit society's well being. Attendance aside, therefore, the Radicals are poor public participants, because they make themselves politically irrelevant.

So where might Campbell fit in such a schematic? Given his view of institutions, both political and ecclesiastical, it is unlikely that Campbell will make Toulouse's "Public Church" hall of fame.¹⁰ Nor does Campbell represent either the "Iconic" or "Priestly" faiths. Perhaps by default,

---

8. Ibid., 153.

9. Ibid., 150–51.

10. See "Resistance to the Steeples" in *Writings in Reconciliation and Resistance*, 90–174.

Toulouse places Campbell in the "Public Christian" category with others from the historic Radical tradition.[11] Toulouse's arrangement, however, highlights an ongoing problem with the historiography of political theology. He pins the title "prophetic" on the "Public Church" because of that way's public mindedness. Notice, however, that the "prophetic" activity of the church described by Toulouse is a negotiated conversation with the pluralistic public, pursuing proximate forms of justice. In other words, the "Public Church's" prophetic activity is proscribed by the very quest of being public, i.e., speaking and acting in ways that are meaningful and relevant to the public square. Shall the litmus test for the "prophetic" be the employment of public reason, or communication in publicly negotiated terms that all peoples understand, appreciate, and perhaps find convincing? Where is the iconoclastic scandal in that? If the social benefit of the *kerygma* can be understood outside the Christian community, how is Christianity prophetic at all?

Campbell and Holloway's "Truth, Language and . . . ," which introduced *Katallagete*'s Summer 1976 issue, illustrates the limitations of Toulouse's "ways" for Radicals. At the height of a national political campaign that saw a Southern Christian successfully attain the highest public office in the "free world," Campbell and Holloway lamented how they could hardly speak either to the church or to society any longer. Because of the way Christians were "hawking" their "jargon," the language of Christianity had become foreign both to the churches *and* the larger American society. They found it nearly impossible to "speak today of truth born in Resurrection," or "of love wrought in Crucifixion, of why the Samaritan is 'good,' of why 'God Alone!'" Then again, they noted, such confusion presented an opportunity. "On several occasions in the journal we have observed that Jesus spoke as he spoke (and did as he did) because the religious language and rhetoric of his time was bankrupt. Burned out. Meaning everything and nothing to everyone and to no one." Consequently, Jesus crafted a new language—a new vocabulary and grammar—to convey his peculiar politics to his new, peculiar community. In Jesus' day the religious leaders were bogged down in thinking that if they could only—through frenetic activity and savvy public leadership—find *the* efficient, effective, miraculous *thing*, then

---

11. In fact, the only mention of Campbell in Toulouse's text is where Toulouse includes Campbell in a list of authors published in what Toulouse classifies as the "Public Christian" periodical, *Sojourners* (p. 132).

they could build the kingdom, transform society, and fulfill their vocation for the world. So today, the steeples presume that if they can only successfully, intelligibly translate the Christian *kerygma* into culture's vernacular, society would have an epiphany. Peace, justice, and progress will prevail.

Time and again, Campbell has cautioned that frenetic involvement and activism are more likely to be idolatry than Christian vocation. Choosing the Radical option, therefore, is not a decision to withdrawal from political involvement. As Tripp York notes, "the crucified Jesus *is* a politic." The strange, objectionable *kerygma* of Christ, Bob Eckblad reminds us, is the political message of the sovereign God who "opposes evil in the world" and "stands with the oppressed and accompanies them in their liberation process." The political scandal of Radicalism is that the sovereign God achieves neither by control or domination, but by "hanging crucified between two dying thieves." Admittedly, "if our politic is truly in the shape of a cross then we should not expect to be well received," York warns. Nevertheless striving "to fail faithfully" should not be seen as political withdrawal, but as the political vocation of *being* what God has already accomplished—an alter-public *polis*.[12]

How does the church do that? How does Christianity create its own culture? The answer is that the church incarnates, in the midst of the world, the politics of Jesus—Christianity's peculiar genius. Radicals need not choose between being against the world, or working to transform it. Nor must Radicals choose between private practices of Christian faith, or the church's collective engagement of the world according to the so-called relevant terms of the public square. As their name suggests, Radicals return to the root of the Christian tradition. As the author of the second-century *Letter to Diognetus* notes, Christians neither withdrawal nor secede from culture to form their own nation or exclusive settlement. In fact, when compared to many aspects of culture, their day-to-day life is not especially eccentric. Instead, Christians "live in Greek and barbarian cities alike, as each person's lot has been cast, and follow the customs of the country in clothing and food and other matters of daily living." Although externally ordinary, Christians nonetheless have a "remarkable and admittedly extraordinary constitution of their own commonwealth."

---

12. York, *Living on Hope While Living in Babylon*, 22, 105; and Eckblad, *A New Christian Manifesto*, 145.

> They live in their own countries, but only as aliens. They have a share in everything as citizens, and endure everything as foreigners. Every foreign land is their homeland, and yet for them every homeland is a foreign land. . . . It is true that they are "in the flesh," but they do not live "according to the flesh." They busy themselves on earth, but their citizenship is in heaven. . . . They love all, and are persecuted by all. They are unknown, and still they are condemned; they are put to death, and yet they are brought to life. They are poor, and yet they make many rich; they are completely destitute, and yet they enjoy complete abundance. They are dishonored, and in their very dishonor are glorified; they are defamed, and are vindicated. They are reviled, and yet they bless; when they are affronted, they still pay due respect. . . . Undergoing punishment, they rejoice because they are brought to life. They are treated by the Jews as foreigners and enemies, and are hunted down by the Greeks; and all the time those who hate them find it impossible to justify their enmity. . . . While Christians are restrained in the world as in a prison, yet they hold the world together.[13]

Like Campbell, Robert Wilken has found the early church to be "a culture in its own right"; with Christians manifesting a culturally untranslatable way of being in the world. The world then and now needs a prophetic Radicalism that incarnates the Christian differences in the world, and for the world. Instead of aligning with, or acquiring the power of those other cultures, Wilken notes, the church should "tell its own story and nurture its own life, the culture of the city of God." To the extent that the church successfully incarnates its difference in the world, "then others will know that there is another city in their midst, another commonwealth whose face is turned toward the face of God."[14]

Instead of contending in the public square according to the terms of public reason, the church is commissioned to incarnate in the world—as the early church did—a different option, a resistance ethic, and/or subversive politics. As the patron saint of the Committee of Southern Churchmen, Jacques Ellul, explained, "We need to remember that the Christian must not act in exactly the same way as everyone else. The Christian has a part to play in this world that no one else can possibly

---

13. In Richardson, *Early Christian Fathers*, 216–18. The translation here was rendered gender inclusive.
14. Wilken, "*Amo, Amas, Amat*: Christianity and Culture."

fulfill."[15] For the church, "to exist is to resist," Ellul announced.[16] This resistance "is to be directed against society, not with the object of changing it but of forming Christian groups independent of it."[17] So, what are disciples supposed to do about those principalities that are, for better or worse, already wielding power? "Let them be," Ellul counseled. Instead, "set up a marginal society which will not be interested in such things" as power, coercion, or control.[18]

Stanley Hauerwas has recently put his finger on the reason why the "Public Church" is insufficient for Radicals like Campbell. Simply stated, the "Public Church" is beholden to the political science of the culture. Fifty years ago, for example, the "Public Church" lobbied the executive, legislative, and judicial branches of the U.S. government to pass and enforce laws that would desegregate American society. The "Public Church" steeples failed both God and society, Campbell has said, by endorsing desegregation via Supreme Court decision or federal mandate. For Christians, racial justice should never be a policy negotiated at city hall or legislated on Capitol Hill. Racial justice is, first and foremost, a Christian doctrine and biblical imperative emerging out of the *sovereignty of God*.[19] To support such a justice issue because society had agreed on it (either by public deliberation, majority rule, or through legislative fiat) is, according to Campbell, an elevation of human privilege that belittles God's sovereignty. "Campbell acknowledges that these humanitarian and egalitarian concerns [e.g., desegregation of schools, equal employment rights] lie within the province of Christian witness," Hauerwas explains. "But when they constitute all that Christians have to say about race, they are not enough. They are not enough because God, not the human, is the only point of reference that matters." Certainly segregation was an evil and inefficient public policy, but Jim Crow was *so* much more than that. Segregation was an affront to the sovereignty of God insofar as segregationists had the audacity to announce that *their wisdom* on race was better than God's.

15. Ellul, *The Presence of the Kingdom*, xi and 3.
16. Ellul, *The Political Illusion*, 222.
17. Heddendorf, "The Christian World of Jacques Ellul," 301.
18. Ellul, *Anarchy and Christianity*, 62.
19. Campbell, "The Sit-Ins: Passive Resistance or Civil Disobedience?" 17. Emphasis added.

But, and here is the punch line, it was no less arrogant for desegregationists to announce that, in *their new-found Constitutional wisdom*, no race was better than another. For Christians, claiming that the principles of liberal democracy would not tolerate racial superiority was no less an offense against God than the racism of the most virulent bigot. The logic was essentially the same. Rather than acting out of humility before the sovereign God who had already resolved this issue once and for all, *both segregationists and desegregationists operated out of public reason*—a human-centered democratic ideology (or political science) seeking the well-being of the U.S. "Nothing is more indicative of such an [egotistical] emphasis than the presumption by modern liberal Christians that the race problem can be solved politically," laments Hauerwas. "Such a presumption serves to legitimate the modern nation-state, which, ironically, has been the primary agent for the categorization of people by race. Christians have quite simply confused humanism with the gospel."[20]

---

20. Hauerwas, "Race: The 'More' It Is About," 98–99. This is a printed version of the address Hauerwas gave for the 2006 Will D. Campbell Lecture at the University of Mississippi.

A CAMPBELL-INSPIRED RADICAL ALTERNATIVE

IF THE NIEBUHR AND Toulouse typologies are unhelpful in creating an accurate and fair understanding of Radicalism's historic contributions, perhaps allowing a Radical like Campbell to define himself—appreciating his quest to incarnate Christianity's own culture in and for the world—will highlight Radicalism's contribution to political theology.

Historically many Christians have employed the political theology of *alignment*, in which they seek, whether individually or as a church, to ally themselves with those in power. The goal is not necessarily to hold and wield power themselves, but for Christians to become "adjuncts," advisors, counselors, or pastors to those who do exercise the power. In such a capacity the Christians would be at least one-level removed from the more problematic aspects of wielding power, and might be less tempted to force their faith agenda on others. Biblical precedent provides plentiful support for such a political theology, with numerous examples of prophets sent to kings, high priests, governors and pharaohs to persuade them to use their sovereign power for the right and the just. John H. Yoder writes, for example, of a "Joseph/Daniel/Mordecai model" found throughout the Hebrew Bible. Although the powers were pagan, the biblical example was for God's people to minister to the principalities, not to replace them via a "theocratic takeover."[1]

This alignment with power allows Christians to take seriously their responsibility for domestic and international neighbors, promoting the peace and well being of the city where they are. They are neither fixated on their own otherworldly spiritual status, nor on their escape from the threats of eternal punishment. Nonetheless, these proponents of the "Align" position often have a utilitarian bent. Moral suasion and mere appeals to conscience ("crying in the wilderness") might elicit

---

1. Yoder, "Exodus and Exile," 307.

sympathy, charity, or brief changes in behavior, but regulatory power can achieve lasting systemic change and behavioral modification. Laws damn evil and proscribe punishments for wrong behavior. Carrots are nice, in other words, but real, sustained progress in this world is unlikely without some coercive stick. In the U.S., as with most nation-states, the government is the institution authorized to wield the power of this stick, and it becomes incumbent on conscientious Christians to sway political outcomes toward desirable ends. Christians, who are already pledged to "the good," thus appeal to those wielding power so that their authority will be used for good outcomes.

In American religious history, several examples the "Align" strategy come to mind. Consider the abolitionist and suffrage movements. Faithful individuals, parachurch groups, and denominations steadfastly petitioned the U.S. government to do the right and just thing. Although far from complete or perfect, the success of these faithful activists in persuading the U.S. to write race and gender justice into its Constitution with the 13th, 14th, 15th, and 19th Amendments have made the U.S. a better nation. The 1908 Federal Council of Churches and its "Social Creed" is another example.[2] Here the FCC sought to honor its theological principles, orchestrate its message, amass its numerical clout, and persuade business and government leaders that they should advance social justice (e.g., reduce the length of the work week, improve industrial safety, provide a living wage, provide suitable retirement for the elderly, and abate poverty). The idea was not for the FCC to enforce these provisions itself, but to have such a sufficiently close relationship with those who did have the power that the FCC could lobby, sway, and support the sovereign leaders to do the right thing. Likewise, many Christians in the modern phase of the civil rights movement worked from this "Align" strategy. They believed that racial justice would come only through federal intervention, legislation, and prosecution. Their job was to lobby and counsel the government to use its full power through the 1954 *Brown v. Board* decision, the Civil Rights Act of 1964, and the Voting Rights Act of 1965, to eradicate egregious bigotry and suppress injustice. Socially responsible Christians, seeking to serve their God and neighbor, in other words, pragmatically and cautiously align themselves with the principalities empowered to get things done.

2. The FCC was the forerunner to the National Council of Churches, for whom Campbell worked in the early 1960s.

A second strategy is the belief that Christians can do better than advise and counsel those in power. Instead Christians (individually and collectively) should *acquire* power for themselves. Why bother with the uncertainties and inconsistencies inherent in any political coalition, where people will inevitably disagree and misunderstand? Remove the political middleman. Christians can best discharge their social responsibilities by attaining and wielding power for themselves. Biblically, this position draws on examples of righteous rulers from the Hebrew tradition, like David or Josiah. Or as a student once explained to me, St. Paul's journey to Rome was an attempt to convert to Christianity someone from the Imperial power structure. "Paul knew that if Christians held important offices, they [powerful Christian political leaders] could make a difference." This is, of course, largely what transpired in the fourth century when Emperor Constantine converted to Christianity, thereby establishing Christendom in Western civilization. The church attained and executed the power of the state in order to affect Christian outcomes.

Although the rationale for the "Acquire" and "Align" strategies is similar, efficiency is a major difference. With the nation-state as the principal actor in the world, getting "things" done in a timely and effective manner requires access to those governmental mechanisms that "make a difference." Moreover, it is "foolhardy" fighting the indefatigable government, a student wrote. Because you cannot beat 'em, "Christians must use the government for the benefit of God's kingdom."

The seventeenth-century Puritans may be one of the better-known examples from Anglo-American religious history of this "Acquire" strategy. At first these English Protestants sought to "align" themselves with monarchs like Elizabeth I and James I, advocating for the greater reformation and purification of the English church and state. When their lobbying attempts failed, some Puritans took the next step and created a "Bible Commonwealth," a political entity through which they exercised power for themselves. Both the Puritans who set up their "City on a Hill" in New England, and those who followed Oliver Cromwell's Roundheads in England assumed the power to administer the legal system and induce behaviors consistent with their godly vision.

This "Acquire" strategy is the intellectual property of neither the right nor the left. In the U.S. populist-progressive era, for example, numerous Christian activists sought to add elected office to their leadership portfolio, to legislate God's will on earth just as God's will is done in heaven.³ Social gospel architects like Washington Gladden saw the acquisition of political power as a natural extension of God's justice in the world, and Walter Rauschenbusch envisioned liberal democracy paving the way for the creation of the kingdom of God on earth. Jerry Falwell's Moral Majority, or the Christian Coalition are, therefore, hardly aberrations in Christian history, and are more accurately recent expressions of this age-old political theology.

In the inaugural issue of *Katallagete*, Campbell and Holloway identified problems with both the "Align" and "Acquire" approaches.⁴ In brief, both political theologies failed the 2 Corinthians 5 benchmark, i.e., any legitimate political theology would be one for which "worldly standards have ceased to count." Both the "Align" and the "Acquire" method, in other words, continue to utilize worldly standards of "race and class, politics, economics, education, geography, dialect, sex, nationality, and above all religion." Those "aligning" themselves with the powers-that-be "serve as Chaplain to the Status Quo," blessing and enabling the divisive standards already at work.⁵ The "Acquire" advocates, on the other hand, often talk of transformation, yet their goal only replaces one set of worldly standards with another. As Campbell told the *Atlanta Weekly*, such a strategy assumes that "we [Christians] are the good people, and if we get the power we'll fix things. You can trust us." Once these Christians actually acquire the power, however, "you can trust us to cut your head off, or drown you, or electrocute you if you start getting in the way of what we say. *That's* what you can trust us to do."⁶

Rejecting the "Align" and "Acquire" options, Campbell hardly withdrawals or isolates himself from society. Instead he envisions a political theology that *incarnates* the countervailing ethics of Jesus in the very midst of society; a living counterpoint to prevailing social and political convention. As Campbell has made manifest in his own life, this incarnational approach may be culturally unorthodox, independent, and marginal. It is, however, anything but isolationist. Certainly no more

---

3. Creech, *Righteous Indignation: Religion and the Populist Revolution*, and Goode, "The Godly Insurrection in Limestone County."

4. June 1965. Campbell and Holloway reprinted this call in *Katallagete*'s Fall 1979 issue as well.

5. In his 1973 interview with *The Wittenburg Door*, Campbell named Elton Trueblood, Billy Graham, and Norman Vincent Peale as "court prophets" and chaplains to the principalities.

6. Shields, "Travels with Brother Will," 32.

isolationist than the incarnation of Christ was an attempt of the divine to withdrawal from the troublesome world. "Social action," for "incarnation" types, "follows as naturally as breathing," Campbell explains.

To help drive home this point, Campbell ran in the inaugural issue of *Katallagete* (1965), William Stringfellow's "The Orthodoxy of Involvement," which dispelled notions of Radical separatism. "The Church of Christ is, quite literally," Stringfellow explained, "the Body of Christ, assuming and engaging in His witness *in this world*." Therefore, the church incarnates

> right now the new society *in the midst of* the old, the new life during the fall, to be the reconciled community when all else is broken and decadent, to be the proof and example of life in the face of death: to be the pioneer and prophet, the witness and foretaste, actually, of God's own terrible accomplishment in Christ in confronting every assault, wile, and fascination of death and overpowering them all in order to restore humanity to life and to all relationships which mean life.... The Church is the very image of what the world is in its essential life; the Church is the society the world, now subject to death, is called to become in that last day when the world is fulfilled in all things, that is, in God.[7]

WILLIAM STRINGFELLOW (1928–1985)

A friend of Campbell's and a kindred spirit with the COSC, Stringfellow was no Southerner. Instead, this Harvard-trained lawyer lived his adult life in the Northeast, manifesting a strong and abiding "option for the poor" in urban settings. Just out of law school, for example, Stringfellow moved to Harlem to serve as an advocate for the voiceless taking on powerful slumlords and pursuing housing rights. He also labored to smash other idols of the "American Babylon." A committed Anglican, Stringfellow challenged his own Episcopal denomination by defending Bishop Pike against the charge of heresy, and labored for the ordination of women. Stringfellow also engaged in his own forms of civil disobedience, staging sit-ins in the late '40s, protesting the Vietnam War in the '60s, and hiding Daniel Berrigan while the Jesuit priest was on the lamb from the FBI for burning draft records at Catonsville, Maryland. Like

---

7. "The Orthodoxy of Involvement," 13. Or, to use Clarence Jordan's language, Radical Christians create a "demonstration plot" showing the world God's peculiar political theology, in living material form.

> Campbell, Stringfellow's lifelong calling was to frustrate all the political, economic, and religious principalities and powers he could. Also like Campbell, Stringfellow was faithful to his vocation.

Because the Christian *kerygma*'s "profoundly political" profession is the proclamation that the world *is* fully and completely reconciled, Christians have nothing but authentic, sacrificial love *for the world*. "To be a Christian is to know and receive and participate in the unconditional, extravagant, inexhaustible, expendable, incredible love of God for all that God has made and called into being." "To be a Christian," Stringfellow later continued, "to be already reconciled, means to love the world—all the world—just as it is—*unconditionally*."[8] Here is the genius of the Radical tradition, so often missed by Niebuhr, Gustafson, Toulouse, and others. Radicals, like Campbell and Stringfellow, never call Christians to withdraw, or isolate themselves away, from the world to which God has reconciled them. To the contrary, Christians are serving the world by *being* God's transfigured people—an alternative to the so-called "worldly" (or divisive) standards. Radical Christians, therefore, are *for the world* precisely insofar as they incarnate the reconciliation God has achieved, and refuse to seek something more by aligning themselves with the world's principalities, or acquire culture's forms of power.

---

8. Ibid.

PROBLEMS WITH THE PRINCIPALITIES AND POWERS

WHAT EXACTLY ARE THE principalities Radicals cannot align with, and why is it that Radicals cannot seek to acquire their power? What is it about these political theologies that Radicals cannot accept? Because these are pivotal questions if we are to understand Will and his Radicalism, this section will delve more extensively into the principalities and powers, exposing them as all too real malevolent and idolatrous forces, preempting God's sovereignty and dealing in death. They are false, illegitimate authorities that seduce our cooperation and allegiance. The extent to which we align with, or seek their power, we vacate the Christian narrative of its distinctive, scandalous, message. We impede Christianity's effort to create its own culture, and deny the world of the very *kerygma* it most needs.

In Christian tradition the "principalities and powers" are much more than fanciful "spirit beings" living in some metaphysical, otherworldly dimension. They are real, this-world entities, earthly structures and systems to be named and engaged. Walter Wink has noted that in the early twentieth century, Latin American theologians were some of the first to call the Christian community back to an awareness of the principalities and powers "not as disembodied spirits inhabiting the air, but as institutions, structures, and systems."[1] Charles Campbell has concurred, asserting that the principalities and powers are "embodied and active in the concrete, structural realities" of our lives. Thus, the principalities and powers are "aggressive actors in the world, shaping human lives in profound ways."[2]

On this point, Will Campbell's associate, William Stringfellow, was a most ardent and articulate critic, eager to warn Christians of the this-world, temporal threats posed by aligning with the principalities and

---

1. Wink, *Powers That Be*, 24.
2. Charles Campbell, *Word against the Powers*, 10.

seeking to acquire their powers.³ First of all, the principalities and powers are material, immediate, and legion, Stringfellow maintained.⁴ They are the "ideologies, institutions, images and systems" we confront in daily life.⁵ More bluntly, "*all* the authorities, corporations, institutions, traditions, processes, structures, bureaucracies, ideologies, systems, sciences and the like" that we routinely and unavoidably encounter are today's manifestation of the principalities and powers described in Scripture.⁶ Stringfellow's classic description comes when he named "all institutions, all ideologies, all images, all movements, all causes, all corporations, all bureaucracies, all traditions, all methods and routines, all conglomerates, all races, all nations, all idols" as the principalities and powers.

> Thus, the Pentagon or the Ford Motor Company or Harvard University or the Hudson Institute or Consolidated Edison or the Diners Club or the Olympics or the Methodist Church or the Teamsters Union are all principalities. So are capitalism, Maoism, humanism, Mormonism, astrology, the Puritan work ethic, science and scientism, white supremacy, patriotism, plus many, many more—sports, sex, any profession or discipline, technology, money, the family—beyond any prospect of full enumeration. The principalities and powers *are* legion.⁷

Updating the list, Bob Eckblad identifies the principalities and powers as:

> Legal systems, laws, racism, U.S. dollar, economic systems and political parties (capitalism, communism, Republican Party, Democratic Party, al-Qaeda), institutions (IMF, WTO, Presbyterian Church (U.S.A.), Catholic Church, NAFTA, World Bank, Pentagon, CIA), multinational corporations (Microsoft, General Mills, Boeing), brand names (Nike, the Gap, iPod), and celebrities (Michael Jackson, Oprah, Brad Pitt, Osama bin Laden, Madonna), ethnic categories such as Caucasian, Hispanic, Semitic, or national identity (United States, France, Japan, Germany).⁸

---

3. Will Campbell illustrates the influence of William Stringfellow on his thinking in *And Also with You* (see pp. 248–49).

4. Stringfellow, *An Ethic for Christians*, 36–37.

5. Stringfellow, *Free in Obedience*, 52.

6. Stringfellow, *An Ethic for Christians*, 27.

7. Ibid., 78.

8. Eckblad, *A New Christian Manifesto*, 101. See also Eckblad, *Reading the Bible with the Damned*, 138.

Making sure that his readers not miss the immediacy of his point, Stringfellow identified the United States and every other nation-state as one of the most common principalities. "America is a demonic principality, or a complex, or a constellation, or a conglomeration of principalities and powers. . . . Though history may vary, though particular facts be different, the same basic theological statement, by virtue of the biblical word, can and must be made about every nation."[9]

Will Campbell agreed. In a 1978 conference at the University of Southern Mississippi, Campbell drew on the work of Jacques Ellul to argue that the principalities and powers impose their logic and their "proper technique" for doing everything. "Whether it is teaching school, being a doctor, or running a road grader," the principalities and powers define our so-called common sense. Their logic regulates civil governments and structures political science. Thus Campbell confessed to the convention that he did not see much difference between respective nation-states, and was disinclined to participate in conventional political processes.

> I was impatient during the recent unpleasantness called the Vietnam War when some of my young friends, and some not so young, would despair or become disgruntled with the stars and stripes—a war which I very much opposed. But then, they would unfurl the banner of Hanoi or Peking or Moscow or Havana, as if anything any different was happening there. There is a technique for running government and that's what runs it. So I don't vote any more.[10]

---

9. Stringfellow, *An Ethic for Christians*, 154.

10. Campbell, "Staying at Home or Leaving," 18. Here Campbell expresses a common Radical critique of the electoral process. As Andy Alexis-Baker has explained, most every political ideology functions according to the "'state-as-savior' mythology" in which "Citizenship rights only intend to take the edge off elite state rulers but never intends to shift sovereignty away from them." Ted Lewis advances this insight, noting that "the politics of Jesus begins with the rejection of conventional power and proceeds with the positive activity of bearing witness to God's core qualities: sacrificial love, covenantal faithfulness, and reconciling justice." Choosing not to vote, continues Lewis, "becomes a confession of faith: we are proclaiming our bond to a different master (to a different king, lord, ruler, or president). We come to confess: 'Life is not about us and our interests. It's not about our thinking that we can make a difference. Life is about something bigger. It's about God's drama in which we are invited to participate.' In this light, indifference about or frustration with politics are never adequate foundations for not voting. Our choice not to vote should always be driven by our deeper motivation to bear witness to the truth." (See Lewis, *Electing Not to Vote*, 14, 107, and 114.)

> ## TO VOTE, OR NOT TO VOTE
>
> The challenge facing Christians, Campbell explained in 1968, is with "principalities and powers—beyond our grasp, beyond the ballot, beyond our understanding. In fact, in recent weeks, I have moved closer and closer to the position that Christians should not even vote. Not because we are righteous or ever will be, but because there are no political solutions to our problems, and to go on pretending that there is, encouraging Christians to 'get out there in the muck and mire of the world of politics' is to perpetuate a myth—the myth that there is any hope at all in the world except a crucified Christ. Maybe the admonition of our Lord to 'render unto Caesar the things that are Caesar's' is speaking to our condition today. Running the state belongs to Caesar. Politics belongs to Caesar. But let it be clear that it is not the world that belongs to Caesar. Only politics belongs to him."
>
> Will Campbell, Untitled manuscript (September 3, 1968). The Papers of Will Campbell, McCain Library and Archives, The University of Southern Mississippi, Box 13, Folder 20.

When Campbell made a similar confession six years earlier to *The Wittenburg Door*, the interviewer inquired whether Campbell was merely "copping out" of his social responsibilities. Campbell balked at the suggestion, noting that the real "cop out" was the person who continued to expend "time, effort, and muscle . . . waving one [political] banner or another and saying that things are going to be different." The real "cop out" was seeking to align oneself with, or acquire the power of the principalities.[11]

In a personal conversation in the summer of 2008, Campbell noted that for about twelve years he did not vote. Confronted with the choice between Ronald Reagan and Jimmy Carter in 1980, Campbell decided to participate in the electoral process once again. He did confess that he has never felt comfortable about voting when he has.

11. "Will Campbell: Door Interview" *The Wittenburg Door*, 8–9. Paul Alexander affirms Campbell's point, explaining, "First Corinthians says that the Jews want power, and Gentiles want wisdom—I want both (I Cor 1:18–31)! But all I have is a murdered God on a cross, Christ crucified, which is weak and stupid, both a stumbling block and foolishness. Abandoning voting, trusting God, and being the church seem weak and stupid to me; these options do not seem like a very good plan to help the world. Unless, of course, noncoercive love is the true grain of the universe." (See Lewis, *Electing Not to Vote*, 90.)

Beyond their ubiquitous temporal reality, Stringfellow was concerned to convey that the principalities and powers are fallen—every one of them malevolent. Humans in general, and Americans in particular, Stringfellow observed,

> persevere in belaboring the illusion that at least some institutions are benign and within human direction can be rendered benign by discipline, reform, revolution, or displacement. The principalities are, it is supposed, capable of being altered so as to respect and serve human life, instead of demeaning and dominating human life provided there is sufficient human will to accomplish this. This view of benign principalities is both too naïve and too narrow, and a stance that is both theologically false and empirically unwarranted. It really asserts that the Fall is not an essential condition of disorientation. At worst, this view sees the Fall as a wayward proclivity or potential corruptibility. It is a remarkable expression of human vanity. This view of the benign nature of the principalities fails to acknowledge the parasitical posture of the principalities toward human life. Principalities restrict, control, consume human life to sustain, extend, and prosper their own survival.[12]

Because the principalities and powers exist in opposition to God, the Christian task is not to discern between good and evil principalities and powers. Nor is the Christian enterprise to liberate the principalities from tyrants, or save the powers from illegitimate rulers. "Leaders are not nitwits, or wicked, so much as *they are puppets to the principalities and powers* to which they are invested," Stringfellow noted. Those who seek to align with the principalities, or acquire their power for themselves become "servile to the survival interest of these powers [which] deletes them as human beings."[13] Stated otherwise, the problem is not with the leaders so much as it is with the intrinsically warped principalities and inherently twisted powers. The Christian vocation, consequently, is not to rank the relative evil of the principalities and powers, but to smash them as the idols they are. They are all equally fallen. They all work from suppositions antithetical to God.

---

12. Stringfellow, *An Ethic for Christians*, 83–84.
13. Ibid., 93. Emphasis added.

> ## LIVING IN BABYLON
>
> By using the biblical metaphor of "Babylon" for "culture," Stringfellow found a stronger way to name and denounce the powers. For him, "Babylon" bears all the nefarious freight attached to it in the book of Revelation. "Babylon" is a "harlot," Stringfellow noted, condemned as the "realm of demons and foul spirits." More importantly, "Babylon" is the "dominion of alienation, slavery, and war," and represents "the essential demonic triumph in a nation"—the "condition of death reigning in each and every nation." "Babylon," therefore, "bespeaks the moral character of every nation and every other principality which is, or which was, or which may be." "Babylon" is the best synonym for the real, immediate, and empirical principalities and powers at work in our everyday world. Whether we live in North America or eastern Asia, whether the prevailing ideology in our corner of the world is capitalist or socialist, the dominant culture is "Babylon." Moreover, according to Revelation all these Babylons are doomed. Rapprochement and detente are not possible. "Babylon" is always laid waste and despoiled, which paves the way for the full fruition of God's glorious Kingdom. For all the metaphorical language, Stringfellow was eager to assert that this contest between "Babylon" and "Jerusalem" was not played out in some "nebulous, ethereal" plane of metaphysical existence between cartoon characters who wear wings on one hand and those who carry pitchforks on the other. "Jerusalem" is not some "spooky, spiritualized, sentimental" reference to an "otherworldly or disembodied church." "Jerusalem" is the church—real, tangible, and fully engaged in liberating the disinherited of this world. The designation "Babylon" refers to all the past, present, and future principalities and powers. Consequently, the church exists as an "embassy among the principalities," a "pioneer community" within the environs of the powers. This prophetic vocation stems not from some contrarian cynicism, but from the fact that in Christ "no estate in secular society can possibly correspond to, or much approximate, the true society of which they are the citizens of Christ. They are—everywhere and in every society—aliens. They are always, in any society, in protest." (*A Keeper of the Word: Selected Writings of William Stringfellow*, ed. Bill Wylie Kellermann, 323.)

Are, however, the principalities and powers really all that bad? Stringfellow thought so, asserting that the principalities and powers are inherently domineering, arrogantly demanding "unequivocal and militant obeisance, a sacrifice of all other supposedly lesser causes and rights."[14] Inverting God's order, the humans who create the principalities and powers end up serving their creation. In the process, the principalities and powers spawn "unjust economic relationships, oppressive political relations, biased race relations, patriarchal gender relations, hierarchical power relations, and the use of violence to maintain them all." To achieve their fallen objectives, the principalities and powers bait persons into becoming minions of their "Domination System," as Walter Wink names it.[15]

If Stringfellow is right, how is it that we fall for the lies of the principalities and powers? What is so alluring about a force so obviously corrupt? Perhaps the attraction goes back to the very ideas of "Align" and "Acquire." To align with the principalities or acquire their power, we must be well integrated into their system. In other words, they offer a powerful package of both history and ethics, narrating not only why things are the way they are, but also how things *ought* to be. That curriculum prepares individuals for service to the principalities and powers. "History is," Stanley Hauerwas has noted, "one of the most influential ways to teach ethics without having to defend that what you are doing is initiating students into discourses" and predetermined narratives.[16] Presuming history to be an objective collection of self-evident facts, few question or analyze the motif and moral of the narrative presented, or how the narration forms students of all ages. Stated differently, the principalities and powers teach self-affirming and self-perpetuating myths. Tenets that fit with and support the tradition are valued and touted as "common sense." Elements contrary to the system are dismissed out of hand as deviant, unrealistic, naïve, perverted, or otherwise obviously wrong. To the extent that the narrative of the principalities and powers orient our lives, we find in them our relative safety, security, prosperity, and fulfillment.

Will Campbell describes how he came to an awareness of the ways the principalities and powers function as a center of value. First it was "Baptistland" when he tried his hand at formal ministry. Then it was "Academe" when he moved to Ole Miss. Both, he realized, were built

---

14. Stringfellow, *Free in Obedience*, 57.
15. Wink, *Powers That Be*, 39.
16. Hauerwas, *The State of the University*, 131.

on "fragile ethical stilts." Moreover those stilts rested on a "quagmire of unfreedom." Every institutional principality and power he encountered had a "credo, a line one is expected to follow, a prescribed channel in which to swim. To assay the banks is to court disfellowship." And, as he experienced, "to challenge the line outright leads directly to the unemployment line." Speaking of himself in the third person, Campbell reflects:

> It was a sad and disillusioning lesson to learn. Why wasn't he told that in the first grade? Or the first day at the university? That *all* institutions, every last one of them—no matter the claim, no matter the purpose, no matter the stated goals—existed sooner or later for their own selves, are self-loving, self-concerned, self-regarding, self-preserving, and are lusting for the soul of all who come near them.[17]

In similar fashion, Charles Campbell has found that the principalities exert their power "*over* others" and for the "control *of* others" by generating "*hierarchies* of dominant and subordinate, winners and losers, insiders and outsiders, honored and shamed."[18] The principalities and powers, therefore, practice the exact opposite of reconciliation, presuming to define who "our" enemy is and how, to maintain "our" way of life, "we" should treat "them." "Under the Domination System, the Power—be it nation, class, institution, etc.—becomes the ultimate good," notes Wink. "All else (life, rights, resources) are subordinated to, or dedicated for the use of the Power." Colonialism provides a classic historical example, as nation-states demand that their citizens sacrifice their own individual vocations and commitments and agree to oppress indigenous people, all to extract the resources that will benefit the colonizing power. The standard operating procedure is that "People become expendable, the principality is not."[19]

Thus, as seen time and again in Will Campbell's experience, principalities and powers assign worth and value, they proclaim what will pass as "good" in their system. "Often they can be quite literal in their preemption of God by their demand for obeisance, service, and glorification from humans," Stringfellow avers. "The principality, insinuating itself in the place of God, deceives humans into thinking and acting

---

17. Campbell, *Forty Acres and a Goat*, 5–6.
18. Charles Campbell, *The Word before the Powers*, 26. Emphasis in original.
19. Wink, *Powers That Be*, 58.

as if the moral worth or justification of human beings is defined and determined by commitment or surrender—literal sacrifice—of human life to the survival interest, grandeur, and vanity of the principality."[20] To the Domination System we concede most everything. The principalities tell us what is "beautiful" and "desirable." The powers assign to us our heroes. They appoint our intellectual ancestors. They tell us not only what our goals are, but how to assess our progress. Sometimes figuratively, but all too often quite literally, the principalities and powers give us marching orders. Because the ends seem worthy, we acquiesce to vulgar means. We shrug off violence, for example, as the cost of doing business in this world, when in reality brutality is the cost of aligning with, or acquiring power.

Death, William Stringfellow noted, is *always* the cost of doing business with the principalities and powers. Indeed, death is the primary enforcement used by the principalities and powers, because without the credible threat of lethal coercion, the principalities could only issue empty threats. None other than Max Weber recognized this characteristic in the nation-state. "The modern state is a compulsory association which organizes domination within a territory," Weber found. Moreover, the nation-state considers itself "the sole source of the 'right' to use violence," and imposes that right of domination via physical force.[21] Describing Thomas Hobbes's political theory, John H. Yoder explains how the nation-state may "moderate or ameliorate" its violence "by a constitutional or a democratic process." Nevertheless, "the definition of the state itself is its monopoly of violence. The state would not exist without that violence at its heart."[22] "Every sanction, or weapon, or policy, or procedure which the state commands against both human beings and against the other principalities carries the connotation of death, implicitly threatens death, derives from and symbolizes death," Stringfellow explains.[23] The death can be social exile or economic retribution, such as "imprisonment, prosecution, persecution, loss of reputation or property or employment, [or other forms of] intimidation."[24] Or, the principalities may impose the power of physical death. Ironically the state will

20. Stringfellow, *An Ethic for Christians*, 80–81.
21. Weber, *Politics as Vocation*, 7 and 2.
22. Yoder, *Christian Attitudes to War, Peace, and Revolution*, 242.
23. Stringfellow, *An Ethic for Christians*, 109–11.
24. Stringfellow, "An Authority over Death," 182–83.

prosecute citizens who murder their personal enemies, yet that same state will order those same citizens to kill the state's enemies, which is glorified as "patriotism."[25]

The smell of death is always on the principalities and powers.[26] "Every value, every goal, every policy, every action, every routine, every enterprise of each and every principality has the elemental significance of death."[27] Why, in God's name, do Christians align with such principalities and seek their power of death dealing?

Walter Wink has shown that by aligning with or seeking to acquire the power of the Domination System we buy into a "myth of redemptive violence" where well-meaning, honest humans socially, economically, and physically kill their neighbors because the principalities and powers tell us that violence achieves just outcomes. The reasoning is all too familiar. To prevail and defeat the evil, good must ultimately play the violent trump card. Villains, in the myth of redemptive violence, threaten truth, justice, and the "American way," until the hero uses violence to control and turn events so that good prevails. A quick survey of narratives, ranging from Disney cartoons and blockbuster films to presidential State of the Union speeches, illustrates how early and often we are socialized to believe this myth. As Wink unmasks the myth, in a world where life is presumed to be a combat, "violence is the story of victory of order over chaos." Therefore,

---

25. One of the standard anti-death penalty questions is "Why do we kill people to teach that killing people is wrong?" Political entities that use the death penalty actually have an answer to that question. Although certainly no deterrent to murder, state killing reminds all citizens who is in charge. The nation-state is the preeminent authority because it alone has the ultimate authority over life and death.

26. Charles Tilley has offered a provocative thesis on this point by teasing out the linkage between the role of violence and the function of nation-states. Governments birth themselves through violence, and also protect themselves by violence. Yet, governments justify their existence to citizens on the promise that they will reduce domestic and international violence. In other words, the very existence of nation-states escalates violence, but nation-states justify themselves by promising to reduce violence. Moreover, the people get to pay for the protection against violence that the state's very presence helps generate. As Tilley illustrates, governments run quite a racket. Their logic is fundamentally that of organized crime. Those who question the "price of protection" are not surprisingly dealt with violently. (See Tilley, "War Making and State Making as Organized Crime.")

27. Stringfellow, *An Ethic for Christians*, 67.

any form of order is preferable to chaos... Ours is never a perfect or perfectible world; is a theater of perpetual conflict in which the prize goes to the strong. Peace through war, security through strength: these are the core convictions that arise from this ancient historical religion [i.e., the myth of redemptive violence], and they form the solid bedrock on which the Domination System is founded in every society.[28]

> ### THE MYTH OF REDEMPTIVE VIOLENCE
>
> In an interview with the *New York Times*, former U.S. Senate majority leader Trent Lott from Mississippi succinctly articulated this myth. Asked how he thought the war in Iraq was progressing, Sen. Lott responded, "There are terrorists in Iraq who have been drawn into that part of the world. Every day we eliminate some of them; that's one more that won't be coming here." Asked for clarification on his use of the term "elimination," Lott said, "They are going to be killed . . . 20 or 30 or 40 at a time are being eliminated." When asked whether it should be U.S. policy to kill everyone who hates America Lott quipped, "We can kill a lot of them." (*The New York Times Magazine*, "All's Fair: Questions for Trent Lott," [June 20, 2004], 15.) Behind the promised violence is not only the presumption that one should beat others into doing the right thing, but also that one's own point of view *is* that right thing.

But Thomas Merton encourages us to demythologize the use of violence as the "unreal concept of authority" that it is. Violence might extort a temporary and begrudging compliance, but it always fails to "elicit intelligent submission of one's inmost personal being." The brigands—even faith-based ones—who violently "put their own interests before anything else are no better than bandits."[29]

Intoxicated with their own might and importance, these rebellious principalities and violent powers demand unwavering devotion and single-minded loyalty from their subjects. Subordinates must pledge their allegiance (a confession of faith), be ready and willing to make any sacrifice, or prosecute any command, upon the principality's order. All life becomes expendable to protect the safety, security, and progress of the

---

28. Wink, *The Powers That Be*, 48. (See especially pages 42–62.)

29. See Thomas Merton, "The Christian in World Crisis: Reflections on the Moral Climate of the 1960s," 20–62.

principalities and powers. Lee Camp tells, for example, of Lt. Col. Garland Robertson, former Air Force chaplain who during the 1991 Gulf War questioned the "justness" of U.S. military objectives. For his caution, the Air Force investigated, accused, indicted, harassed, and otherwise pressured Robertson to conform. Chaplains, the Air Force explained, were commissioned not only to sanctify announced policies, but to convince soldiers to prosecute the commands. "Robertson experienced a very old move of the principalities and powers," Camp explains. "The powers find it useful to fashion a god in their own image, a god that supports their own agenda, that rallies around their own imperialistic purposes. This god is then set forward as 'God,' and the citizenry told to bow the knee."[30] Lee Camp is correct. Whether self-delusional or intentionally misleading, the principalities and powers promote themselves as a "grotesque parody" of God, and demand deference and fidelity from their subjects. "They do everything in their power to create the illusion that they, not God, are the divine regents in the world," writes Charles Campbell.

> The beast in the book of Revelation first and foremost seeks to receive the *worship* of human beings. Idolatry is the fundamental sin of the fallen powers. . . . The powers, in short, have become demonic. . . . Everything else is expendable: human beings, compassion, humanity, the land, preaching—everything. For the powers, finally, the only morality that matters is their own survival, and they will use any means necessary to ensure that survival.[31]

From a lifetime of eloquent writing, one of Thomas Merton's most incisive pieces questioned the sanity of the principalities and powers. At the Nuremburg war crimes trials, for instance, the prosecution put psychiatrists on the stand to affirm Adolf Eichmann's sanity and, thus, legal culpability. Such testimony led Merton to ponder the implications. Merton found the gravity of such evaluations not in what the psychiatrists said about Eichmann, but in what the testimony said about the sanity of the principalities and powers. If society, in other words, cannot write Eichmann off as a pathological aberration or a bizarre social deviant, what is revealed about society? Is something not learned about a world in which the industry of mass murder is not accidental, but intentional? Surely something is revealed about the mindsets of principalities

---

30. Camp, *Mere Discipleship: Radical Christianity in a Rebellious World*, 43.
31. Charles Campbell, *Word before the Powers*, 24–25.

and powers that logically, rationally, and systematically plot holocausts of their enemies via nuclear, biological, chemical, or "conventional" means. "It begins to dawn on us," Merton notes,

> that it is precisely the *sane* ones who are the most dangerous. It is the sane ones, the well-adapted ones, who can without qualms and without nausea aim the missiles and press the buttons that will initiate the great festival of destruction that they, *the sane ones*, have prepared. . . . No one suspects the sane, and the sane ones will have perfectly good reasons, logical, well-adjusted reasons, for firing the shot.

Then one wonders, in a world that separates love from sanity, what business have we to equate "sanity" with "Christianity?" Merton rhetorically asked. "The worst error," he retorted, "is to imagine that a Christian must try to be 'sane' like everybody else, that we *belong* in our kind of society. That we must be 'realistic' about it." In a world ordered by the provincial political 'science' of the principalities and powers, perhaps the "worst insanity is to be totally 'sane.'"[32]

Charles Campbell has outlined the steps principalities and powers take to make their insanity sensible.[33] First, they impose "negative sanctions" (ostracism, punishment, death) on those who fail to serve them, while conversely celebrating with "rewards and promises" those who compromise and accommodate. Second, implementing a divide-and-conquer strategy, the principalities and powers "isolate and divide" dissenters from the rest of society. In other words, the principalities and powers wear down and demoralize resisters until the nonconformists are unable to withstand. Third, whether through public entertainment, grand spectacles, or other busyness, the principalities and powers divert attention away from themselves and what they are up to, and "ritualize"

---

32. Merton, "A Devout Meditation in Memory of Adolf Eichmann," 45–49. According to Will Campbell, the issue of sanity and insanity cuts both ways. On the one hand, Campbell recounts sage advice his brother Joe gave him in 1956, in the midst of Will's contest with the powers of Ole Miss and the principalities of Mississippi. Beware "how fast," Joe warned, "they go from lunacy to reality and nobody knows which is which." (*Brother to a Dragonfly*, 124.) On the other hand, citing the work of the mercurial James Bevel in Mississippi, Campbell argues that to resist the principalities and powers "creative insanity" is often necessary. (Campbell, *Robert G. Clark's Journey to the House*, 49.) Dorothy Day's "Are the Leaders Insane?" raises similar questions of the principalities and powers (*Catholic Worker* [April 1954]).

33. Charles Campbell, *Word before the Powers*, 33–43.

its order—again, co-opting and taming resistance.[34] Martin Luther King Jr., for example, gave his life criticizing American racism, militarism, and economic exploitation. How do the principalities and powers respond? They make King's birthday a national holiday. Corporations, institutions, universities, and municipal governments that refuse to pay a living wage, take the third Monday in January as a holiday in honor of the architect of the Poor People's Campaign. The largest purveyor of militarism in the world, the U.S. military, holds MLK Day ceremonies in honor of America's best-known advocate of nonviolence. These ritualized observances enable the principalities and powers to tame King's message and recast his legacy in more palatable (less threatening) terms.[35] Fourth, "the powers use language and image to delude and capture minds and hearts." This is the most important step in creating the idolatry because "language shapes the way we see the world." Herein lays the portentous role of history and historians, for they write the "catechism" used by principalities and powers to form, integrate, or otherwise graft their desired community together. Under the guise of impartiality, the discipline of history assumes the right to name, and "a name is shorthand for a story of who you are and what you care about," writes Stanley Hauerwas. "A name is power to determine memory for how the story continues to be told." Thus, history is an exercise in privileging some stories with the "language of objectivity" yet simultaneously "silencing other voices." These authorized stories "become what anyone would believe" we are told, "if they thought about it or were better 'educated.'"[36] Historians are some of the most loyal priests of the principalities and powers, for example, especially when they codify the myth of redemptive violence. Visit the history section at the local bookstore, flip to the History Channel, or sit in on a required history class. Military history often dominates the

---

34. Elizabeth McAlister attributes much of America's epidemic of "civil obedience" to the pacification of our preoccupations. "Pacification takes many forms," McAlister notes. "In the ghetto all around our home, people are savagely addicted. It is part of the pacification. They are consumed with the next fix and if they kill one another in the process there is no weeping in government or corporate offices. For those not addicted to drugs, there is TV, shopping, sports, soap operas, prurient preoccupation with the rich and famous—you know the litany. They are today's answer to bread and circuses." (McAlister "Preach the Good News and Cast Out Demons: On Civil Disobedience.")

35. The principalities' extreme makeover of Martin Luther King Jr. is only superseded by what these powers do to the image of the scandalous Christ.

36. Hauerwas, *After Christendom*, 136 and 140.

offerings.[37] Fifth, "secrecy" or silence can powerfully communicate what is off limits, what the "sacred cows" may be, or whose history is not worthy of inclusion. Ignorance—i.e., simply being unaware—is a powerful sedative. Together, these strategies of the principalities and powers promote a seductive, even sensible, idolatry.

Admittedly, the foregoing is a bleak character assessment of the principalities and powers. The very principalities and powers in which billions of people invest their lives and resources stand starkly and arrogantly in opposition to the sovereign God. The entire enterprise of the principalities and powers is selfish, greedy, lustful, prideful, oppressive, idolatrous, domineering, and violent. The principalities and powers are fallen. They rebel against every value attributed to God, and are inimical to Christ. Moreover, there is no hope for them. Their divisive character defines their essential being, and to change their character would be to end their existence. They are what they are. They will always and only be what they are and always have been.

Seriously? Is there no hope for the principalities and powers? "The categorical answer is 'no,'" Stringfellow asserted. "The answer informed by the biblical witness is 'no.' The answer for those who are Christians is 'no,' and therefore, the answer which Christians commend to other human beings is 'no.'"[38] Christians can neither become chaplains to, nor seek the powers of the principalities, but we have an alternative.

In Revelation the idolatrous and violent Domination System is routed. Christ "dethrones," "defeats" and "disarms" the principalities and powers—an occasion for great rejoicing in heaven. Christ strikes the weapons from the hands of the tyrannical principalities. Christ exposes the divisive myth of redemptive violence for the fiction it is. Christ pulls back the curtain and reveals the principalities and powers' illusions of "ultimate certainty, ultimate direction, ultimate happiness, and ultimate duty."[39] They are not "glorious, autonomous, everlasting powers, but in fact are themselves vassals, or serfs, acolytes, or surrogates, apparitions, or agents of death."[40] Once *this* reality comes to light, humanity is finally

---

37. See "Resistance to the Academy" in *Writings on Reconciliation and Resistance*, 205–32. Also see, Goode, "The Radical Idea of Christian Scholarship: Plea for a Scandalous Historiography."

38. Stringfellow, *An Ethic for Christians*, 155.

39. Berkhof, *Christ and the Powers*, 39.

40. Stringfellow, *An Ethic for Christians*, 81.

liberated to discover hope in the only *real* source—God. Thus, although the diagnosis for the principalities and powers is devastatingly grim, the prognosis for humanity is bright.

Even though Christ has proven the principalities impotent and pronounced them terminal, they continue their pretense of power. They have, however, only the power humans confer upon them. After Easter, the principalities derive whatever illegitimate power they have from the consent of their beguiled subjects. Withhold cooperation and the principalities wither. Live by the Kingdom's reality and the powers fade. We are, therefore, constantly challenged to choose whom we will serve: the illegitimate principalities and powers and their Domination System of *realpolitik*, or God and the reality of reconciliation. God's reconciliation is made manifest by the meek and merciful, the forgiving peacemakers, and the disinherited outcast—"the poor, the sick, the prisoners, and those socially discriminated against."[41] That is Easter realism. "God builds the City of Salvation," Stringfellow pledges.

> It is not some never-never land, some alabaster city beyond the realm of time, but a City, whatever be the final shape and reality of its fulfillment at the end of time, which has form and actuality here and now in the midst of this history. The City which God builds is a society which lives in this history in the midst of death, surrounded, as it were, by all the cities and societies of the world which are places of death. . . . Christ is revealed [on the Cross] as the embodiment, in his own person, of the City of Salvation.[42]

The problem with that Easter realism is not in God's design, but in the church's incarnation. Will Campbell's Radical jeremiad is that Christians keep voluntarily trading their Easter birthright for a mess of pottage from the principalities and powers. God's politics of loving peace, God's ethics of restorative justice, God's reconciled and reconciling community *can* thrive on earth, as in heaven, but only as God's people incarnate an unending, irrepressible conflict with—an antagonistic resistance to—the principalities and powers.

---

41. Stringfellow, *Free in Obedience*, 46.
42. Ibid., 32.

WHAT IS THE RADICAL DIFFERENCE BEING INCARNATED?

FROM THE GOSPELS WE know that Jesus foreswore the use of power to push circumstances in his favor. As Charles Campbell notes, "Jesus says 'no' to making his own survival the top priority and to using his power to meet his own needs.... Jesus does not use his power to destroy even the devil by means of violence or domination."[1] We also know that Jesus refused the temptation to become a military messiah. Given the two-dimensional nature of the "fight or flight" syndrome, therefore, the presumption is that since Jesus chose not to fight, by default he embraced apolitical withdrawal.

Granted, Jesus shunned violent revolution and governmental domination, but it does not necessarily follow that his nonviolence represents a vote for passive submission or pragmatic accommodation. In refusing to play the hand dealt him he allowed neither circumstances nor opponents to dictate, delineate, or dominate his options for engagement. Instead, Jesus seized the initiative to invoke what Walter Wink often calls "the third way," a nonviolent assault on the principalities and powers. In the tradition of the bold, undaunted Shadrach, Meshach, and Abednego, who walked confidently into the fiery furnace, Jesus assertively performed his public ministry and in so doing assailed all the political orders of the day.[2] Jesus' nonviolence "seeks out conflict, elicits conflict, even initiates conflict," Wink correctly announces, in order to expose the illegitimacy of the rebellious principalities. Jesus created conflict with the violent powers with the "same alacrity as the most hawkish militarist."[3] Because he was patently offensive, scandalous, and notorious, being objectionable—even

---

1. Charles Campbell, *Word before the Powers*, 46.
2. Berkhof, *Christ against the Powers*, 50.
3. Wink, *The Powers That Be*, 121.

to the point of martyrdom—is Radicalism's political incarnation of the Christian *kerygma* in and for the world.[4]

Palm Sunday is one of the best examples of Jesus' confrontational approach, challenging notions that disciples are called to align with the principalities or acquire their power. Jesus' charisma could have arguably generated sufficient numerical support either to force concessions from the Roman and Jewish principalities, or to attain the power of political revolution. Instead of the triumphal conquering hero entering Jerusalem on a war steed, however, Jesus enters the city on a donkey. Charles Campbell finds in this Palm Sunday scene a

> carefully orchestrated piece of street theater. Jesus enacts a parody of the world's understanding of power and domination, as well as a challenge to the religious community's expectations about the messiah. . . . Jesus goes on to take possession of Jerusalem unarmed and on a donkey. . . . He is turning the world's notions of power and rule and authority on their heads. His theater is a wonderful piece of political satire. In his 'triumphal entry,' Jesus lampoons all the powers of the world and their pretensions to glory and domination, and he enacts an alternative to the way of the Domination System. . . . Jesus enacts the subversive, nonviolent reign of God in the midst of the city. . . . Jesus intentionally chooses the way of nonviolence, for the purposes of God cannot be fulfilled through violent means. . . . Finally, the cross itself becomes a subversion of the world's understandings of power and dominion. . . . The victim of the world's injustice is ironically the ruler. . . . The violence of the powers is thoroughly subverted as God identifies not with those who inflict the violence but with the one who is its victim.[5]

Stringfellow explored the question whether Jesus' "resistance and renunciation of temptation to political authority on Palm Sunday counsels

---

4. As Tripp York writes, "Martyrdom is a manner of missionary work that is inescapably public and political. For the church, historically speaking, martyrdom is the political act because it represents the ultimate imitation of Christ, signifying a life lived in obedience to, and participation in, the triune God. . . . The church is, inescapably, a body politic that produces [incarnates] a different kind of political agent, namely, the martyr." (See *The Purple Crown: The Politics of Martyrdom*, 22–23.)

5. Charles Campbell, *Word before the Powers*, 60–61. Wink asserts that "nothing deflates them [the powers-that-be] more effectively than deft lampooning. By refusing to be awed by their power, the powerless are emboldened to seize the initiative, even where structural change is not immediately possible. This message, far from counseling an unattainable otherworldly perfection [or withdrawal], is a practical, strategic measure for empowering the oppressed." (See Wink, *The Powers That Be*, 105.)

Christians to withdraw from the political life of the world." Far from an example of withdrawal or isolation, Stringfellow found Palm Sunday "the example of utter and radical involvement in the existence of the world, an involvement which does not retreat even in the face of the awful power of death." Christ's example, in other words, compels "involvement, not indifference; realism, not withdrawal; knowledge, not ignorance."[6]

Palm Sunday, therefore, dramatizes Christ's political theology of confrontational incarnation. He enters Jerusalem divested of domineering designs, violent intention, manipulative strategies, or selfish intent. He will not use his power to check militaristically the power of the principalities. He simply interjects himself into the arena of the principalities and powers certain of the subversive nature of his self-donation. Jesus walks forthrightly among the first century principalities and powers—his own fiery political furnace—without "fear of contamination," or lust for domination. He announces that the principalities and powers can scheme to kill him if they desire, but he will not withdraw, accommodate, nor violently strike back.

A "real test" of incarnating the Christian difference in the world, according to Will Campbell, is the level to which our "Christian love will hurt those we love." "Because Moses, an outside agitator and organizer, loved his people he let the status quo have no peace until his people were free." Likewise, "Christian love may mean constant agitation and opening the sore of racial segregation, freeing those who are bound and those who bind." Consequently, "my Christian love means this constant disturbance of what seems to be and what we are told is 'getting along fine.'"[7]

Having confronted, rejected, and resisted the status quo of the principalities and powers, Christ's love compels us to privilege the disenfranchised. As Howard Thurman rightly proclaims:

> The solution Jesus found for himself and for Israel, as they faced the hostility of the Greco-Roman world, becomes the word and work of redemption for all the cast-down people in every generation and in every age. I mean this quite literally. . . . Wherever his spirit appears, the oppressed gather fresh courage; for he announced the good news that fear, hypocrisy, and hatred, the three

---

6. Stringfellow, *Free in Obedience*, 38–39.
7. Campbell, "Christian Concern: Fourteenth Amendment or First Commandment?"

> hounds of hell that track the trial of the disinherited, need have no dominion over them.[8]

As Thurman maintains, the ongoing Christian story is of society's disinherited, living audaciously with allegiance to none, knowing that the existence of this impudent community—that loves indiscriminately—exposes the illegitimacy of the principalities and powers.[9] "The inherent, invariable, unavoidable, intentional, unrelenting posture of the Church in the world," Stringfellow notes, "is one of radical protest and profound dissent toward the prevailing status quo of the secular society." Yet the most telling radical protest is through the church's "actual existence as the new society, beseeching the end of the world."[10] This is, to use the language of Will Campbell, Christianity being "its own culture."

"Jesus," Yoder reminds us, "defeated the Powers not by being better than they at their trade of domination, but by refusing to meet them on that terrain, at the cost of his life."[11] "The way beyond the principalities and powers is by dying? Will it work?" people ask warily. That is, of course, for Radicals the wrong question. Like Christ, the politics of nonviolent resistance may get disciples killed, and their deaths may hardly deter the principalities and powers from their course. "Folks who are determined enough to hold on to unlimited love usually wind up on a cross, like Jesus," Clarence Jordan warned.

> Their goods get plundered and they get slandered. Persecution is their lot. Surely nobody would be inclined to call this practical.

---

8. Thurman, *Jesus and the Disinherited*, 28–29.

9. Phil Kenneson has offered one of the best, prophetic articulations of this perspective. "The church is different from the world because its life is animated by a different Spirit—a difference manifested in its material practices and institutions, as well as in the narratives and convictions that give them shape and intelligibility." Radical Christians are not seeking to withdrawal from society, but to "order" their lives "by a set of narratives, practices, and convictions at odds with those narratives, practices, and convictions the church is called to embody. . . . Part of what it means to be a Christian is to 'read' all stories, all practices, all convictions with reference to our discipleship to Jesus and our loyalty to his emerging kingdom. Churches are rightly understood as alternative communities to the extent that they offer [or incarnate] a way of ordering life—an alternative way of telling and embodying their stories that locates who they are and what they should do within a framework" dominated by the principalities and powers. Such Christian narration, Kenneson concludes, requires "a conscious resistance." (See Kenneson, *Beyond Sectarianism*, 83–104.)

10. Stringfellow, *Dissenter in the Great Society*, 142–43, and 162.

11. Yoder, "On Not Being In Charge," 85.

> Yet in its final stages, unlimited love seems to be the only thing that can possibly make any sense. Crucifixions have a way of being followed by resurrections. Only one who is foolish enough to lose one's life, finds it. It is the grain of wheat that falls into the ground and dies, that lives. Jesus didn't tell his followers to love their enemies because love would work, or would not work. . . . Christians are at the complete mercy of their enemies, since by complete surrender to the divine will they no longer have the freedom to cease being what they are. Bound by this higher loyalty, the argument of practicality is irrelevant.[12]

Living a holy indifference toward efficiency and effectiveness, Jordan instead committed his life to creating a "demonstration plot." Jesus, instead of lobbying legislators or mobilizing masses for marches to sway the powers, formed a community whose very existence called into "question the legitimacy of the so-called norm." In like manner, Jordan created Kononia as an "alternative community," an active case in point, "whose very presence in the world offers the world an alternative to the world," Tripp York explains. Jordan did not mobilize for "a different kind of government; rather, he participated in a movement that attempted to *be* that which we may hopefully call both good and just." Jordan helped generate "alternative economies" and "alternative relationships" that "required far more than carrying signs and gathering around municipal buildings."[13]

As Jordan's own life illustrated, however, if the preeminent goal is quickly to stop the principalities and powers from dealing in death, this incarnated Christian resistance may seem ineffective. "To risk confronting the Powers with such harlequinesque vulnerability, simultaneously affirming our own humanity and that of those whom we oppose, and daring to draw the sting of evil by absorbing it in our own bodies—such behavior is not likely to attract the faint of heart," Wink confesses. Disciples, however, are Easter realists. They have pledged their lives to the proposition that "God can bring out of voluntarily assumed suffering" (e.g., Good Friday) "the precious seeds of a new reality." Because Radicals are more concerned about *kairos* than efficiency, Merton explained that they are more likely to sing "This is the day of the Lord, and whatever may happen to us, God will overcome" than "We Shall Overcome." Deferring control to God, disciples acknowledge, "the cross

---

12. Jordan, *Sermon on the Mount*, 48–49.
13. York, *Living on Hope While Living in Babylon*, 78–80.

means not necessarily winning. The Principalities and Powers are so colossal, entrenched and determined that the odds for their overthrow or repentance are miniscule, whatever means we use." Yet Wink correctly senses the existence of a "whole host of people simply waiting for the Christian message to challenge them, for once, to a heroism worthy of their lives. Has Jesus not provided us with that word?" Is that not a Radical's pledge in the taking of the Eucharist?[14]

Because Christians are the living "real sign of the sacrifice of the Lamb of God," a real presence "constantly renewed in the midst of the world," Ellul counseled, it is "essential that Christians not be wolves—that is people who try to dominate others." Instead, "Christians must accept the domination of other people, and offer the daily sacrifice of their lives."[15] To be the offspring of the Lamb of God, therefore, means that "No one created in God's image and for whom Christ died can be for me an enemy whose life I am willing to threaten or take," Yoder reminded. Any willingness to claim the power and dominate circumstances—even with the best, most sincere and altruistic of intentions—means "I am more devoted to something else—to a political theory, to a nation, to the defense of certain privileges, or my own personal welfare—than I am to God's cause."[16] The fight of faith, therefore, is not a battle to defeat enemies and dominate circumstances—to eradicate evil and impose good. Instead of a quest to rule, the fight of faith is sacrificial. "The fight of faith demands sacrificing one's life, success, money, time, and desires," Ellul explains.

> The fight of faith is perfectly peaceable, for it is fought by applying the Lord's commandments. Humanly speaking, to fight thus is to fight nakedly and weakly. It is not by sequestering ourselves in our churches to say little prayers that we fight, but by changing human lives. And it is truly a fight—not only against our own passions and interests and desires, but against power that can be changed only by means which are opposite of its own. Jesus over-

---

14. Merton, "Peace and Revolution: A Footnote from *Ulysses*," 70–75. Wink, *Violence and Nonviolence in South Africa*, 34 and 69. As Wink notes a few pages later, "It takes far more courage to walk into a situation voluntarily, knowing that suffering is inevitable, choosing to draw the poison of that violence with one's own body rather than perpetuating the downward spiral of hate. But that is what we celebrate in every Eucharist as Jesus' way" (72).

15. Ellul, *The Presence of the Kingdom*, 4.

16. Yoder, *He Came Preaching Peace*, 20.

came the powers of state, authorities, rulers, law, etc. not by being more powerful, but by surrendering himself even to death.[17]

Jesus' Way is to exist in an unending, irrepressible conflict with—an antagonistic resistance to—the principalities and powers. "I say that Jesus was, according to the testimonies of the gospels," Stringfellow reminds us, "a criminal: not a mere nonconformist, not just a protester, more than a militant, not only a dissident, not simply a dissenter, but a criminal. He was a criminal revolutionary, whose existence threatened the nation in a revolutionary way."[18] Although most Americans like to engage in a little revisionist history so that Jesus comes off as falsely accused, denied due process, and unjustly executed, Stringfellow rightly asserts that Jesus *was* guilty of the charges leveled at him. Jesus *was* a traitor, and Jesus' Way *is* to commit treason. Not in the Benedict Arnold sense of betraying one principality for another, or supplanting one power with another, but treason in the sense of renouncing *all* principalities and powers. For Radicals, treason is a spiritual discipline in the sense that reconciled people have no enemies to defend against.[19] "The way of the cross *is* the way of treason against the principalities and powers," Charles Campbell argues, in which

> Jesus challenges not only the idolatrous claim of the powers but also their reliance on violence to ensure their own survival and domination. . . . He is calling us not simply to bear the burdens of life or practice ascetic self-denial but to take up the way of resistance to the Domination System. He is calling us not passively to accept violence or abuse but actively to resist the powers of domination without resorting to their violent means. Jesus is calling us not to suffer for the sake of suffering but to bear the suffering that may come when we stand in solidarity with the victims of the powers and engage in nonviolent resistance against their oppression.[20]

17. Ellul, *Violence*, 165.

18. Stringfellow and Towne, *Suspect Tenderness: The Ethics of the Berrigan Witness*, 60.

19. Richard Hughes has described the "long tradition of treason" that defines the Christian witness to the nation-states. (See his *Christian America and the Kingdom of God*, 84.)

20. Charles Campbell, *Word before the Powers*, 63–64. Several authors have recently stressed the anti-imperial nature of the Christian *kerygma*. Mark Finney, for example, has described how in I Corinthians, Paul "makes a deliberate effort to deracinate social norms and to present a new and radical paradigm for life as a Christ follower." (See Finney, "Christ Crucified and the Inversion of Roman Imperial Ideology

"The very presence of the church in a world ruled by the Powers is a superlatively positive and aggressive fact," Berkhof notes. "All resistance and every attack against the gods of this age will be unfruitful, *unless the church herself is resistance and attack*, unless she demonstrates in her life and fellowship how people can live freed from the Powers."[21] "The world will think you an idiot for trusting God more than men or idols," Stringfellow warned, because everyone knows that the principalities only respect—and yield to—power.[22]

As Will Campbell explained in his 1991 response to the questions of the *New Oxford Review* editors, Christian anarchists refuse to operate according to what "everyone knows." Vernard Eller, a contributor to *Katallagete*, explained that Christian anarchists are "unimpressed with, disinterested in, skeptical of, nonchalant toward, and uninfluenced by highfalutin claims of any and all arkys." These "arkys" are the epistemologies, principalities, and powers that claim to be preeminent, sovereign, and normative. "Precisely because Jesus is THE ARKY," Eller argues, "the Prince of Creation, the Principal of All Good, the Prince of Peace and Everything Else, Christians dare never grant a human arky the primacy it claims for itself." Thus Christian anarchists are "unarchical" insofar as their confession of Christ as the one *archos* (master) rejects the legitimacy and normativity of all other contenders.[23] Although some will hear the term "anarchism" and think of violent revolutionaries, "Christian anarchism" is qualitatively different. "Christian anarchism rejects the very presuppositions that make the idea of revolution, and, perhaps, even liberation itself, intelligible," Tripp York explains. Because "Jesus is neither exemplified in Che Guevera or Simon the Zealot," Christian anarchists do not seek to replace a bad government with our good one. Instead, Jesus "established a community of believers who developed and reside in the *altera civitas* on earth: the church."[24]

---

in I Corinthians," 20–33.) See also Elliott, "The Anti-Imperial Message of the Cross;" and Horsley, *Jesus and Empire: The Kingdom of God and the New World Disorder*, especially pages 79–104 and 129–49. Not to be left out, Stanley Hauerwas has asserted that the Christian *kerygma* should be so scandalous to the principalities that those powers would perceive Radicals as a terrorist threat—a rather dangerous plea in light of events occurring the year after the publication of Hauerwas's essay. See his "The Nonviolent Terrorist: In Defense of Christian Fanaticism."

21. Berkhof, *Christ against the Powers*, 51.
22. Stringfellow, *Free in Obedience*, 47.
23. Eller, *Christian Anarchy: Jesus' Primacy over the Powers*, 2.
24. York, *Living on Hope While Living in Babylon*, 30.

Many have dismissed self-professed Christian anarchists and Radicals as tradition-less, irresponsible, withdrawal-minded sectarians, who lack concern and compassion for their neighbors. As Jacques Ellul noted, however, "there has always been a Christian anarchism. In every century there have been Christians who have discovered the simple biblical truth, whether intellectually, mystically, or socially." Comprising this storied tradition, Ellul lists Tertullian, Francis of Assisi, John Wycliffe, Felicite Robert de Lamennais, Charles de Foucauld, and Christopher Blumhardt.[25] Others making the list should include the thirteenth-century Brothers and Sisters of the Free Spirit, who denied the authority of both the state and institutional church to proscribe behavior and belief for individual Christians. In 1381, England's King Richard II executed John Ball for his anarchical message that social rank and economic privilege intentionally flouted God's social design and Christ's egalitarian message. In the fifteenth century, Peter Chelcic likewise denounced government as a principality that divided humans according to inequities of property and the fictions of social rank. Gerrard Winstanley helped inspire the seventeenth-century English Digger movement, arguing that Christ's message was one of universal liberty. All forms of power, including male domination of women in society and marriage were intrinsically unchristian. Not surprisingly, Winstanley's ideas continued on through George Fox and the Quakers. Then in the late eighteenth century, William Godwin influenced many later anarchists with his 1793 book, *Enquiry Concerning Political Justice*. In the nineteenth-century U.S., William Lloyd Garrison and Adin Ballou carried the Christian anarchist mantle,[26] and at the beginning of the twentieth century David

---

25. Ellul, *Anarchy and Christianity*, 7.

26. In 1838, for example, Garrison declared: "We cannot acknowledge allegiance to any human government; neither can we oppose any such government by a resort to physical force. We recognize but one King and Lawgiver, one Judge and Ruler of mankind. We are bound by the laws of a kingdom which is not of this world; the subjects of which are forbidden to fight; in which Mercy and Truth are met together, and Righteousness and Peace have kissed each other; which has no state lines, no national partitions, no geographical boundaries, in which there is not distinction of rank, or division of caste, or inequality of sex; the officers of which are Peace, its exactors Righteousness, its walls Salvation, and its gates Praise. . . . Our country is the world, our countrymen are all mankind. . . . The interests, rights, liberties of American citizenship are no more dear to us than those of the whole human race. Hence we can allow no appeal to patriotism, to revenge any national insult or injury. The Prince of Peace, under whose stainless banner we rally, came not to destroy, but to save, even the worst of enemies. He has left us with an example, that we should follow his steps." On July 4, 1854, Garrison dramatized his

Lipscomb's *Civil Government* made the case as well.[27] Here we find the legacy of Will D. Campbell. Much more than a "bootleg preacher," troubadour, or priest of a Southern civil religion, Will Campbell has carried forward a vital and relevant Radicalism in Christian history.

Christian anarchism by denouncing the U.S. Constitution as a "covenant with death and an agreement with hell." He then burned a copy of the Constitution, grinding the ashes under his heel, announcing "so should perish all compromises with tyranny." (Cain, *William Lloyd Garrison and the Fight against Slavery*, 101–5, and 35–36.)

Adin Ballou also denounced the role that the principalities and powers serve for the Christian. Does the state, he asked, offer something the disciple cannot find in a purer, higher form in the Christian *kerygma*? Ballou answered his rhetorical question noting that the state offered only inferior versions of what God had already offered. Thus, "the will of man (human government) whether in one, a thousand, or many millions, has no intrinsic authority—no moral supremacy—and no right to claim the allegiance of man." What then becomes of this principality and institution known as government? "When it opposes God's government it is *nothing*; when it agrees with God's government it is *nothing*; and when it discovers a new item of duty—a new application of the general law of God—it is *nothing*." Institutions, principalities, and governments are merely "dross." But what about making a difference in the world? one might ask. Should we not align with the principalities or acquire their power in order to make a difference in the world? "It is not by getting into places of worldly power that Christians are to promote human welfare," Ballou asserted. "Away then with the intrigues and tricks of political ambition, the petty squabbles of partisans and officeholders, the hallow bluster of demagogues, and the capricious admiration of a tickled multitude. Let us obey God, declare the truth, and walk in love." (Ballou, "Non-Resistance: A Basis for Christian Anarchism," 141–49.)

27. David Lipscomb, *Civil Government*. See also Lipscomb's "Christian Appeal to the Confederacy" in Polner and Woods' *We Who Dared to Say No to War*, 61–66. Lipscomb was undoubtedly influenced by Alexander Campbell. On the verge of the American Civil War, Campbell wrote, "It is worthy of special note that in the numerous and various allusions to the Christian virtues in the Christian scriptures, and in the summaries given of them on some occasions, patriotism, is not once named, or alluded to, in any one of them." Continuing on, Campbell explained, "In the Christian's optics the whole earth is his country, and its whole population his natural brotherhood. He is unworthy of the name Christian who exclusively appropriates that name to his own party, or to the clique of his special election, merely because of his and their concurrence in some special theory or creed of their own." (*Millennial Harbinger*, [June 4, 1861], 366.)

RETHINKING SECT

We now see what Niebuhr, Gustafson, and others have failed to appreciate. One of the most under-appreciated forms of resisting the principalities and powers is the embodied witness of Jesus' reconciled people—an incarnated alternative community living in opposition to the domination system of the principalities and powers. This is the challenge Ellul proposed when he retorted,

> If the Christian is to contend against violence (whatever its source), he will have to be absolutely intransigent, he will have to refuse to be conciliated. The Christian faith implies rejection and condemnation of both revolutionary violence and the violence of the established powers. . . . All the demands implied in these words—faith in Jesus Christ, love of enemy, the overcoming of evil by love—must be affirmed, taught, and lived with the most absolute intransigence. There can be no accommodation. The Christianity that accommodates itself to the culture in the belief that it will thus make itself more acceptable and better understood, and more authentically in touch with humanity—this is not half-Christianity; it is a total denial of Christianity.[1]

To portray the Radical's incarnation as apolitical withdrawal would be to miss in an absolute way the bold political vocation and ecclesiastical vision of this reconciled and reconciling community.

Will Campbell once recalled how he had been in a Southern city on Easter morning, the day after a "mob of local citizenry" had beaten activists for trying to desegregate local transportation. "I listened to several sermons on the radio that day," Campbell recounted. "Not one reference was made to what had happened the day before, not one word to indicate that their city was in chaos and on the verge of a blood bath." Such *social conformity is apolitical withdrawal*. For Campbell, by contrast, Luke 4:18 *is* politics. "Yes, that is exactly what it is. And when our Lord said," he continued, "'Yea, they bind heavy burdens . . . and lay them

---

1. Ellul, *Violence*, 145.

on men's shoulders,' He was talking in clear unmistakable terms about working conditions and labor-management relations. AND THAT'S POLITICS." "But let us not be now confused," Campbell warned. "The message of Easter is not, 'Clear up the slums, get the rich off the poor, and quit segregating one another into ghettos.' The message of Easter is 'You *are* reconciled. God has done it.' Our living faith is to *be* reconciled, to *be* what we *are* in the New Creation."[2] Thus the charge of apolitical withdrawal utterly misses the reality that Radical Christianity *is* political engagement, but it is politics that intentionally resists conventional political science of both the "right" and the "left."[3]

Recall that James Gustafson indicted sectarian Radicals for being "idolatrous" about their identity. As Gavin D'Costa has warned, however, the dominant superpower is often a more malicious sectarian force because it presumes the right to impose its views on others.[4] Stringfellow surely would have agreed. The principalities and powers are the ones who position themselves as the political and ethical "north star" "in relation to which the moral significance of everything and everyone else is determined." That is the definition of idolatrous "sectarianism."[5]

> Each principality claims a man's loyalty, service, and worship; each makes essentially the same demands that a man regard it as his god, as the one in the idolatry of which a man's life will gain moral significance. Each makes the same claim, but a man is beset by the several claims of the principalities of class, race, nation, profession, and family; all made more or less at the same time and each insistent upon taking precedence over everything else. . . . Each principality boasts that men will find the meaning and fulfillment of human life in service to the principality and to that which abets its survival; a profound concern for self-survival is the governing morality of every principality. This comes first. To this all other interests must be sacrificed; from this all else, including individual's life and work, takes its significance; by this a man is judged. The principalities claim, in other words, sovereignty over human life and history.[6]

---

2. Campbell, "My Living Faith," Emphasis in original.

3. See the section "Resistance to Political Principalities and Powers" in *Writings on Reconciliation and Resistance*, 175–204.

4. D'Costa, *Theology in the Public Square*, 82 and 87.

5. Stringfellow, *An Ethic for Christians*, 51.

6. Stringfellow, *Free in Obedience*, 60–61.

Who, therefore, are the real advocates of passivity? Is it the Radicals, or those seeking to align with the principalities, hoping to acquire their power? As Thomas Merton claimed, real inactivity and resignation is exhibited in subservient opportunism, the mass mind, obedience amenable to any crime that will retain one's favorable position, mechanical submission, blind fidelity to authority, making survival the chief criterion, abdication of responsibility, or simply following orders without question.[7] Those who buy into the political science of the principalities and their ways of power are the ones who manifest withdrawal. A "politicized mind," Ellul finds, is an "invaded, crushed, passively submissive mind," because the myths of the principalities and powers limit the range of possibilities and alternatives.[8] Far from apolitical passive withdrawal, therefore, the Radical Christian—who is "everywhere, in every society, an alien"[9]—is pledged to an authentically liberated politics, always treasonous to the nation-state and everywhere in conflict with orthodox political science. Or, as Elizabeth McAlister has argued, "'Exile' is an image that might enlighten us concerning the truth of our status anywhere, at any time—aliens, wanderers. . . . There is no hope in government; the hope is in exiles."[10] Exiles are the ones who incarnate the imperative reality of *katallagete*.

---

7. See Merton, "Passivity and Abuse of Authority," 129–33.
8. Ellul, *The Political Illusion*, 24.
9. Stringfellow, *Dissenter in the Great Society*, 162.
10. McAlister, "Preach the Good News and Cast Out Demons: On Civil Resistance."

CONCLUSION

Will Campbell has often confessed his discomfort with the word "ministry," believing the term can convey a presumptuous and arrogant attitude. Instead, he much prefers to be called a "preacher," a vocation that—he believes—leaves the grand designs and measurable outcomes to God.[1] From that perspective, the description of preaching offered by Stanley Saunders and Charles Campbell fits the life and Radical iconoclasm of Will D. Campbell quite well. Preaching at its heart is the annunciation of a notorious, treasonous message. "In the midst of death, in the face of the powers, in the power of the Word," Saunders and Campbell announce,

> Christians take a stance of resistance—often "audacious, extemporaneous, fragile, puny, foolish" resistance. . . . Because of the verbal nature of the powers' tactics, preaching, as the counter-speech of the Word of God, can be a particularly important form of resistance. . . . This homiletical resistance to the principalities and powers takes two forms: *exposing* and *envisioning* the alternative of God's redeemed creation. Essential to this twofold resistance is the gift of discernment, the most basic gift of the Holy Spirit to the church, which enables Christians to expose and rebuke the powers of death while also affirming the living, promising Word of God. . . . On the cross Jesus *exposes* the principalities and powers for what they are—not the divine regents of the world, but rather the violent purveyors of death. In the resurrection Jesus is victorious over the powers of death and gives a vision of the promised future, which can be glimpsed even now in the living word made incarnate in the midst of death. The gift of discernment enables Christians to see this crucified and risen

---

1. Here recall Merton's famous "Letter to a Young Activist." In this letter, Merton encouraged Jim Forest "Do not depend on the hope of results. When you are doing the sort of work you have taken on, you may have to face the fact that your work will be apparently worthless and even achieve no results at all, if not perhaps results opposite to what you expect. . . . The real hope, then, is not in something we think we can do, but in God who is making something good out of it in some way we cannot see."

Jesus in the world. Preaching that is shaped by the story of Jesus and empowered by the Spirit of discernment will engage in this two-fold exposing and envisioning. . . . In the midst of babel, Christian preaching, first of all, exposes the powers of death. The preacher names the powers and rebukes them. Like the cross of Jesus, this "No!" to the powers, which uncovers their false claims and deadly lies, marks the beginning of human freedom from bondage to death. This "No!" takes away the "mirrors" by which the powers delude us into thinking they are the divine regents of the world. The powers are exposed as emperors without any clothes, a disarming humiliation for those who rely so heavily on their pretensions of dignity and control.[2]

Hope is the second element of preaching's shocking vocation. People of faith can beat their swords into plows, and their spears into pruning hooks. The marginalized lambs *can* lie down with the powerful lions. *Shalom* (i.e., justice and mercy) is not just a blissful dream for the afterlife. Because of Easter morning, a "new heaven and a new earth" exists. "The good news to the world is that we can stop living in thrall to the powers now, even under the conditions of death," Wink writes. "The gospel is that God sets us free from the dread of death, the cajolery of death, and the seductiveness of death."[3] If we need a contemporary face to put on this vocation of preaching, we could hardly do better than Will Davis Campbell.

A trusted friend and mentor once expressed appreciation for Campbell's courageous bipartisan spirit, and admiration for his mediation between hostile parties. Despite his respect for Campbell, however, my friend wondered what Campbell leaves us with at the end of the day. Campbell may be able to walk comfortably, even sacrificially, in diverse communities, but "Does he ever bring those groups any closer together? What will be Campbell's legacy? What changes has he made in the world? Has he changed the world's power dynamics? Is his life replicable? Can anyone, in other words, ever use Campbell's life and work as a model for engaging the problems they face in their world?"

Although understandable, perhaps asking such questions illustrates a failure to grasp Campbell's vocation. These questions, like so many we ask, focus on some sort of doing. What has Campbell accomplished? Has he made the world a better, more just, place? What are his successes,

---

2. Stanley Saunders and Charles Campbell, *The Word on the Street*, 74–76.
3. Walter Wink, "Stringfellow on the Powers," 20.

and is his approach broadly replicable? What has he done in his life that I can do in my own to achieve progress? Campbell, however, might retort, "Why are you imposing *those* questions on my life? '*Do* nothing. *Be* what you are, reconciled.'" A biography of his life is fine, but I do not believe he expects us to look to his life for a strategy, a tactic, or a model of social activism. The particulars of his life have been as unique as his sense of fashion. Will is irreplaceable and beyond imitation, with one important exception. Campbell's vocation, as with any other Radical Christian, is to collapse the idolatrous principalities that tempt us to seek their powers. Yet the strategy for resisting and smashing the icons is not via a political science or an effective use of power. As Campbell illustrates, we crash the idols by incarnating the Christian difference in the world—by being a peculiar, reconciling, alternative community in the midst of an all too normal world.

BIBLIOGRAPHY

CAMPBELL'S BOOKS

Campbell, Will D. *And Also with You: Duncan Gray and the American Dilemma.* Franklin: Provident House, 1997.

———. *Brother to a Dragonfly.* New York: Continuum, 1977.

———. *Cecelia's Sin: A Novella.* Macon: Mercer University Press, 1983.

———. *The Convention: A Parable.* Grand Rapids: Eerdmans, 1988.

———. *Forty Acres and a Goat.* Atlanta: Peachtree, 1986.

———. *The Glad River.* Eugene: Wipf and Stock, 2000.

———. *God on Earth: The Lord's Prayer for Our Time.* New York: Crossroad, 1983.

———. *Providence.* Atlanta: Longstreet, 1992.

———. *Race and the Renewal of the Church.* Philadelphia: Westminster, 1962.

———. *Robert G. Clark's Journey to the House: A Black Politician's Story.* Jackson: University Press of Mississippi, 2003.

———. *Soul among the Lions: Musings of a Bootleg Preacher.* Louisville: Westminster John Knox, 1999.

———. *The Stem of Jesse: The Costs of Community at a 1960s Southern School.* Macon: Mercer University Press, 1995.

———. *Writings on Reconciliation and Resistance.* Edited by Richard Goode. Eugene: Cascade, 2010.

Campbell, Will D., and James Y. Holloway. *"And the Criminals with Him": Luke 23:33.* New York: Paulist, 1973.

———. *Callings!* New York: Paulist, 1974.

———. *The Failure and the Hope: Essays of Southern Churchmen.* Grand Rapids: Eerdmans, 1972.

———. *Up to Our Steeples in Politics.* New York: Paulist, 1970.

CAMPBELL'S ARTICLES AND ADDRESSES

Campbell, Will D. "Brer Fox and Brer Tarrypin and the Crisis at Ole Miss." *Christianity and Crisis* 37 (October 17, 1977) 232–36.

———. "Class of '79." *Katallagete* (Fall 1979) 24–33.

———. "Commie-killing: Ethics, Law, and Geography." *Christianity and Crisis* 43 (May 14, 1984) 174–76.

———. "The Day of Our Birth." *Katallagete* 1 (June 1965) 3–5.

———. "Faith of a Fatalist." *New South* 23 (Spring 1968) 51–57.

———. "The Death of Willie Gene Carreker." *Race Relations Reporter* 5 (September 1974) 31–37.

———. "He Ate Yesterday." *The Other Side* 19 (October 1983) 11.
———. "How Much Love Is Loving Too Much?" *Christianity and Crisis* 44 (October 14, 1985) 388–90.
———. "I Love My Country: Christ Have Mercy." *Motive* 30 (December 1969) 42–47.
———. "If We Should Get Serious." *Katallagete* (Winter 1967–68) 1–2.
———. "The Inner Life of Church and Synagogue in Race Relations." In *Race: Challenge to Religion*, edited by Mathew Ahman, 9–27. Chicago: Henry Regnery, 1963.
———. "July 19, 1959." *Katallagete* (Fall 1975) 28–32.
———. "Last Act in a Tragedy: Where to Sit in Scottsboro." *Christianity and Crisis* 37 (August 17, 1977) 189–91.
———. "Law and Love in Lowndes." *Katallagete* (December 1965) 11–14.
———. "A Little More Memphis." *New South* 24 (Summer 1969) 28–34.
———. "A Man Had Two Sons." *Christianity Today* 9 (April 10, 1964) 36–38.
———. "Milestones into Millstones." *Katallagete* (Winter 1966–67) 2–4.
———. "Movement Hangover." *Christianity and Crisis* 45 (March 17, 1986) 77–78.
———. "The Nature of the Problem." *New South* 17 (June 1962) 3–8.
———. "Nit-picking on a Fine Book." *Christianity and Crisis* 42 (February 20, 1984) 42–43.
———. "On Getting Sick Together." *Christianity and Crisis* 45 (April 1, 1985) 100–2.
———. "On Silencing Our Finest." *Christianity and Crisis* 44 (September 16, 1985) 340–41.
———. "Our Adolescent History." In *Retrospect: 25 Years of School Desegregation (1954–1979)*, edited by Walter J. Leonard, Will D. Campbell, and Robert E. Eaker, 39–48. The School Law Symposium Series. Murfreesboro, TN: Middle Tennessee State University, 1980.
———. "Perhaps and Maybe." *The Christian Century* 79 (September 19, 1962) 1133.
———. "A Personal Struggle for Soul Freedom." *Christian Ethics Today* (December 1995). Online: http://www.christianethicstoday.com/cetart/index.cfm?fuseaction=Articles.main&ArtID=430.
———. "Pudor Sit Academia." *Christianity and Crisis* 44 (June 25, 1984) 246–47.
———. "Quit Picking on Paul." *Christianity and Crisis* 46 (December 8, 1986) 428–30.
———. "Religion in Nashville, A.D. 2050." In *Nashville: An American Self-Portrait*, edited by John Egerton and E. Thomas Wood. Nashville: Beaten Biscuit, 2001.
———. "The Role of Religious Organizations in the Desegregation Controversy." *Union Seminary Quarterly Review* 16 (January 1961) 187–96.
———. "Rumblings of Rebellion among Southern White Clergy." *Dialogue* 3 (Spring 1964) 124–29.
———. "The Sit-Ins: Passive Resistance or Civil Disobedience?" *Social Action* 27 (January 1961) 14–18.
———. "Staying at Home or Leaving." In *Sense of Place: Mississippi*, edited by Peggy Prenshaw and Jesse O. McKee, 14–23. Jackson: University Press of Mississippi, 1979.
———. "Summit Wishes." *Christianity and Crisis* 45 (December 23, 1985) 508–10.
———. "Symposium on Transcending Ideological Conformity." *New Oxford Review* 58 (October 1991) 7–8.
———. "Tennessee Disinherits the Wind." *Christianity and Crisis* 27 (July 10, 1967) 165–66.
———. "There Is Hope." *Christian Ethics Today* (1995). Online: http://www.christianethicstoday.com/cetart/index.cfm?fuseaction=Articles.main&ArtID=431.

———. "The Time Twelve Women Priests Rewrote the Prayer Book." *Katallagete* (Summer 1976) 42–44.

———. "Tourist Notes." *Christianity and Crisis* 46 (March 16, 1987) 85–86.

———. "Used and Abused: The Redneck's Role." In *The Prevailing South: Life and Politics in a Changing Culture*, edited by Dudley Clendinen. Atlanta: Longstreet, 1988.

———. "Vocation as Grace." *Katallagete* (Fall-Winter 1972) 80–86.

———. "The West Virginia Controversy: Whose Code Do We Follow?" *Christianity and Crisis* 31 (March 31, 1975) 68–73.

———. "When History Is All We Have." *Christianity and Crisis* 49 (September 24, 1990) 285–87.

———. "Which Is the Real Evil—Snake-Handling or the Establishment Church?" *Southern Voices* 1 (March/April 1974) 41–48.

———. "Which Way for Southern Churches: Footwashing or the New Hermeneutic?" *Katallagete* (Summer 1966) 1–6.

———. "The World of the Redneck." *Katallagete* (Spring 1974) 34–40.

Campbell, Will D., and James Y. Holloway. "Can There Be a Crusade for Christ?" *Katallagete* (Summer 1973) 2–6.

———. "The Good News from God in Jesus Is Freedom to the Prisoners." *Katallagete* (Winter-Spring 1972) 2–5.

———. "An Open Letter to Dr. Billy Graham, or, About This Issue." *Katallagete* (Winter 1971) 1–4.

———. "Our Grade Is 'F.'" *Katallagete* (Fall 1969) 3–10.

———. "Up to Our Steeples in Politics." *Katallagete* (Fall 1968) 2–9. Also reprinted in *Christianity and Crisis* (March 3, 1969) 36–40.

Ligon, Herschel [Will D. Campbell]. "The Pragmatics of Parity." *Christianity and Crisis* 37 (Feburary 6, 1978) 6–8.

CAMPBELL ARCHIVAL MATERIAL

Campbell, Will D. "Christian Concern: Fourteenth Amendment or First Commandment?" (dated 10 November 1963). The Papers of Will Campbell, McCain Library and Archives, University of Southern Mississippi, Box 13, Folder 43.

———. "My Living Faith," (dated 1966). The Papers of Will Campbell, McCain Library and Archives, University of Southern Mississippi, Box 10, Folder 10.

CAMPBELL INTERVIEWS

Bowman, Norman. "Prophet, Poet, Preacher-at-Large." *The Student*. (December 1970) 29ff.

Caudill, Orley B. "An Oral History with Will D. Campbell." University of Southern Mississippi. Center for Oral History and Cultural Heritage. Volume 157 (1976).

Clancy, Walter B. "Jesus in the Brush Arbor: An Interview with Will Campbell." *The New Orleans Review* 4:3 (1974) 228–31.

Flynn, Bob. "Interview with Will D. Campbell." *The Wittenburg Door* (November/December 2006) 6–10.

Gibble, Kenneth L. "Living Out the Drama: An Interview with Will Campbell." *Christian Century* 101 (May 30, 1984) 570–74.

Houston, Benjamin. "An Interview with Will D. Campbell." (2003) *The Journal of Southern Religion*. 10 (2007). No pages. Online: http://jsr.fsu.edu/Volume10/Houston.htm.

Lloyd, Jeremy. "Radical Grace: An Interview with Will D. Campbell." *The Sun* (May 2000) 8–16.

Wray, Harmon. "Interview of Will D. Campbell." (2002 and 2003) Nashville Public Library. Civil Rights Oral History Project.

"Will Campbell: Door Interview." *The Wittenburg Door* (June/July 1973) 5–13.

"The Futility of Fighting Over What We Believe: Interview with Will Campbell." *The Wittenburg Door* (March/April 1990) 12–15.

SECONDARY MATERIALS: BOOKS

Berkhof, Hendrikus. *Christ and the Powers*. Translated by John Howard Yoder. Scottdale, PA: Herald, 1977.

Bradstock, Andrew, and Christopher Rowland. *Radical Christian Writings: A Reader*. Oxford: Blackwell, 2002.

Branscomb, Bennett Harvie. *The Contribution of Moral and Spiritual Ideas to the Making of the American Way of Life*. Madison: University of Wisconsin, 1952.

Bryan, G. McLeod. *These Few Also Paid a Price: Southern Whites Who Fought for Civil Rights*. Macon: Mercer University Press, 2001.

Burgess, David. *The Fellowship of Southern Churchmen: Its History and Promise*. No publication data. James Y. Holloway Papers. University of Mississippi, Department of Archives and Special Collections.

Burkholder, John Richard, and Barbara Nelson Gingerich. *Mennonite Peace Theology: A Panorama of Types*. Akron: Mennonite Central Committee, 1991.

Camp, Lee. *Mere Discipleship: Radical Christianity in a Rebellious World*. Grand Rapids: Brazos, 2003.

Campbell, Charles. *The Word before the Powers*. Louisville: Westminster John Knox, 2002.

Carter, Craig. *Rethinking Christ and Culture: A Post-Christendom Perspective*. Grand Rapids: Brazos, 2007.

Connelly, Thomas L. *Will Campbell and the Soul of the South*. New York: Continuum, 1982.

Creech, Joe. *Righteous Indignation: Religion and the Populist Revolution*. Urbana: University of Illinois Press, 2006.

Dark, David. *The Gospel according to America: A Meditation on a God-blessed, Christ-haunted Idea*. Louisville: Westminster John Knox, 2005.

———. *The Sacredness of Questioning Everything*. Grand Rapids: Zondervan, 2009.

D'Costa, Gavin. *Theology in the Public Square: Church, Academy, and Nation*. Malden, MA: Blackwell, 2005.

Dunbar, Anthony P. *Against the Grain: Southern Radicals and Prophets, 1929–1959*. Charlottesville: University Press of Virginia, 1981.

Eckblad, Bob. *A New Christian Manifesto: Pledging Allegiance to the Kingdom of God*. Louisville: Westminster John Knox, 2008.

———. *Reading the Bible with the Damned*. Louisville: Westminster John Knox, 2005.

Egerton, John. *A Mind to Stay Here: Profiles from the South*. New York: Macmillan, 1970.

Eller, Vernard. *Christian Anarchy: Jesus' Primacy over the Powers*. Grand Rapids: Eerdmans, 1987.

Ellul, Jacques. *Anarchy and Christianity*. Trans. Geoffrey W. Bromiley. Grand Rapids: Eerdmans, 1988.

———. *The Political Illusion*. Trans. Konrad Kellen. New York: Vintage, 1972.

———. *The Presence of the Kingdom*. Trans. Olive Wyon. Colorado Springs: Helmers and Howard, 1989.

———. *Violence: Reflections from a Christian Perspective*. Trans. Cecelia Gaul Kings. New York: Seabury, 1969.

Findlay, James F. Jr. *Church People in the Struggle: The National Council of Churches and the Black Freedom Movement, 1950–1970*. New York: Oxford University Press, 1993.

Friedland, Michael B. *Lift Up Your Voice Like a Trumpet: White Clergy and the Civil Rights and Antiwar Movements, 1954–1973*. Chapel Hill: University of North Carolina Press, 1998.

Frady, Marshall. *Billy Graham: A Parable of American Righteousness*. Boston: Little, Brown, 1979.

———. *Southerners: A Journalist's Odyssey*. New York: New American Library, 1980. Includes a reprint of Frady's "Travels with Brother Will: Fighter for Forgotten Men." *Life* 72 (June 16, 1972) 57ff.

Halberstam, David. *The Children*. New York: Random House, 1998.

Hatch, Nathan O. *The Democratization of American Christianity*. New Haven: Yale University Press, 1989.

Hauerwas, Stanley. *The State of the University: Academic Knowledges and the Knowledge of God*. Illumiations: Theory & Religion. Malden, MA: Blackwell, 2007.

Hawkins, Merrill M. Jr. *Will Campbell: Radical Prophet of the South*. Macon, GA: Mercer University Press, 1997.

Horsley, Richard A. *Jesus and Empire: The Kingdom of God and the New World Disorder*. Minneapolis: Fortress, 2003.

Hughes, Richard T. *Christian America and the Kingdom of God*. Urbana: University of Illinois Press, 2009.

Inchausti, Robert. *Subversive Orthodoxy: Outlaws, Revolutionaries, and Other Christians in Disguise*. Grand Rapids: Brazos, 2005.

Jordan, Clarence. *Sermon on the Mount*. Valley Forge, PA: Judson, 1952.

Kenneson, Philip D. *Beyond Sectarianism: Re-Imagining Church and World*. Harrisburg, PA: Trinity, 1999.

Lewis, Ted, editor. *Electing Not to Vote*. Eugene, OR: Cascade, 2008.

Lindbeck, George A. *The Nature of Doctrine: Religion and Theology in a Postliberal Age*. Philadelphia: Westminster, 1984.

Lipscomb, David. *Civil Government*. Nashville: McQuiddy, 1913.

Lohfink, Gerhard. *Does God Need the Church? Toward a Theology of the People of God*. Translated by Linda Maloney. Collegeville, MN: Liturgical, 1999.

———. *Jesus and Community: The Social Dimension of Christian Faith*. Translated by John P. Galvin. Philadelphia: Fortress, 1984.

Lovett, Bobby L. *The Civil Rights Movement in Tennessee: A Narrative History*. Knoxville: University of Tennessee Press, 2005.

Martin, Robert F. *Howard Kester and the Struggle for Social Justice in the South, 1904–77*. Charlottesville: University Press of Virginia, 1991.

Matthiessen, F. O. *American Renaissance: Art and Expression in the Age of Emerson and Whitman*. New York: Oxford University Press, 1941.

Niebuhr, H. Richard. *Christ and Culture*. New York: Harper & Row, 1951.

Paton, Alan. *Cry, the Beloved Country*. New York: Charles Scribner's Sons, 1948.

Polner, Murray, and Thomas E. Woods, Jr. *We Who Dared to Say No to War: American Antiwar Writing from 1812 to Now*. New York: Basic Books, 2008.

Ramsey, G. Lee, Jr. *Preachers and Misfits, Prophets and Thieves: The Minister in Southern Fiction*. Louisville: Westminster John Knox, 2008.

Richardson, Cyril C. *Early Christian Fathers*. New York: Macmillan, 1970.

Saunders, Stanley, and Charles Campbell. *The Word on the Street: Performing the Scriptures in the Urban Context*. Grand Rapids: Eerdmans, 2000.

Schipani, Daniel, editor. *Freedom and Discipleship: Liberation Theology in an Anabaptist Perspective*. Maryknoll, NY: Orbis, 1989.

Silver, James W. *Running Scared: Silver in Mississippi*. Jackson: University Press of Mississippi, 1984.

Sokol, Jason. *There Goes My Everything: White Southerners in the Age of Civil Rights, 1945–1975*. New York: Knopf, 2006.

Stringfellow, William. *An Ethic for Christians and Other Aliens in a Strange Land*. Waco: Word, 1973.

———. *Dissenter in the Great Society: A Christian View of America in Crisis*. New York: Holt, Rinehart, and Winston, 1966.

———. *Free in Obedience*. New York: Seabury, 1964.

———. *A Keeper of the Word: Selected Writings of William Stringfellow*, edited by Bill Wylie Kellermann. Grand Rapids: Eerdmans, 1994.

———. *My People Is the Enemy: An Autobiographical Polemic*. New York: Holt, Rinehart and Winston, 1964.

Stringfellow, William, and Anthony Towne. *Suspect Tenderness: The Ethics of the Berrigan Witness*. New York: Holt, Rinehart and Winston, 1971.

Thurman, Howard. *Jesus and the Disinherited*. Nashville: Abingdon, 1949.

Toulouse, Mark G. *God in Public: Four Ways American Christianity and Public Life Relate*. Louisville: Westminster John Knox, 2006.

Wink, Walter. *The Powers That Be: Theology for a New Millennium*. New York: Doubleday, 1998.

———. *Violence and Nonviolence in South Africa: Jesus' Third Way*. Philadelphia: New Society, 1987.

Woodward, C. Vann. *The Strange Career of Jim Crow*. New York: Oxford University Press, 1955.

Yoder, John H. *Christian Attitudes to War, Peace, and Revolution*. Grand Rapids: Brazos, 2009.

———. *He Came Preaching Peace*. Scottdale, PA: Herald, 1985.

———. *Nevertheless: Varieties of Religious Pacifism*. Scottdale, PA: Herald, 1971, 1992.

———. *The Original Revolution: Essays on Christian Pacifism*. Scottdale, PA: Herald, 1971.

York, Tripp. *Living on Hope While Living in Babylon: The Christian Anarchists of the Twentieth Century*. Eugene: Wipf and Stock, 2009.

———. *The Purple Crown: The Politics of Martyrdom*. Scottdale, PA: Herald, 2007.

SECONDARY MATERIALS: ARTICLES AND CHAPTERS

Adamson, June N. "Few Black Voices Heard: The Black Community and the Desegregation Crisis in Clinton, Tennessee, 1956." *Tennessee Historical Quarterly* 53 (Spring 1994) 30–41.

Ballou, Adin. "Non-Resistance: A Basis for Christian Anarchism." In *Patterns of Anarchy: A Collection of Writings on the Anarchist Tradition*, edited by Leonard Krimerman and Lewis Perry. New York: Anchor, 1966.

Baxter, Michael J. "'Blowing the Dynamite of the Church': Catholic Radicalism from a Catholic Radicalist Perspective." In *The Church as Counterculture*, edited by Michael L. Budde and Robert W. Brimlow, 195–212. SUNY Series in Popular Culture and Political Change. Albany: State University of New York Press, 2000.

Bevel, James. "Caught Not Praying." *Katallagete* (Winter 1968–69) 8–11.

Boers, Arthur. "Will Campbell: In the Great Company of God's Grace." *The Other Side* (September 1987) 40–44.

Boomershine, Tom. "Theological Education: Rich Man's Slave or Poor Man's Servant?" *Katallagete* (Fall 1969) 34–40.

Eagles, Charles W. "The Closing of Mississippi Society: Will Campbell, The $64,000 Question, and Religious Emphasis Week at the University of Mississippi." *Journal of Southern History* 67 (May 2001) 331–72.

Egerton, John. "Black Judge in the Halls of Ivy." *Katallagete* (Fall 1969) 11–15.

———. "Starting Over." *Katallagete* (Fall 1977) 15–20.

Eller, Vernard. "How the Kings of the Earth Land in the New Jerusalem: 'The World' in the Book of Revelation." *Katallagete* (Summer 1975) 21–27.

Ellul, Jacques. "The Betrayal of the Individual: The Executioner." *Katallagete* (Spring 1978) 17–22.

Elliott, Neil. "The Anti-Imperial Message of the Cross." In *Paul and Empire: Religion and Power in Roman Imperial Society*, edited by Richard A. Horsley, 167–83. Harrisburg, PA: Trinity, 1997.

Elshtain, Jean Bethke. "With or Against Culture." *Books and Culture* 12/5 (2006) 30.

Finney, Mark T. "Christ Crucified and the Inversion of Roman Imperial Ideology in I Corinthians." *Biblical Theology Bulletin* 35 (2005) 20–33.

Garrison, William Lloyd. "Declaration of Sentiments Adopted by the Peace Convention. September 28, 1838." In *William Lloyd Garrison and the Fight against Slavery: Selections from The Liberator*, edited by William E. Cain, 101–5. Boston: Bedford, 1995.

Goode, Richard C. "The Godly Insurrection in Limestone County: Social Gospel, Populism and Southern Culture in the Late Nineteenth Century." *Religion and American Culture: A Journal of Interpretation* 3:2 (1993) 155–69.

———. "The Political Scandal of Christian Anarchism." *Leaven: A Journal of Christian Ministry* 10 (2002) 85–90.

———. "The Radical Idea of Christian Scholarship: Plea for a Scandalous Historiography." In *Restoring the First-century Church in the Twenty-first Century: Essays on the Stone-Campbell Restoration Movement*, edited by Warren Lewis and Hans Rollmann, 227–42. Studies in the History and Culture of World Christianities. Eugene, OR: Wipf & Stock, 2005.

Gray, Duncan M. Jr. "In Defense of the Steeple." *Katallagete* (Winter 1968–69) 29–31.

Gustafson, James. "The Sectarian Temptation: Reflections on Theology, the Church, and the University." In *Moral Discernment in the Christian Life: Essays in Theological Ethics*, edited by Theo A. Boer and Paul E. Capetz, 142–55. Library of Theological Ethics. Louisville: Westminster John Knox, 2007.

Hauerwas, Stanley. "Autobiography and Politics." Review of *Brother to a Dragonfly*, by Will D. Campbell, and *Once to Every Man*, by William Sloan Coffin. *Worldview* 21 (1977) 49–51.

———. "The Nonviolent Terrorist: In Defense of Christian Fanaticism." In *The Church as Counterculture*, edited by Michael Budde and Robert W. Brimlow, 89–104. SUNY Series in Popular Culture and Political Change. Albany: SUNY Press, 2000.

———. "The Politics of Witness: How We Educate Christians in Liberal Societies." In *After Christendom? How the Church Is to Behave If Freedom, Justice, and a Christian Nation Are Bad Ideas*, 133–52. Nashville: Abingdon, 1991.

———. "Race: The 'More' It Is About: Will D. Campbell Lecture: University of Mississippi, 2006." In *Christianity, Democracy, and the Radical Ordinary: Conversations between a Radical Democrat and a Christian*. Theopolitical Visions 1. Eugene, OR: Cascade, 2008.

Heddendorf, Russell. "The Christian World of Jacques Ellul." *Christian Scholars Review* 2:4 (1973) 291–307.

Henley, Wallace. "The Backwoods Guru." In *Dixieland This Week* (January 5, 1969). Clipping in James Y. Holloway Papers. University of Mississippi, Department of Archives and Special Collections.

Holloway, James Y. "For Three Transgressions and for Four." *Katallagete* (December 1965) 3–10.

———. "Politics and Baal." *Katallagete* (Winter 1966–67) 5–10.

———. "Violence and Snopes." *Katallagete* (Winter 1967–68) 3–6.

Koontz, Gayle Gerber. "Peace Theology in Transition: North American Mennonite Peace Studies and Theology, 1906–2006." *Mennonite Quarterly Review* 81 (2007) 77–96.

Lewis, John. "Reflections." *Katallagete* (Summer 1967) 14–16.

Lipscomb, David. "Race Prejudice." *Gospel Advocate* (21 February 1878), 120–21.

McAlister, Elizabeth. "Preach the Good News and Cast Out Demons: On Civil Disobedience." No pages. Online: http://www.thewitness.org/agw/mcalister022704.html.

Merton, Thomas. "The Christian in World Crisis: Reflections on the Moral Climate of the 1960s." In *The Nonviolent Alternative*, 20–62. New York: Farrar, Straus, and Giroux, 1980.

———. "The Church in World Crisis." *Katallagete* (Summer 1967) 30–36.

———. "A Devout Meditation in Memory of Adolf Eichmann." In *Raids on the Unspeakable*, 45–52. New York: New Directions, 1964.

———. "Events and Pseudo-Events: Letter to a Southern Churchman." *Katallagete* (Summer 1966) 10–17.

———. "Hot Summer of Sixty-Seven." *Katallagete* (Winter 1967–68) 28–34.

———. "Passivity and Abuse of Authority." In *The Nonviolent Alternative*, 129–33. New York: Farrar, Straus, Giroux, 1980.

———. "Peace and Revolution: A Footnote from Ulysses." In *The Nonviolent Alternative*, 70–75. New York: Farrar, Straus, and Giroux, 1980.

Percy, Walker. "The Failure and the Hope." *Katallagete* (December 1965) 16–21.

———. "Stoicism in the South." *Commonweal* 79 (July 6, 1956) 342–44.

Shields, Mitchell J. "Travels with Brother Will." *Atlanta Weekly* (April 19, 1981) 30ff.

Smith, Kelly Miller. "Trek Toward the Dawn." *Katallagete* (December 1965) 1–2.

Stringfellow, William. The American Importance of Jacques Ellul." *Katallagete* (Spring 1970) 47–48.

———. "*Authority over Death*: The Arrests of Peter and John . . . and Daniel Berrigan." *Christianity and Crisis* 30:15 (1970) 181–83.

———. "The Orthodoxy of Involvement." *Katallagete* 1 (June 1965) 12–17.

———. "The Shadow of Judas." *Christianity and Crisis* (March 3, 1969) 40–41.

Sweat, Joseph. "Nothing Sacred." *Nashville Scene* (December 1, 2005). No pages. Online: http://www.nashvillescene.com/Stories/Cover_Story/2005/12/01/Nothing_Sacred/.

Tilley, Charles. "War Making and State Making as Organized Crime." In *Bringing the State Back In*, edited by Peter B. Evans, Dietrich Rueschemeyer, and Theda Skocpol, 169–91. Cambridge: Cambridge University Press, 1985.

Weber, Max. *Politics as a Vocation*. Trans. H. H. Gerth and C. Wright Mills. Facet Books: Social Ethics Series 3. Philadelphia: Fortress, 1965.

Wilken, Robert Louis. "*Amo, Amas, Amat*: Christianity and Culture," *Reflections* 7 (2003). No pages. Online: http://www.ctinquiry.org/publications/reflections_volume_7/wilken.htm.

Wink, Walter. "Stringfellow on the Powers." In *Radical Christian and Exemplary Lawyer: Honoring William Stringfellow*, edited by Andrew W. McThenia, 17–30. Grand Rapids: Eerdmans, 1995.

Yoder, John Howard. "Exodus and Exile: The Two Faces of Liberation." *Cross Currents* 23 (Fall 1973) 297–309.

———. "How H. Richard Niebuhr Reasoned: A Critique of Christ and Culture." In *Authentic Transformation: A New Vision of Christ and Culture*, edited by Glen Stassen, D. M. Yeager, and John Howard Yoder, 31–89, 271–84. Nashville: Abingdon, 1996.

———. "On Not Being in Charge." In *The Jewish-Christian Schism Revisited*, by John Howard Yoder, edited by Michael Cartwright and Peter Ochs, 168–80. Grand Rapids: Eerdmans, 2003.

———. "The Free Church Syndrome." In *Within the Perfection of Christ: Essays on Peace and the Nature of the Church*, edited by Terry L. Brensinger and E. Morris Sider, 169–78. Nappanee, IN: Evangel, 1990.

Yoder Neufeld, Thomas R. "Varieties of Contemporary Mennonite Peace Witness: From Passivism to Pacifism, From Nonresistance to Resistance." *Conrad Grebel Review* 10 (1992) 243–57.

———. "Christian Counterculture: *Ecclesia* and Establishment." *Mennonite Quarterly Review* 63:2 (1989) 193–209.

———. "Resistance and Nonresistance: The Two Legs of a Biblical Peace Stance." *Conrad Grebel Review* 21:1 (2003) 56–81.

York, Tripp. "Thinking Through Jon Sobrino's 'Rethinking' of Martyrdom." *Mennonite Quarterly Review* 78:2 (2004) 213–34.

Young, Pete. "A Few Soft Words for the Ku Klux Klan." *Esquire* 72 (July 1969) 104–5, 134–37.

———. "Saints, Maniacs and Hypocrites." *Christianity and Crisis* (March 3, 1969) 42–43.

SCRIPTURE INDEX

Genesis
1:11–12	87–88
1:21	88
1:24–25	88
1:26	88
22:2	98
22:6	98
22:10	98

Exodus
16:3	126

Deuteronomy
4:39	118
32:15	128
32:39	118

Joshua
24	146

Judges
4:8	139

2 Samuel
17:26	119

2 Kings
19:15	119

Psalms
51:17	107
100:3	88

Proverbs
16:4	116-117

Isaiah
40:22–24	117
61:1–2	xi, 70, 79

Matthew
5–7	153n11
10:37	99
23:37	106
25	66, 153n11

Luke
4	66, 153n11
4:18	40, 199
4:18–19	xi, 40, 79
4:23	101
23:33	45

John
1:12	107

Acts
2:36	119
17:26	119

Romans
7:19	121

1 Corinthians
1:18–31	176
9:16	112
12:21–22	79

2 Corinthians
5	45, 53, 61, 66, 170
5:15–20	43
5:16	79

5:17 102
5:19 78, 103
10:4 3

Galatians
3 66
3:28 103

Philippians
2 37

Hebrews
13:8 145

1 John
2:9 108
2:18–29 108
3:14 137

Revelation
1:8 119

SUBJECT INDEX

Abbey of Gethsemani, 23, 44
Aberdeen, SD. *See* South Dakota
Abolition, 168
Alabama, 37, 83, 111, 133; Birmingham, 13n6, 24–25, 27, 102, 124, 132; Dothan, 132; Fairhope, 48; Hayneville, 48; Lowndes County, 48; Montgomery, x, 15, 21, 23, 69, 83, 94, 124, 126; Selma, 42, 45, 49
Albany, GA. *See* Georgia
Albany Movement, 29, 30
Allegiance, 54–55, 86, 146, 147, 149, 173, 183, 192, 197n26, 198n26
Alexander, Paul, 176
Alexis-Baker, Andy, 175
American Baptist College, 20
American Civil Liberties Union, 40
American Nationalists, 84
American Renaissance, 115, 115n1
Americus, GA. *See* Georgia
Amish, 151
Amite County, MS. *See* Mississippi
Amite River, 4
Amstel River, 66n10
Amsterdam, 66n10
Anabaptist, ix n6, xii, 1, 8, 37, 47, 57, 66, 66n10, 142, 143, 143n7, 146, 151, 161
Anarchist, 57, 152, 196, 197
Anarchism, 153n10, 196, 197, 198n26
Anarchy, 10
. . . and the criminals with him . . . Luke 23:33, 45
Anderson County, TN. *See* Tennessee
Anglicans, ix n6
Anthropology, 53

Apartheid, 17
Aquinas, Thomas, 147
Arkansas, 50; Little Rock, x, 19, 34, 40, 66n10, 69, 76, 98–99, 126, 133
Arkansas National Guard, 20
Army, 5, 6, 7, 8
Atlanta, GA. *See* Georgia
Atlanta Weekly, 170
Augustine, 114, 148
Auschwitz, 31, 75

Baal, 39, 45. *See also* Idol; Idolatry
Babylon, 171, 178
Bachelor of Divinity Degree, 8
Bagby, Grover, 27
Bainton, Roland, 8
Baker, Ella, 20
Ball, John, 197
Ballou, Adin, 197, 198n26
Baptist, ix, 4–5, 13, 59, 61, 123, 137
Baptist Sunday School Board, 5
Baptize, ix, 20, 60, 61
Barrett, Annie, 23
Barrett, George, 22, 23
Barth, Karl, 44, 62, 71, 114, 117
Barth, Markus, 45
Basel, Switzerland, 44
Baxter, Michael, 150n5
Be Good to God Week. *See* Religious Emphasis Week
Beatitudes, 36
Beisswenger, Don, 62, 63
Belle Meade Country Club, 28
Beloved Community, xi, 16, 58, 64, 70, 130. *See also* Community
Berea College, 44

Berea, KY. *See* Kentucky
Berrigan, Daniel, 45, 171
Berry, Marion, 20
Bevel, James, 20, 185n32
Bigot, xi, 26, 27, 35, 54, 69, 166, 168
Bigotry, 7, 32, 64, 84, 141
Biloxi, MS. *See* Mississippi
Birmingham, AL. *See* Alabama
Black Church, 159
Black Monday, 11
Black Muslims, 83, 89, 127, 133
Black Nationalist, 102
Black Panthers, 61
Black Power, 50
Blasphemy, xi, 6, 56, 70
Blumhardt, Christopher, 197
Book of Discipline, 57
Born of Conviction Statement, 38
Borosage, Robert, 65
Bowman, Norman, 61
Brady, Tom, 11
Branscomb, Harvie, 22, 92–93
Branscomb, James, 43
Brattain, Miriam, 29
Braxton, Beth, 47
Brother to a Dragonfly, ix n3, 14
Brothers and Sisters of the Free Spirit, 197
Brown, H. Rap, 50
Brown v Board of Education, 10, 11, 17, 168
Brownell, Herbert, 19
Buffalo, NY. *See* New York
Bunche, Ralph, 32
Bunt, Grandpa, 4, 48
Bush, George, W., 155
Bryan, G. McLeod, 14, 70–71

Cady, Linell, 160n4
Caesar, 6, 46, 47, 60, 61, 62, 176
California, 83; Inglewood, 84; Los Angeles, 84, 124
Callings!, 45
Calvin, John, 78, 114, 118, 148
Camp, Lee, 184
Campbell, Alexander, 198n27

Campbell, Brenda. *See* Fisher, Brenda
Campbell, Charles, 173, 180, 184, 185, 189, 190, 195, 203
Campbell, Hancie Bea "Ted" Parker, 3, 4–5
Campbell, Joe, 5, 7, 14, 48, 185n32
Campbell, Luther, 4
Canada, 47, 55
Canterbury, 54, 138
Capitalism, 174
CARE, 11
Carmichael, Stokely, 50
Carter, Billy, 61
Carter, Jimmy, 61, 176n10
Cash, Johnny, 61
Cash, W. J., 16
Catholic, ix, ix n6, 17, 26, 78, 85, 111, 112–13, 124, 138, 174
Catonsville, MD. *See* Maryland
Cecelia's Sin, 1
Central High School, x, 19
Charlotte Observer, 61
Chelcic, Peter, 197
Cheney, James, 49
Chicago, IL. *See* Illinois
Christ, 5, 6, 18, 19, 37, 44, 49, 52, 55, 57, 61, 63, 70, 74, 76–79, 84, 87, 95, 96, 99, 101, 102, 103, 108, 112, 115–17, 119–20, 128, 138, 142, 145–50, 151n8, 152–53, 155, 158, 163, 171, 176, 176n11, 178, 186n35, 187–88, 190n4, 191, 194, 195n20, 197, 199. *See also* Jesus; Messiah
Christ and Culture, 145, 148–50, 154
Christendom, 73, 138, 148, 151n8, 169
Christian Century, The, 29–30
Christian Coalition, 156, 170
Christian Nationalist Crusade, 84
Christianity and Crisis, 46
Christianity Today, 157
Church(es), ix, x–xi, 18, 19, 26, 27, 28, 29, 31, 35, 38, 39, 43, 45, 46, 52, 59–60, 61, 64, 65, 66, 70, 71, 73–81, 85–87, 89, 90, 92–99,

Subject Index   221

100–104, 105–6, 107–9, 111–14,
  119–20, 121–25, 127–28, 130,
  133–39, 149, 150n5, 152, 155–56,
  156n3, 157–59, 162–65, 167, 169,
  171, 178, 188, 190, 192n9, 194,
  196, 203
Church of Christ, 95
Citizens' Council of America, 85, 102
Citizenship, x, 69, 116, 153n1,
  175n10, 197n26
Civil Government, 198
Civil Religion, x, 69, 141, 143, 198
Civil Rights, ix, 14, 15, 16, 19, 23–24,
  30, 33, 34, 37, 39, 41, 46, 48, 69,
  83, 96, 100, 134
Civil Rights Acts, 34, 168
Civil Rights Movement, 14, 16, 21,
  22, 23, 24, 28, 30, 34, 38, 49, 51,
  66, 168
Civil War, 27, 198n27
Claiborne, Shane, 61
Clancy, Walter, 53
Clark, D. W., 37
Clark, Jim, 45
Class, viii, xi, 28, 34, 102, 114, 120,
  133, 170, 180
Clinton, TN. *See* Tennessee
Coleman, Thomas, 48
College Degree, 5
Collins, Davis, 3
Colonialism, 180
Committee of One Hundred, 13
Committee of Southern Churchmen
  (COSC), 23, 40–47, 59, 164, 171
Committee of Younger Churchmen,
  40
Common Sense, 84
Commonweal, 35
Communion, 112, 137
Communion of Saints, 29, 56, 146
Community, xi, xii, xiii, 1, 7, 12–13,
  16, 17, 21, 28, 32, 33, 35, 40–42,
  43, 58, 63, 64, 67, 70, 74, 78, 84,
  86, 94, 122, 123, 125, 130, 132,
  133, 135, 144n8, 153–54, 162,
  171, 173, 178, 186, 190, 192,
  196, 199, 205. *See also* Beloved
  Community
Connecticut; New Haven, 8
Connelly, Thomas, 141
Conservative, ix, 22, 37, 85, 95,
  134–35, 156
Constantine, 150, 169
Constantinian, 156n3
Constantinianism, 156
Constitution of the United States, 31,
  107, 156, 168, 198n26
Cosby, Gordon, 142
Country Music, ix
Crary, Stephen, 6
Cromwell, Oliver, 169
Cross, 38, 54, 176n11, 188, 190, 192,
  193, 195, 203–4
Cry, the Beloved Country, 75

Dabbs, James McBride, 44
Daniels, Jonathan, 48
Davenport, Eugene, 37
Davidson, Donald, 17
Day, Dorothy, 48, 142, 185n32
D'Costa, Gavin, 200
de Foucauld, Charles, 197
de la Beckwith, Byron, 49n16
de Lamennais, Felicite Robert, 197
Debs, Eugene V., viii
Decalogue, 36
Deification, 115–17, 119
Democracy, xi, 63, 73, 74, 96, 100,
  117, 126–27, 133, 166, 170
Department of Racial and Cultural
  Relations, 15, 31
Depression Era Mississippi, 4
Desegregation, 11, 19–20, 22, 34, 113,
  124, 125, 127, 134–35, 165
Detroit, MI. *See* Michigan
Dialogue, 37
Director of Religious Life, 10. *See also*
  University of Mississippi
Disciples, xi
Discipleship, x, 37, 43, 66, 148, 149,
  152, 192n9
Divinity School, ix

Subject Index

Division of Christian Life, 15
Dixon, Thomas, 8
Dodds, Robert C., 35
Dolan House, 47
Domination System, 179–83, 187–88, 190, 195, 199
Dothan, AL. *See* Alabama
Douglass, Frederick, 7
Dunbar, Tony, vii, 46, 65

Eakes, T. J., 24, 38
East Fork Baptist Church, 3, 4, 62
East Fork Consolidated High School, 4
East, P. D., 48
Easter, 44, 66, 188, 193, 199–200, 204. *See also* Resurrection
Ecclesiology, 52
Eckbald, Bob, xi, 163, 174
Eckford, Elizabeth, x, 69
Eddy, Sherwood, 40
Edwards, Jonathan, 71, 108
Egerton, John, 62
Eichmann, Adolf, 31, 75, 184
Eisenhower, Dwight, 19, 20
Elizabeth, LA. *See* Louisiana
Eller, Vernard, 196
Ellul, Jacques, 39, 44, 142, 164–65, 175, 194, 197, 199, 201
Elshtain, Jean Bethke, 150n6
Emancipation Proclamation, 31, 96
Enola Gay, 6
Enquiry Concerning Political Justice, 197
Epsy, Edwin, 38
Eucharist, 194, 194n14
Evers, Medgar, 49n16
Exile, 26, 181, 201

F. W. Woolworth, 28
Fabus, Orval, 20
Failure of Hope: Essays of Southern Churchmen, The, 45
Fairhope, AL. *See* Alabama
Faith, 6, 22, 34, 38, 45, 80, 81, 86, 98, 100, 122, 130, 136, 149, 156, 156n3, 158, 160, 167, 183, 194, 199, 200

Falwell, Jerry, 170
Farmer, ix, 8, 89, 105
Fast, Howard, 7
Fayette Country, TN. *See* Tennessee
Federal Council of Churches (FCC), 168
Federal Government, x
Fellowship of Reconciliation, 21, 40
Fellowship of Southern Churchmen (FSC), 23, 40–41, 44
Finney, Mark, 195
Fisher, Brenda, 8, 10, 59, 70
Fisk University, 17, 20
Ford Motor Company, 174
Forest, Jim, 203
Fort Benning, 62
Forty Acres and a Goat, ix n3
Fox, George, 197
Frady, Marshall, 59, 65
Francis of Assisi, 197
Freedom, xi, 18, 37, 55, 63, 73, 79, 80, 122, 127, 128, 133, 134, 193, 204
Freedom Rides, 20, 23, 39
Freedom Road, 7, 48, 54

G.I. Bill, 8
Gandhi, Mahatma, 21, 22, 127
Garrison, William Lloyd, 197, 197n26
Gass's Tavern, 60
Geneva, 54, 148
Georgia, 11, 30, 37, 46, 123, 155n1; Albany, 29–30; Americus, 11–12; Atlanta, 30, 108, 113, 124, 138; Sumter County, 12, 123
Germany, Horace, 38
Geronymus, Cecelia, 1, 66
Gibble, Kenneth, 4
Glad River, The, viii n2
Gladden, Washington, 170
God in Public: Four Ways American Christianity and Public Life Relate, 155
Godwin, William, 197
Good Friday, 66, 193
Goodman, Andy, 49

Gospel, x, xi, 3, 18, 27, 34, 36, 39, 41, 45, 46, 54, 65, 69, 74, 101, 103, 105, 107, 109, 112, 117, 131, 150n5, 166, 170, 204
Gospel Advocate, 95
Government, x, xi, 23, 24, 49, 55, 62, 69, 73, 92, 96
Grace, x, 18, 39, 44, 88, 101, 102, 112, 115, 139
Grafman, Milton, 13n6
Graham, Billy, 45, 62, 170
Grambling University, 9
Gray, Duncan, 38
Greenleaf, Richard, 32
Gustafson, James, 160, 160n4, 161, 172, 199, 200

Hall, Tom T., 61
Hamer, Fanny Lou, 42
Handbook of Denominations in the United States, 59
Harding, Vincent, 45
Harlem, NY. *See* New York
Harvard University, 56, 171, 174
Hauerwas, Stanley, xii, 61, 156n3, 159, 165, 166, 179, 186, 196n20
Hayes, Rutherford B., 7
Hayneville, AL. *See* Alabama
Henry, Carl F. H., 157
Heresy, 45, 76, 81, 171
Higher Education, 5
Highlander Folk School, 23, 40
Hiroshima, 6
Hitler, Adolf, 71
Hobbes, Thomas, 181
Holloway, James, 33, 43–46, 162, 170
Holmes County, MS. *See* Mississippi
Hoover, J. Edgar, 23
Hope, 12, 16, 33, 39, 59, 63, 112, 128, 137, 141, 155, 176, 187–88, 201, 203n1, 204
Horne, Lena, 32
Horton, Myles, 22, 40
Humanism, 100, 166, 174
Humanist, 39, 100, 101, 104, 111, 127
Humanitarian, 36, 39, 41, 113, 147, 165

Humanitarianism, x, 69, 96, 116, 128
Hutchins, Robert, 121

Ichausti, Robert, 142
Iconoclasm, x, 63, 64, 69, 154, 203
Iconoclast, ix, 3, 23, 30, 63, 64
Iconoclastic, 30, 143, 153, 162
Idol, x, 26, 29, 34, 63, 66, 67, 126, 171, 174, 177, 196, 205. *See also* Baal
Idolatry, 29, 46, 78, 152, 163, 186–87, 200
Illich, Ivan, 39
Illinois; Chicago, 31, 32, 38, 102, 124, 136
Incarnate, 26, 42, 55, 58, 64, 66, 115, 142, 144, 163, 164, 167, 170, 171, 172, 188, 189, 190n4, 192n9, 193, 199, 201, 203
Incarnation, 65, 115–17, 142, 171, 188, 190, 191
Incarnational, 45, 170
Inglewood, CA. *See* California
Institution, 9, 27, 28, 37, 38, 39, 41, 42, 46, 54–58, 59–60, 64, 65, 76–78, 89, 92, 121, 123, 127, 132, 134–35, 136, 156, 161, 168, 173, 174, 177, 180, 186, 192n9, 198n26
Institutional Church, xi, 37, 42, 101, 124, 130, 197. *See also* Steeple
Integration, 50, 85, 134
Integrationists, ix, 31, 87, 93, 114, 119

Jackson Daily News, 12
Jackson, Jimmie Lee, 49
Jefferson, Thomas, 147
Jennings, Waylon, 61
Jerusalem, 89, 103, 106, 146, 178, 190–91
Jesus, 19, 37, 38, 44, 47, 49, 50, 57, 60, 65, 75, 89, 95, 96, 106, 108, 112, 115, 119–20, 127, 128, 131, 143, 145–47, 149, 150n5, 151, 153, 160, 162, 170, 175n10, 189–94, 194n14, 195–96, 199, 203–4. *See also* Christ; Messiah
Jew, ix, 7, 26, 35, 118, 134, 164, 176

Subject Index

Jim Crow, 7, 17, 19, 115, 165
John Birch Society, 85, 86, 112, 122
Johnson, Charles S., 17
Jordan, Clarence, viii, 11–12, 22, 26, 123, 141, 171n7, 192–93
Judgment, 18, 19, 87, 90, 103, 106, 107, 108, 109, 119, 136, 153
Justice, xi, 7, 16, 18, 21, 26, 28, 42, 46, 66, 73, 87, 93, 96, 101, 116, 124–26, 128, 135, 136, 145n3, 157, 158, 161, 162, 163, 165, 168, 170, 175n10, 182, 188, 204

Kasper, John, 17, 18
Katallagete, xii, 6, 23, 43, 45, 46, 47, 52, 142, 162, 170, 171, 196, 201
Keck, Leander, 45
Kennedy, Robert, 23
Kenneson, Phil, 192n9
Kenosis, 37. *See also* Incarnation
Kentucky; Berea, 44; Louisville, 11
Kersey, Gerald, 37
Kershaw, Alvin, 11–13
Kerygma, xi, xii, 19, 35, 36, 39, 64, 67, 146, 153, 156n3, 158, 162, 163, 172, 173, 190, 195n20, 198n26
Kester, Howard "Buck," 19, 40–41
King, Coretta Scott, 65
King, Martin Luther, Jr., 13n6, 14, 16, 19, 21, 63, 186, 186n35
Kingdom of Christ, 115. *See also* Kingdom of God
Kingdom of God, 28, 52, 101, 107, 115, 139, 145, 153, 158, 163, 169, 178, 188, 197n26
Klansmen, ix, 35, 86
Klansmen, The, 8
Kluxer, 50, 53
Knapp Lecture, 92
Koinonia Farm, 11–12, 26, 123, 142, 193
Kristofferson, Kris, 61
Ku Klux Klan (KKK), 3, 7, 17, 46, 54, 61, 83, 86, 133. *See also* Klansmen; Kluxer
Kudzu, 61

Lafayette, Bernard, 20, 22
Lasch, Christopher, 45
Lawson, James M., Jr., 20, 21–22, 93
Lee, Oscar, 70
Letter from a Birmingham Jail, 13n6
Letter to Diognetus, 163
Lewis, John, 20, 45
Lewis, Ted, 175n10
Liberal, ix, 33–35, 39, 52, 53, 70, 95, 125, 134, 135, 156, 166, 170
Liberalism, 95, 115, 117
Liberty, MS. *See* Mississippi
Lindbeck, George, 159
Lippmann, Walter, 45
Lipscomb, David, 95–96, 198, 198n27
Little Rock, AR. *See* Arkansas
Lloyd, Jeremy, 60
Locke, John, 147
Lordship, 79, 119
Los Angeles, CA. *See* California
Lott, Trent, 183
Louisiana, 10; Elizabeth, 9; New Orleans, 8, 76, 85, 94, 113, 126; Pineville, 5; Taylor, 9, 10
Louisiana College, 5, 8
Louisville, KY. *See* Kentucky
Love, ix n6, 4, 10, 18, 37, 42, 44–45, 48, 53, 55, 64, 75, 79–80, 81, 83, 85, 87, 89, 90, 95, 97, 99, 102, 113, 136, 137, 139, 154, 162, 164, 172, 175n10, 176n11, 185, 191–93, 198n26, 199
Lowndes County, AL. *See* Alabama
Lucy, Autherine, x, 69
Luther, Martin, 147
Lynch, 53
Lynching, 40

Mansfield, TX. *See* Texas
March Against Fear, 47
Marching Orders, 5
Marlette, Doug, 61
Martyr, 66, 190n4
Martyrdom, 1, 149, 190, 190n4
Maryland; Catonsville, 171
Matthiessen, F.O., 115–16

Maurin, Peter, 48
Mays, Benjamin, 19
McAlister, Elizabeth, 186, 201
McCarthyism, 9
McComb, MS. *See* Mississippi
McCormick, Richard, 160
Means of Grace, 112
Meharry Medical College, 20
Memphis, TN. *See* Tennessee
Mennonites, 146
Mercer University, 43, 44
Meredith, James, 47
Meridian, MS. *See* Mississippi
Merton, Thomas, vii, 23, 44, 45, 142, 183, 184–85, 193, 201, 203n1
Messiah, 6, 189, 190. *See also* Christ; Jesus
Methodist Laymen's League, 111
Michigan; Detroit, 124
Milbank, John, 159
Military, 6
Military Service, 5
Miller, J. Quinter, 16
Mind of the South, The, 16
Ministry of Reconciliation, xi, 16, 154
Mission, xi, 38, 45, 76, 79, 80–81, 87, 111, 130, 148, 156n3
Mississippi, 7, 10–12, 25, 27, 33, 37, 47, 83, 84, 183, 185n32; Amite County, 3, 5; Biloxi, 108; Holmes County, 11, 25; Liberty, 3; McComb, 5, 22; Meridian, 14; Neshoba County, 49; Oxford, x, 11, 13, 14, 69; Sumerall, 8; Vicksburg, 132
Mississippi Baptist Association, 3
Mississippi Citizen's Council, 12, 85
Missouri; St. Louis, 16
Monteagle, TN. *See* Tennessee
Montgomery, AL. *See* Alabama
Montgomery Improvement Organization, 14
Montpelier, VT. *See* Vermont
Moore, D. Elisha, 4
Moral Majority, 156, 170
Morris, Willie, 141
Morrow, Jimmy, Jr., 12

Moscow, 75, 76, 175
Mt. Juliet, TN. *See* Tennessee
Musil, Robert, 65
Muste, A. J., 21, 62
My Bondage and My Freedom, 7

Narrative, xii, 39, 148, 153, 154, 173, 179, 182, 192n9
Nash, Diane, 20
Nashville Banner, The, 22
Nashville Christian Leadership Conference, 19
Nashville Civil Rights Oral History Project, 21
Nashville Community Relations Conference, 17
Nashville Scene, ix
Nashville, TN. *See* Tennessee
Nation-State, 55, 56, 101, 115, 156, 166, 168, 169, 174, 175, 178, 180–81, 182n25, 182n26, 195, 195n19, 201. *See also* State
National Association for the Advancement of Colored People (NAACP), 11, 12, 40, 124, 136
National Catholic Welfare Conference, 31
National Conference on Religion and Race, 31, 35
National Council of Churches (NCC), 14, 15–16, 21, 26–29, 31–33, 35, 38–39, 41, 46, 49, 59, 60, 65, 70, 131, 168n2. *See also* Department of Racial and Cultural Relations; Division of Christian Life; National Conference on Religion and Race; Southern Project
Nationalism, 73
Nazi Germany, 51
Nelson, J. Robert, 22
Neshoba County. *See* Mississippi
New Christian Manifesto, A, xi n10
New Deal, 40
New Haven, CT. *See* Connecticut
New Jersey; Union, 84
New Orleans, LA. *See* Louisiana

New Oxford Review, 196
New York; Buffalo, 124; Harlem, 102, 136, 171; New York City, 7, 29, 54, 108, 124, 138; Westchester County, 83, 133
New York City, NY. *See* New York
Newsweek, 52
Niebuhr, H. Richard, 44, 70, 114, 145–50, 150n7, 151–52, 154, 155, 158, 160, 161, 167, 172, 199
Niebuhr, Reinhold, 40, 45, 57, 62, 150n5, 150n7
Nixon, Richard, 19
Nonviolence, 6, 21–22, 32, 63, 93, 127, 149, 151, 186, 189, 190, 195
North Carolina, 8; Winston-Salem, 8

O'Connor, Flannery, 41, 141
Ole Miss. *See* University of Mississippi
Oniki, Garry, 49
Ordination, 4-5
Oxford, MS, x, 11, 13, 14

Pacifism, 12, 150n5
Pacifist, 6
Palm Sunday, 190–91
Parks, Judy, viii
Parks, Rosa, 15
Paton, Alan, 75
Patriotism, 5, 55, 174, 182, 197n26
Patterson, Robert B., 85
Paul (St. Paul the Apostle), 49, 52–53, 61, 62, 78, 79, 114
Peace, ix n6, 38, 40, 47, 84, 96, 134, 135, 139, 152, 156n3, 157, 163, 167, 183, 188, 191, 196, 197n26
Peale, Norman Vincent, 170
Penn, William, Jr., 152n9
Pennsylvania, 152n9; Philadelphia, 79, 132
Peoples' Party, 3
Percy, Walker, 35–36, 45, 65, 141
Philadelphia, PA. *See* Pennsylvania
Pineville, LA. *See* Louisiana
Piney Woods, 3

Pittsburgh Theological Seminary, 24
Plato, 147
Pneumonia, 4, 105
Political Theology, xii, 145, 148, 149, 150, 152n9, 153, 154, 155–62, 167, 170, 171n7, 173, 191
Politics, 10, 16, 40, 45, 46, 134, 143, 146, 148, 150n5, 153n10, 155n2, 157, 162, 163, 164, 170, 175n10, 176, 188, 190n4, 192, 199–200, 201
Poor, 3, 7, 28, 34, 36, 37, 53, 54, 59, 79, 153, 164, 171, 188, 199
Pope, Liston, 8
Preacher, ix, 4, 5, 8, 9, 10, 43, 59, 60, 61, 86, 100, 102, 153, 203
Prison, viii, 4, 63, 64, 164
Prisoners, 46, 188
Pritchett, Laurie, 29, 30
Prophet, 8, 12, 16, 42, 62, 100, 106, 115, 123, 130, 136, 139, 167, 171
Prophetic, 29, 36, 38, 39, 61, 62, 64, 71, 108, 130, 134, 136, 139, 143, 158, 162, 164, 178, 192n9
Protestant, 17, 26, 36, 70, 85, 86, 92, 95, 101, 111, 113, 115–16, 121–24, 130–31, 134–36, 138
Protestantism, 86, 95, 111, 112, 115, 116, 121–24, 134, 136
Providence, 10–11
Providence Farm, 11, 26, 27, 40
Pulpit, ix, 3, 10, 17, 38, 42, 43, 62, 86, 103, 112, 135
Pur, Uncle, 5
Puritans, 169, 174

Quaker, 152n9, 197

Race, xi, 7, 8, 18, 28, 31, 35, 38, 66, 74–77, 79, 83–85, 87–89, 92, 94–98, 100–101, 102, 106, 107, 112–15, 120, 122, 133, 137, 138, 139, 143n7, 165, 166, 168, 170, 174, 197n26
Race and the Renewal of the Church, x–xi, 29, 32, 36–37, 69–140

Race Relations, 7, 11, 15–16, 33, 34, 35, 53, 56, 73–78, 89, 95, 100, 101, 102, 103, 107–8, 111–12, 117–19, 121, 123, 134, 137, 179
Race Relations Institute, 17
Racism, 3, 35, 55–56, 81, 86, 87, 103, 104, 115, 121, 125, 130, 166, 174, 186
Racist, xi, 17, 18, 19, 24, 27, 33, 36, 69, 81, 89, 90, 96–97, 99, 102, 108, 117, 159
Radical, ix, ix n6, xi, 37, 39, 66, 66n10, 142–43, 143n7, 144, 144n8, 146, 150, 150n6, 150n7, 151–54, 161–62, 163, 165, 167, 171, 171n7, 172, 173, 175n10, 188, 192, 192n9, 193, 194, 195, 196n20, 197, 199, 200, 201, 203, 205
Rauschenbusch, Walter, 159, 170
Reagan, Ronald, 155, 176n10
Reconciled, ix, 28, 43, 44, 49–50, 52, 53, 61, 67, 171, 172, 188, 199, 200, 205
Reconciler, 61
Reconciliation, xi, 18, 19, 28, 29, 32, 34, 35, 39, 43–45, 46, 49, 52, 58, 61, 70, 78, 79, 107, 136, 153, 156n3, 161, 172, 180, 188. *See also* Ministry of Reconciliation
Reconciling, x, 18, 41, 51, 56, 63, 64, 66, 78, 102, 175n10, 188, 199, 205
Reconstruction, 7, 96
Redemption, 18, 25, 77, 81, 97, 101, 102, 103, 105, 107, 108–09, 119, 141, 191
Redneck, ix, 26, 27, 48, 53, 54
Reeb, James, 49
Reeves, Thomas, 37
Reformation, 45, 123–24, 143, 169
Religious Emphasis Week, 11–13, 29
Repentance, 6, 31, 107, 194
Resurrection, 43, 162, 193, 203. *See also* Easter
Revolt Among the Sharecroppers, 41
Ritschel, Albrecht, 147

Riverbend Maximum Security Prison (RMSI), vii, viii, xiii, 66
Robertson, Garland, 184
Rome, 54, 138
Roosevelt, Franklin D., 40
Rustin, Bayard, 19

Salvation, 5, 107, 115, 157, 188, 197n26
Saunders, Stanley, 203
Scarritt College for Christian Workers, 19
School of the Americas, 62
Schwerner, Mickey, 49
Sectarian, 150, 150n5, 151, 160–61, 200
Sectarianism, 150n5, 160, 200
Segregation, 12, 50, 74, 76, 80, 86, 87, 92, 93, 98, 112, 113, 114, 122, 131, 165, 191
Segregationist, 11, 12, 18, 19, 24, 26, 27, 31, 34, 49, 79–80, 83–84, 87–89, 93, 97–98, 100–102, 105–7, 113–14, 116, 117, 118, 119, 131, 165, 166
Seigenthaler, John, Sr., 17
Selma, AL. *See* Alabama
Selma March, 49
Seminary Degree, 5
Sermon on the Mount, 66
Sharp, Tom, 5
Shields, Mitchell J., 49–50
Simmons, W. J., 85
Sin, 27, 29, 30, 43, 49, 55, 74, 75, 78, 79, 90, 95, 103, 104, 106, 108, 109, 112–14, 119, 126, 128, 130, 133, 137, 143, 156, 159, 184
Sixteenth Avenue Baptist Church, 24
Slave, 7, 37, 54, 125
Smiley, Glenn, 22
Smith, Frank E., 65
Smith, Gerald, L. K., 84
Smith, Kelly Miller, Jr., 17, 20, 43
Smith, Wofford, 38
Social Gospel. *See* Gospel
Social Justice. *See* Justice

Socrates, 147
Sojourners, 157, 162n11
South Africa, 17, 74, 75, 133
South Dakota; Aberdeen, 132
South Pacific Medic Corps, 6
South, The, 6, 7, 8, 11, 15, 27, 36, 39, 40–41, 46, 53, 69, 84, 85, 86, 89, 93, 99, 104, 108, 123, 141–43
Southern Baptist, 4, 8, 9, 26, 59, 71
Southern Baptist Theological Seminary, 11
Southern Christian Leadership Conference (SCLC), 19
Southern Churchmen Speak Column, 42
Southern Farmers' Alliance, 3
Southern Prison Ministry, vii, 46
Southern Project, 15
Southern Tenant Farmers Union (STFU), 40
Sovereign, xi, 37, 115, 116, 118, 119, 120, 163, 166, 167–68, 187, 196
Sovereignty, 31, 45, 66, 70, 93, 99, 114–19, 126, 127, 137, 165, 173, 175n10, 200
St. Louis, MO. *See* Missouri
Stahlman, James, 22
Standard Oil, 5
State, xi, 6, 11, 39, 61, 64, 74, 75, 85, 92, 94, 97, 99, 156n3, 157, 169, 176, 181–82, 195, 197, 197n26, 198n26. *See also* Nation-State
Steeple, 9, 17, 26, 37, 38, 39, 41–42, 46, 54, 59, 60, 62, 64, 65, 66, 163, 165. *See also* Institutional Church
Stoic, 36, 142
Strange Career of Jim Crow, The, 115
Stringfellow, William, vii, 32, 35, 44, 171–72, 173–74, 174n3, 175, 177, 178, 179–81, 187–88, 190–92, 195, 196, 200
Student Nonviolent Coordinating Committee, 20
Suffrage Movement, 168
Sumerall, MS. *See* Mississippi
Sumter County, GA, 12

Supreme Court, 10, 41, 74, 84, 92, 94, 96, 101, 127, 165
Surgery, 7
Surgical Technician, 5–6
Synagogue, 31, 35
Synagogue Council of America, 31

Taylor, Alva, 40
Taylor, LA. *See* Louisiana
Teamsters Union, 174
Ten Commandments, 155, 155n1
Tennessean, The, 62
Tennessee, 32, 46, 93; Anderson County, 17–18; Clinton, x, 17–18, 34, 37, 69, 135; Fayette County, 105, 108, 133; Memphis, 56, 113; Monteagle, 40; Mt. Juliet, vii, 47, 59, 60; Nashville, vii, x, 16–17, 18, 19–22, 34, 39, 43, 54, 59, 62, 65, 66, 69, 87, 113, 124, 138
Tennessee Federation for Constitutional Government, 17
Tennessee National Guard, 20
Tennessee Society for the Maintenance of Segregation, 83–84
Tennessee State University, 20, 23
Tertium Genus, 77. *See also* Third Race
Tertullian, 146, 151, 197
Texas, 95; Mansfield, 37
Third Race, 77, 102, 137
Thurman, Howard, 191–92
Tilley, Charles, 182n26
Time, 32
Tolstoy, Leo, 146, 151
Toulouse, Mark, 155–59, 161–62, 162n11, 167, 172
Towne, Anthony, 23
Tracy, David, 160, 160n4
Treason, 74, 195, 195n19
Tragedy, 7, 30, 54, 62, 63, 90, 99, 106, 137
Tragic, 6, 42, 103, 130
Trueblood, Elton, 170
Tubman, Harriet, 63

Tulane University, 8
Turner, Paul, 17–18, 37
Tyranny, 55

UNICEF, 11
Union, NJ. *See* New Jersey
Union Seminary Quarterly Review, 36
Union Theological Seminary, 7
University of Alabama, x, 69
University of Chicago, 121
University of Georgia, 11
University of Mississippi, 10–14, 22, 29, 179, 185n32
University of Southern Mississippi, 175
University of Wisconsin, 92
Up To Our Steeples in Politics, 46

Vanderbilt Divinity School, viii, 21, 22, 40
Vanderbilt Program in Faith and Criminal Justice, viii
Vanderbilt University, viii, 21, 22, 44, 92, 93
Vaughn, James Willis, 37
Vermont; Montpelier, 132
Vicksburg, MS. *See* Mississippi
Vietnam War, 46, 47, 171, 175
Vivian, C. T., 20
Vocation, 11, 14, 20, 29–30, 39, 46, 49, 61, 65, 66, 70, 158, 163, 172, 177, 178, 180, 203, 204, 205
Voting Bill, 34
Voting Rights Act of 1965, 168

Waits, Jim, 45
Wake Forest College, 8, 14, 70
Walker, John, 4
Walking with the Wind, 20
Wallace, George, 65
Wallis, Jim, 157
Washington DC, 75, 113, 138
Weathersby, Dean, 5
Webb, Lee, 3
Weber, Max, 181
Westchester County, NY. *See* New York

Westfeldt, William, 22
Westmoreland, Lynn, 155
White Citizens Councils, 11, 83, 84, 85, 86, 94, 122, 133
White Property Owners' Association, 102
Wilken, Robert, 164
Will Campbell and the Soul of the South, ix n4
Will Campbell: Radical Prophet of the South, ix n4
Williams, J. D., 12
Williams, P. Edgar, 32
Williams, Roger, 57, 63
Wilmore, Gayraud, x, 69
Wink, Walter, 173, 179, 180, 182, 189, 190n5, 193, 194, 194n14, 204
Winstanley, Gerrard, 197
Winston-Salem, NC. *See* North Carolina
Witness, 27, 38, 45, 104, 106, 111, 112, 114, 125, 130, 136, 165, 171, 175n10, 195n19, 199
Wittenburg Door, ix, x, 51, 58, 170, 176
Wolf, Janet, viii, xiii
Wood, Dorothy, 21
Woodward, C. Vann, 115
World War II, 5, 80
Wray, Harmon, vii–viii, xii, xiii, 22
Writings on Reconciliation and Resistance, xii n12, xiii, 45n9
Wycliffe, John, 197

Yale Divinity School, 8, 9, 10, 62
Yale University, 44
YMCA, 14, 47
Yoder, John Howard, xii, 142, 149, 150n7, 151–52, 152n9, 153, 167, 181, 192, 194
Yoder Neufeld, Tom, 143n7
Yoderwasians, xi
York, Tripp, 163, 190n4, 193

www.ingramcontent.com/pod-product-compliance
Lightning Source LLC
Chambersburg PA
CBHW020407230426
43664CB00009B/1218